WOMEN'S STUDIES QUARTERLY

VOLUME 47   NUMBERS 3 & 4   FALL/WINTER 2019

An educational project of the Feminist Press at the City University of New York, the College of Staten Island, City University of New York, Hunter College, City University of New York, and LaGuardia Community College, City University of New York, with support from the Center for the Study of Women and Society at the Graduate Center, City University of New York

WSQ: Women's Studies Quarterly, a peer-reviewed, theme-based journal, is published in the summer and winter by the Feminist Press at the City University of New York.

COVER ART
Azabache by Mildred Beltré

WEBSITE
feministpress.org/wsq

EDITORIAL CORRESPONDENCE
WSQ: Women's Studies Quarterly, The Feminist Press at the City University of New York, The Graduate Center, 365 Fifth Avenue, Suite 5406, New York, NY 10016; wsqeditorial@gmail.com.

PRINT SUBSCRIPTIONS
Subscribers in the United States: Individuals—$60 for 1 year; $150 for 3 years. Institutions—$85 for 1 year; $225 for 3 years. Subscribers outside the United States: Add $40 per year for delivery. To subscribe or change an address, contact *WSQ* Customer Service, The Feminist Press at the City University of New York, The Graduate Center, 365 Fifth Avenue, Suite 5406, New York, NY 10016; 212-817-7915; info@feministpress.org.

FORTHCOMING ISSUES
Inheritance, Maria Rice Bellamy, College of Staten Island, City University of New York, and Karen Weingarten, Queens College, City University of New York

RIGHTS & PERMISSIONS
Fred Courtright, The Permissions Company, 570-839-7477; permdude@eclipse.net.

SUBMISSION INFORMATION
For the most up-to-date guidelines, calls for papers, and information concerning forthcoming issues, write to wsqeditorial@gmail.com or visit feministpress.org/wsq.

ADVERTISING
For information on display-ad sizes, rates, exchanges, and schedules, please write to *WSQ* Marketing, The Feminist Press at the City University of New York, The Graduate Center, 365 Fifth Avenue, Suite 5406, New York, NY 10016; 212-817-7918; sales@feministpress.org.

ELECTRONIC ACCESS AND SUBSCRIPTIONS
Access to electronic databases containing backlist issues of *WSQ* may be purchased through JSTOR at www.jstor.org. Access to electronic databases containing current issues of *WSQ* may be purchased through Project MUSE at muse.jhu.edu, muse@muse.jhu.edu; and ProQuest at www.il.proquest.com, info@il.proquest.com. Individual electronic subscriptions for *WSQ* may also be purchased through Project MUSE.

ISSN: 0732-1562   ISBN: 978-1-936932-72-6 $25.00

Contents

Editors' Note

In 2019 we are celebrating the fiftieth anniversary of influential U.S. movements—such as the gay liberation movement following the Stonewall uprising (1969) and the launch of the New York chapter of the Young Lords Organization (1969)—that demonstrated the power of alliances to successfully shift and challenge seemingly entrenched heteronormative, racialized, and gendered social structures. Yet, as many anniversary event organizers and movement veterans have reminded us at recent celebrations, it is also critical to recognize the differential power relations, exclusions, and uneasy relationships among the various participants within these movements. The insights of Miss Major and Victoria Cruz as well as recent films and articles celebrating the legacies of Marsha P. Johnson and Sylvia Rivera attest to the frequently unacknowledged role of trans women of color in the Stonewall uprising and the struggles that trans women of color faced and continue to experience within the queer and feminist movements that they helped initiate. Likewise, Sylvia Rivera's participation in the Lesbian and Gay Caucus of the Young Lords and the founding of the Women's Caucus of the Young Lords by Iris Morales, Denise Oliver-Velez, and fellow organizers following the launch of the Young Lords Organization in 1969 illustrate that the Puerto Rican and Third World liberation movements that brought activists together also included an ongoing struggle to address sexuality and gender hierarchies within the movements.

Guest editors Ujju Aggarwal and Linta Varghese and contributors to *WSQ: Together* offer a timely dialogue that helps us better understand and critically assess the limits and possibilities of past and current calls to come together for liberation and justice. Aggarwal and Varghese's careful

WSQ: Women's Studies Quarterly 47: 3 & 4 (Fall/Winter 2019) © 2019 by Jillian M. Báez and Natalie Havlin.

curation of case studies of gendered violence, migration, reproduction, solidarities, and welfare rights, as well as activist reflections on Critical Resistance and INCITE!'s "Statement on Gender Violence and the Prison Industrial Complex" (originally released in 2001), offer analytical frameworks and methodologies to push us to "expand our political horizons by foregrounding the relationality of struggle" (Aggarwal and Varghese 2019, 13).

"Together" is a fitting theme and capstone to end our term as general editors of the journal. We began our editorship in January 2017 in the context of the beginning of the Trump administration. Our challenge immediately became how to curate content, including both scholarly and creative contributions, that would speak to the multiple crises we are currently facing from various perspectives. During this liminal time, we edited the issues *Precarious Work*, *Beauty*, *Protest*, and *Asian Diasporas*. The issues *Beauty* and *Protest* revisited some of the most debated issues in women's and gender studies surrounding beauty politics and resistance while also asking important questions about our contemporary realities. *Precarious Work* offered thoughtful inquiry into today's insecure and exploitative global labor conditions. That issue also included more visual art than any other previous issue. *Asian Diasporas* offered meditations on the impact of global gendered migration and a number of entry points into understanding today's current immigration crisis. Throughout all of these *WSQ* issues, we, the guest editors, as well as the poetry editor, fiction and prose editor, peer reviewers, contributors, board members, and Feminist Press staff, have contemplated what it means to work with, against, and in tension with one another in these liminal and turbulent times. Women's and gender studies has long debated what sisterhood and feminist solidarity means and how it is practiced. Who is included in calls for "sisterhood" and feminist solidarity? How are solidarities formed and reworked, and how do they sometimes end? *WSQ: Together* intervenes in these debates, asking what it means to work through solidarity, dissent, and nontraditional forms of organizing across institutions and locales.

The issue's theme is also particularly apt at the level of production of the journal. Since 1972 *WSQ* has not only published scholarship, activist thought, and creative expression probing the limits and possibilities of calls to come together to address gender inequality, but the journal has also served as a venue for putting into practice the work of feminist collaboration. It has been our pleasure as general coeditors to work with *WSQ*

Editorial Board members and guest editors to shape each issue. Because of the deeply collaborative process that *WSQ* requires, everyone involved in an issue is constantly in conversation and negotiation. Unlike many other women's and gender studies journals, every issue of *WSQ* is a themed issue curated by guest editors. Because of this, each issue has its own unique energy, logistical challenges, and working relationships. We also work closely with our publisher, the Feminist Press, a publishing house that is committed to editing and printing a wide range of feminist works, many of them very accessible to the public. From this wide array of talents and visions, each issue came *together* under the auspices of a collaborative dedication to pursue each theme in thoughtful and creative ways that spoke to some of the most pressing issues of our time.

We thank guest editors Ujju Aggarwal and Linta Varghese for their careful curation of academic and artistic works that encourage new feminist inquiry about calls to come together. We also extend our gratitude to *WSQ* Editorial Board member Rupal Oza for serving as a consulting editor to support and move the issue forward. We are very grateful to have had the opportunity to feature art by Mildred Beltré on the cover and inside this issue. We also extend our appreciation to all of the contributors in this issue and the peer reviewers for their time and expertise.

We thank *WSQ* Editorial Board members for their time and labor providing feedback on issue themes, conducting peer reviews, and offering guidance. In *Together*, for example, we are pleased to feature *WSQ* Editorial Board member and National Women's Studies Association president Premilla Nadasen's response to Wilson Sherwin and Frances Fox Piven's article "The Radical Feminist Legacy of the National Welfare Rights Organization." During the production of *Together*, we also experienced the loss of a generous and insightful collaborator with the passing of longtime Editorial Board member Dr. Meena Alexander in November 2018. Alexander's role as an Editorial Board member, creative writer, and faculty member at Hunter College and the CUNY Graduate Center exemplifies a praxis of probing fissures and imagining new horizons for feminist politics.

During our tenure as general coeditors, we have had the pleasure of reading the creative prose and poetry selections carefully curated by *WSQ*'s creative prose editor Rosalie Morales Kearns and poetry editor Patricia Smith. We thank Rosalie and Patricia for assembling prose and poetry for *Together* and past issues that creatively probe the heart of feminist debates about personal and collective feminist projects.

We also deeply appreciate the collaboration and generous commitment of the graduate students who work as editorial and social media assistants for *WSQ*. A special thank-you goes to *WSQ*'s editorial assistant Melina Moore for careful attention to the many details of *Together*. We would also like to extend our deep-felt thanks to *WSQ* editorial assistant Elena Cohen for her commitment and work for *WSQ* throughout the years. In fall 2018, we welcomed our newest team member, Kirsten Corneilson, as *WSQ*'s first social media assistant. We would like to thank Kirsten for increasing the visibility and circulation of *WSQ* via Twitter and Facebook.

We also appreciate the tremendous support *WSQ* receives from the Feminist Press, especially from Jamia Wilson, Lauren Rosemary Hook, Nick Whitney, Jisu Kim, Drew Stevens, Lucia Brown, Dorsa Djalilzadeh, and Crystal Song.

The ongoing support of the CUNY Graduate Center has been essential for supporting the editorial assistant positions and the newest social media assistant position. Thank you to the Office of the Provost at the CUNY Graduate Center for continued support of the editorial assistant positions. We would also like to extend a very special thank you to Dr. Dána-Ain Davis and the Center for the Study of Women and Society (CSWS) staff for the opportunity to expand the collaboration between *WSQ* and CSWS in the past few years.

Finally, we would like to recognize the generosity of the Office of the Dean of Humanities and Social Sciences at the College of Staten Island, the School of Arts and Sciences at Hunter College, and the Office of the Provost at LaGuardia Community College. The support of multiple campuses demonstrates CUNY's commitment to advancing women's, gender, and sexuality research both within CUNY and globally.

Jillian M. Báez
Associate Professor of Africana
   and Puerto Rican/Latino Studies
Department of Africana
   and Puerto Rican/Latino Studies
Hunter College
City University of New York

Natalie Havlin
Associate Professor of English
Department of English
LaGuardia Community College
City University of New York

Works Cited

Aggarwal, Ujju, and Linta Varghese. 2019. "Introduction." *WSQ* 47, nos. 3/4: 13–24.

Introduction

Ujju Aggarwal and Linta Varghese

In recent years, a diverse range of actors have emphasized the need to come together, to join forces in and against the context of escalating ecological disaster, permanent war and empire, violence against women, growing economic precarity, the prison industrial complex, and heightened state-sanctioned racism and xenophobia. On one hand, calls to come together can expand our political horizons by foregrounding the relationality of struggle that moves us beyond single issues and allyship. Indeed, unlikely, subversive alliances have disrupted power relations and in doing so, expanded liberatory paths and political futures. However, appeals to come together can also do the opposite and reinscribe structures and logics of hierarchical differentiation. For example, as scholars who challenge the limits of reform demonstrate, efforts that claim to contest structured inequalities through a joining of mutual interests are often circumscribed by their failure to uproot the foundations that have produced these injustices (Gorz 1964; Bell Jr. 1980; Gilmore and Gilmore 2008; Berger, Kaba, and Stein 2017). Likewise, feminist theory calls attention to the contradictory nature of collective action that does not transform power as well as the limits and significance of situated knowledge (Alexander 1994; Boris 1989; Collins 2002; Crenshaw 1991; Lorde 1984; Rajan 2003).

This volume's focus on the possibilities and limitations of coming together is rooted in our commitment to traditions of organizing that center the gendered dimensions of local and global structural violence. These have included struggles against settler colonialism and Black freedom, anticolonial, and internationalist struggles. This commitment informs how we approach our scholarship: educational justice for Ujju and domestic

WSQ: Women's Studies Quarterly 47: 3 & 4 (Fall/Winter 2019) © 2019 by Ujju Aggarwal and Linta Varghese.

worker organizing for Linta. In the United States, where we both conduct our research, domestic work and education have been sites through which the significance of race, gender, class, and region are articulated. They have also been sites where protracted efforts have expanded notions of citizenship, social reproduction, and solidarity. As scholars who have, to varying degrees, been involved in work to advance these struggles, we have noticed the increased promotion of tactics which foreground cohesion and mutuality as partial solutions to the crises in education and care. In our work, we questioned how these solutions, grounded in logics of voluntarism and pragmatism, might be indicative of a (Gramscian) commonsense that constrains our political imaginary; and what thinking through the contradictions that we encountered might illuminate about our particular historical conjuncture.

Linta began her research in the early 2000s examining domestic worker organizing in the South Asian community in New York City at Workers Awaaz, a now-defunct South Asian workers' center. Workers Awaaz emerged in 1999 from a rupture at the anti–domestic violence group, Sakhi for South Asian Women. This was caused by the perceived inability of the regional/racial identity "South Asian" (around which Sakhi mobilized) to adequately address the various divisions within the community, particularly the gendered class subjectivities produced through low-wage domestic labor, and the structural violence that shaped this. Once Workers Awaaz became an independent organization, leadership instituted bylaws cognizant of class divisions within the community, including one stating that no member could employ a domestic worker as the worker-employer relationship was a "naturally" antagonistic one, and thus antithetical to the organization's mission.

A decade later, Linta briefly worked at a national nonprofit, Hand in Hand: The Domestic Employers Network (HiH), which was part of the broader domestic worker movement in the United States. HiH focused on people who employed domestic workers, or domestic employers in the organization's parlance. Emerging in 2005 from an employer engagement strategy that was critical to the passing of the New York State Domestic Worker Bill of Rights, a campaign led by the member based organization Domestic Workers United, HiH eventually moved from an allyship model to one of mutual interest between the employer and the domestic worker. In this theory-of-change the two parties could come together through the shared experience of care—the giving of it and the need for it. This manifested most frequently in the mantra "quality care for the employer and quality work for the worker" and the oft repeated statement that we all have needed or will need care at some point in our lives. Both statements highlight the reality of interdependence that marked most human life.

While not diminishing the market and labor realities that structured the relationship between domestic employers and domestic workers, the frame of mutual interest sought to show that both parties could make common cause. Many feminists scholars of waged social reproduction have shown how domestic work taken up by women of color and immigrant women has played a role in racialized and classed constructions of womanhood (Palmer 1989; Duffy 2007) and continues to facilitate the entry of middle-class (mainly) white women into the labor market (or *productive labor*) through easing the burden of care work (Glenn 1992; Parreñas 2001). It remains to be seen if the focus on care—as an experience and need—can bridge this long-existing structural divide.

For just under a decade, Ujju had worked to build the Center for Immigrant Families (CIF), a neighborhood-based, member-led social justice organization of poor and working-class immigrant women of color and community members. Throughout this work, she grew increasingly curious about some of the contradictions she encountered in the course of their organizing. The school district that CIF organized in (and that Ujju later came to study) was one of the most diverse yet segregated school districts in the nation's largest school system, and one that provided the most choice, or options to parents about which public elementary school to send their child. In her work, Ujju traces the contestations over public schools that emerged in the aftermath of the great recession when a number of middle- and upper-middle income families re-assessed their finances and decided to switch from private to public schools in this district. While this migration was often narrated as an investment in civic life, the common good, and democracy, Ujju found that this period was characterized by intensified competition, consumer citizenship, and differential rights claims to the shared resource of public schools. These claims were undergirded by the production of raced- and classed-political subjectivities of motherhood, care, and citizenship and bound together by the contradictions inherent to liberalism's universalism.

Six years later, in 2015, the district hit a tipping point and became the focus of contentious zoning wars. In the context of the growing Movement for Black Lives, state and municipal officials and education policy advocates—along with a growing number of parent-based groups—clamored for solutions that might squelch the controversies that had garnered national and international press. What bound these various efforts together were appeals from and to largely white parents with economic wealth that if they made the right choice and did the right thing, no "harm" would be inflicted that might disrupt the security that they had assumed would mark their children's lives. As power brokers determined what types of changes were possible and legitimate, difference was rendered as something to be "addressed" through, for example, exposure to "others" and an overcoming of individual bias.

Bonnie Honig (2017) reminds us that public infrastructures such as education—"public things," as she puts it—have historically worked as sites of racialized dispossession. Yet, she notes, they also present a terrain of struggle over what our social relations and understandings of citizenship and belonging might be. As this case demonstrates, the role of the state in structuring the "fatal coupling of power and difference" (Hall 1992; Gilmore 2002) was obfuscated, thus contracting the terrain of struggle and reinforcing the enclosure, dispossession, and differentiation that racial capitalism relies upon.

It is from these experiences and inspired by the freedom dreams that have guided social movements—that we approached this issue.

We invited contributors to reflect on long-standing debates and theorizations about the limitations and possibilities of coming together by addressing some of the following questions: What historical formations and legacies of struggle can we draw upon to enliven contemporary struggles? What assumptions of subject positions—and exclusions—do calls to come together rely upon, and how, as Roediger (2016) propels us to question, might we make solidarity uneasy? What might examining efforts and appeals to come together through transfeminist critiques, Indigenous feminisms, Black feminisms, Marxist feminisms, third world feminisms, and/or U.S. women of color feminisms illuminate about specific political conjunctures? What subjectivities, affective registers, affinities, political formations, and temporalities are imbricated in calls to come together? What determines the possibilities or the limits of coalition or solidarity to enliven liberatory futures?

The responses that we received answered these queries through various disciplines and engaged a range of geographic sites and historical moments. They provide commentary on contemporary flashpoints ranging from attacks on reproductive justice; the prison industrial complex and its carceral feminist imbrications; the growing crisis of mobility and migration as well as heightened forms of exclusion in the context of global right-wing ascendency and nationalism; the possibilities that politics as embodied poetics might present as radical alternatives to the limitations of capitalism and liberalism; and emergent formations of self-determination, solidarity, and social reproduction.

We open the issue with artwork by Mildred Beltré. Her print *Azabache* adorns the cover, and her piece *Constellation 1*, made of crocheted human hair, follows this Introduction. Beltré is a Brooklyn-based artist who works in print, drawing, and participatory, politically engaged practice to explores facets of social change. These and the six other of Beltré's works that are placed throughout the issue are meditations on the structures and formations of power, histories, realities, and dreams that have shaped liberation struggles and social movements.

Gendered Violence / Gendered Crisis

The articles by Jennifer C. Nash, Renu Pariyadath, and Eman Ghanayem explore the gendered vulnerabilities produced by state-sanctioned, structural, and interpersonal violence, and what these vulnerabilities—and their attendant solutions—illuminate about articulations and formations of power. In her article, "Birthing Black Mothers: Birth Work and the Making of Black Maternal Political Subjects," Nash explores the current conjuncture in which the crisis of Black maternal and infant mortality in the United States has gained mainstream recognition. Drawing on ethnographic research with doulas, Nash explores what we might learn by taking a closer look at the discourse of crisis, how it is managed, and "how black women seem to only come into political view through their proximity to death"? As she cautions, we must consider how the increasing number of initiatives addressing Black maternal and infant mortality that position doulas as "agents of crisis-mitigation." In her article, "Unhomely Alliances: The Coalitional Possibility of Migrant Homes," Pariyadath illustrates how reconsiderations of spaces produced partially through notions of comfort and inclusion can move us toward nontraditional alliances. Through ethnographic analysis of the Indian diasporic organization, Association for India's Development, Pariyadath shows how two high-profile cases of violence against women in India—the torture and rape of Soni Sori, an Adavasi human rights activist, and the gang-rape and resulting death of a young woman in Delhi—challenged the organization's "imagining [of] home as a space of stability and comfort."

In "Colonial Loops of Displacement in the United States and Israel: The Case of Rasmea Odeh," Ghanayem employs discourse analysis to examine the linkages between Odeh's torture, imprisonment, expulsion from Israel, and her eventual deportation from the United States. Ghanayem develops the framework of "colonial loops of displacement" to join Odeh's experiences that span over three decades, and provides insight into the ways that the United States and Israel, as settler colonial nation-states, require the consistent production, exclusion, and expulsion of racialized and gendered subjects.

Border Crossings

The article by Ruben Zecena and the photo-essay by Mizue Aizeki turn our attention to migration, surveillance, and resistance on the U.S.-Mexico border. Each piece considers visual engagement with the border, a space that has long served as a site of imperial enforcement and nation building by the United States. In "Migrating Like a Queen: Visuality and Performance in the Trans Gay Caravan," Zecena explores the political strategy of coming together in and through border crossings that he terms "migrating like a queen," a "form of performative political intervention" that "consider[s] the fierce relationalities that trans women and gay men create in the process of migration." Zeneca examines the 2017 Trans Gay Caravan in order to consider the visual and performative strategies that the Arcoíris 17—as the group called itself—employed to disrupt the immigration and surveillance regimes that mark the U.S.-Mexico border.

The seven photos that comprise Mizue Aizeki's photo-essay, "Remembrance and Resilience: Resisting the Violence of the U.S.-Mexico Border," were taken between 2001 and 2005. These images, part of a larger series which focused on the thousands of deaths that occurred as a consequence of Bill Clinton's 1994 radical build-up of the border-policing apparatus, remind us of the long histories of opposition—and connection—that have always been present in the violence of borders.

Revisiting the Radical Potential of the National Welfare Rights Organization

In their piece, "The Radical Feminist Legacy of the National Welfare Rights Organization," Wilson Sherwin and Frances Fox Piven argue that existing scholarship on this movement has missed the radical tendencies which were practiced and deployed. Working from archival and firsthand accounts, the authors contest the centrality of gendered social roles to the NWRO's demands that previous scholars have highlighted. They argue that the movement's demands "forged a subversive feminist politics which . . . is deeply relevant to today's political landscape," including guaranteed income, social reproduction, and bodily autonomy.

As Sherwin and Piven's piece engaged in a rereading of existing scholarship, we invited Premilla Nadasen, author of two works on the NWRO and *WSQ* editorial board member, to compose a response. Through a focus on the politics of citation, Nadasen discusses what is at stake in the multiple feminist readings of the movement. The section also includes a brief response to Nadasen from Sherwin and Piven.

Insurgent Solidarities

Crystal A. Jackson and Mamyrah A. Dougé-Prosper engage questions of scale to consider how practices of friendship, mutuality, and reciprocity undergird concepts of solidarity and provide a foundation to the political potential of insurgent solidarities.

In her article, "'Sex Workers Unite!': U.S. Sex Worker Support Networks in an Era of Criminalization," Jackson draws on fieldwork and interviews from the 2010 Desiree Alliance conference to explore how the formation of support networks are a critical form of activism for sex workers. Through a detailed discussion of relationships that are built through friendship and knowledge sharing, Jackson argues that "emotionality and community" must been seen as "central to [sex worker] organizing and activism." Jackson also illustrates how "sex worker support networks are a vibrant form of resistance and care" that hold lessons for the contemporary labor and feminist movements.

Through her detailed examination of Limonade Women's Association for the Development of Agricultural and Craft Production's seed bank and transformation center, Dougé-Prosper proposes that the Haitian *konbit*, "a mode of nonmonetized exchange of labor and resources between family members and neighbors occupying a given territory" is an articulation of a solidarity economy. She asks us to consider the political possibilities and potential of "reconfigur[ing] woman, family, and nation in and beyond extractive zones." As she illustrates, these alternative understandings of kinship, gender, and belonging that are brought to life through practices of reciprocity and solidarity are far from new, but rather, rooted in "communalist practices [that] not only endured the plantation system, they weathered the so-called postcolony, the long durée of U.S. imperialism, dictatorship, and globalization."

Poetics of Embodied Politics

Turning to literary analysis, Jennifer Hayashida and Davy Knittle each consider embodiment as a method and site of knowledge that might indicate limitations as well as possibilities of collectivity, translation, and alliance. Hayashida, in her essay-as-poem, "*Tillsammans* Means Overlapping Edges, as in Tiles or Scales: *Feeling Translation*," begins with the translation, or the problem-question of translation as it relates to Claudia Rankine's 2014 book *Citizen*, to ask: What does it mean to see translation as a condition of being, and what are the politics—and practices—involved, or required, in turn, to translate that condition? Hayashida leads us through her exploration of these questions as she dwells on their implications, articulations, and feelings, "while also scanning the increasingly neoliberal, racist, and xenophobic terrain of the Swedish welfare state as a site for reading race in translation."

In "Public Sexuality and the Feminist Poetics of Redevelopment in Leslie Scalapino and Adrienne Rich," Knittle analyzes Scalapino's and Rich's embodied accounts of sexualized experiences of urban public space juxtaposed against the physical transformation of their cities. Through a critical examination of feminist anti-pornography activism, Knittle's work provides a lens through which we might understand urban sexual history and planning history as a coarticulation of one another.

Classics Revisited

For our classics revisited, we chose Critical Resistance and INCITE!'s (2006) "Statement on Gender Violence and the Prison-Industrial Complex." We reprint the statement nearly twenty years after the two organizations joined forces to issue a call to social justice movements "to develop strategies and analysis that address both state AND interpersonal violence, particularly violence against women," noting the need to develop shared analysis and work directed toward "build[ing] movements that not only end violence, but that create a society based on radical freedom, mutual accountability, and passionate reciprocity . . . based on a collective commitment to guaranteeing the survival and care of all peoples" (2006). Since the statement was issued in 2001, the work of both abolitionist organizations has inspired grounded work which has taken multiple forms and shapes. We asked three organizations to reflect on the impact of the statement on their work, and what praxis-based lessons they might add. The three responding organizations—Freedom, Inc., BreakOUT!, and Justice for Muslims Collective—work at the intersections of gendered and/or sexual violence to build anti-carceral projects in their respective communities, building upon the CR-INCITE! call to end state, interpersonal, and gendered violence.

As this volume goes to press, we find ourselves amid multiple local and global crises. In the United States, the buildup of the perpetual war machine, the manufactured crisis at the border, and the concentration camps in which migrants are being held must be understood as part of long-standing U.S. capitalist projects of imperialism, nationalism, and the carceral state. These developments are also part of the global ascendency of right wing power and its attendant structured violence. For example, the elections of Narendra Modi in India and Jair Bolsonaro in Brazil have further emboldened attacks on Dalit, Muslim, Black, poor, queer, trans, and other marginalized communities. In this context, clarity of intention and political purpose through which we come together holds even greater stakes.

We draw inspiration, most recently, from the Queer Liberation March and Rally organized by Reclaim Pride Coalition on the fiftieth anniversary of the Stonewall uprising. By standing in strong opposition to rainbow capitalism and enlivening the legacy of abolition and anti-imperialism that has grounded radical queer and trans organizing, the march—and the organizing that led to it—offers a powerful example of formations of coming together that signal a liberatory future. We hope that this volume contributes to that political project.

Acknowledgments

This issue, like all work, could not have been done without the support, insight, and labor of many people.

We would like to thank the *WSQ* general editors Jillian M. Báez and Natalie Havlin, whose guidance, patience, and encouragement were invaluable throughout this past year. Thank you to editorial assistant Melina Moore for your consistent and careful work at every stage of this process. We are grateful to prose and fiction editor Rosalie Morales Kearns and to poetry editor Patricia Smith for their keen eye, as well as to the members of the *WSQ* board for their suggestions which helped us sharpen our vision of what *Together* entailed. We would also like to thank the team at the Feminist Press.

We thank Mildred Beltré and Mizue Aizeki for generously sharing their artwork with us.

We are grateful to M Adams and Freedom Inc., Collette Carter and BreakOUT!, and Darakshan Raja and Justice for Muslims Collective, who took time from their already overpacked schedules and work to engage our classics revisited. Thanks also to Alisa Bierria, Mimi Kim, Soniya Munshi, and Lee Ann Wang for sharing your expertise and recommendations.

We are indebted to a number of friends and colleagues, as well as members of the *WSQ* editorial board, who served as peer reviewers. Thank you for your time and expertise. We also extend our appreciation for the time, work, and effort of our contributors.

We thank our colleagues at the Borough of Manhattan Community College, CUNY, and The New School, with special appreciation to Tania Aparicio for providing invaluable editing support.

Finally, we are indebted to the organizations and individuals we have worked with/continue to work alongside for their role—intended and unintended—in shaping our thinking. These organizations include: Center for Immigrant Families, Hand in Hand: The Domestic Employers Network, INCITE!, Parent Leadership Project, and Workers Awaaz (especially Shahbano Aliani, whose leadership was integral to the life of the organization and whose recent passing is mourned by many). We would also like to Nicole Burrowes, Eve Dunbar, Caroline Hong, Laura Liu, Corinna Mullin, Soniya Munshi, and Mitra Rastegar for your encouragement and critical feedback on this (and many other) projects. We thank Rupal Oza for her mentorship, support, and feedback throughout the course of this project.

And last but far from least, we thank everyone in the multiple formations of togetherness that we inhabit.

Ujju Aggarwal is an assistant professor of anthropology at The New School. She is currently completing her first book, *The Color of Choice: Raced Rights, the Structure of Citizenship, and Inequality in Education*. Her next project focuses on epistemologies of enclosure in relation to constructions of insurgent citizenship, urban spatial imaginaries, and visions for an urban commons. She can be reached at aggarwau@newschool.edu.

Linta Varghese is an assistant professor in the Center for Ethnic Studies at the Borough of Manhattan Community College. She is currently finishing a project analyzing employer engagement and the caring economy in the domestic workers' movement in the United States. Her prior research focused on domestic work in the South Asian American community and the economic cultures forged in the relationships between the Indian state and the Indian diaspora. She can be reached at lvarghese@bmcc.cuny.edu.

Works Cited

Alexander, M. Jacqui. 1994. "Not Just (Any) Body Can Be a Citizen: The Politics of Law, Sexuality and Postcoloniality in Trinidad and Tobago and the Bahamas." *Feminist Review* 48, no. 1: 5–23.

Bell Jr., Derrick A. 1980. "*Brown v. Board of Education* and the Interest-Convergence Dilemma." *Harvard Law Review* 1: 518–33.

Berger, Dan, Mariame Kaba, and David Stein. 2017. "What Abolitionists Do." *Jacobin*, August 24, 2017. https://www.jacobinmag.com/2017/08/prison-abolition-reform-mass-incarceration.

Boris, Eileen. 1989. "The Power of Motherhood: Black and White Activist Women Redefine the Political." *Yale Journal of Law and Feminism* 2: 25–49.

Collins, Patricia Hill. 2002. *Black Feminist Thought: Knowledge, Consciousness, and the Politics of Empowerment*. New York: Routledge.

Crenshaw, Kimberle. 1991. "Mapping the Margins: Intersectionality, Identity Politics, and Violence Against Women of Color." *Stanford Law Review* 43: 1241–99.

Critical Resistance and INCITE! Women of Color Against Violence. 2006. "Gender Violence and the Prison-Industrial Complex." In *Color of Violence: The INCITE! Anthology*, edited by INCITE! Women of Color Against Violence, 223–26. Durham, NC: Duke University Press.

Duffy, Mignon. 2007. "Doing the Dirty Work. Gender, Race, and Reproductive Labor in Historical Perspective." *Gender & Society* 21, no. 3: 313–36.

Gilmore, Ruth Wilson. 2002. "Fatal Couplings of Power and Difference: Notes on Racism and Geography." *The Professional Geographer* 54, no. 1: 15–24.

Gilmore, Ruth Wilson, and Craig Gilmore. 2008. "Restating the Obvious." In *Indefensible Space: The Architecture of the National Insecurity State*, edited by Michael Sorkin, 141–61. New York: Routledge.

Glenn, Evelyn N. 1992. "From Servitude to Service Work: Historical Continuities in the Racial Division of Paid Reproductive Labor." *Signs* 18, no. 1: 1–43.

Gorz, André. 1964. *A Strategy for Labor*. Boston: Beacon Press.

Hall, Stuart. 1992. "Race, Culture, and Communications: Looking Backward and Forward at Cultural Studies." *Rethinking Marxism* 5, no. 1: 10–18.

Honig, Bonnie. 2017. *Public Things: Democracy in Disrepair*. Oxford, UK: Oxford University Press.

Lorde, Audre. 1984. *Sister Outsider: Essays and Speeches*. Trumansburg, NY: The Crossing Press.

Palmer, Phyllis. 1989. *Domesticity and Dirt: Housewives and Domestic Servants in the United States, 1920–1945*. Philadelphia: Temple University Press.

Parreñas, Rhacel Salazar. 2001. *Servants of Globalization: Women, Migration and Domestic Work*. Palo Alto, CA: Stanford University Press.

Rajan, Rajeswari Sunder. 2003. *The Scandal of the State: Women, Law, and Citizenship in Postcolonial India*. Durham, NC: Duke University Press.

Roediger, David. 2016. "Making Solidarity Uneasy: Cautions on a Keyword from Black Lives Matter to the Past." *American Quarterly* 68, no. 2: 223–48.

Mildred Beltré, *Constellation 1*, 2014. Human hair, approx. 3 x 6 in. Image courtesy of the artist.

PART I. **GENDERED VIOLENCE / GENDERED CRISIS**

Birthing Black Mothers: Birth Work and the Making of Black Maternal Political Subjects

Jennifer C. Nash

Abstract: This paper traces three tensions that undergird contemporary doula practice: questions about training and professionalization, questions about the meanings of medicalization, and questions about the exceptionality of birthing. In all three cases, while doulas are called upon to be agents of crisis mitigation, particularly in relationship to black women, and to use togetherness to mediate obstetric violence, these tensions complicate efforts to "resolve" the crisis black mothers face, and at times further suture black maternal bodies to crisis, placing black maternal bodies as the space in need of remediation, repair, and transformation. **Keywords:** birth work, doulas, maternal health, reproductive politics

By all accounts, black mothers are in crisis.[1] In a 2018 *New York Times* article describing the "life or death crisis" facing black mothers and black infants, Linda Villarosa writes, "Black women are three to four times as likely to die from pregnancy-related causes as their white counterparts, according to the CDC—a disproportionate rate that is higher than that of Mexico, where nearly half the population lives in poverty—and as with infants, the high numbers for black women drive the national numbers." A few weeks later, the *New York Times* editorial board reported that black women delivering babies in New York City are twelve times as likely to die from childbirth-related causes than white women are, which is "triple the rate of white New Yorkers, and roughly comparable to complication rates in Sierra Leone" (2018). If this is the condition of black mothers, black infants fare similarly: they are more than twice as likely to die as white infants are. Villarosa starkly notes, "In one year, that racial gap adds up to more than 4,000 lost black babies" (2018). Here, the specter of "lost black babies" is

WSQ: Women's Studies Quarterly 47: 3 & 4 (Fall/Winter 2019) © 2019 by Jennifer C. Nash. All rights reserved.

not the result of black women's imagined pathological reproductivity—as infant mortality was often cast in previous eras—but newly described as the result of medical apartheid (see Lane 2008). The black maternal body has become a symbol—or *the* symbol—for the deathly work of antiblackness and misogyny, and black motherhood itself is constituted by its imagined proximity to trauma, injury, precarity—by its location as *the* crisis.

Lauren Berlant suggests we treat crisis as a genre, one which "can distort something structural and ongoing within ordinariness into something that seems shocking and exceptional" (2007b, 7). Crisis discourse performs its work by obscuring the quotidian and persistent nature of violence, treating it as a rupture with rather than a constitutive element of the ordinary. As black motherhood is increasingly situated as ground zero of antiblackness, as the Mothers of the Movement are increasingly the public face of Black Lives Matter, as the state increasingly describes black mothers as its most vulnerable citizens, black mothers have been increasingly sutured to crisis discourse, a discursive project that performs myriad forms of political work for the varied subjects who mobilize it. The genre of black maternal crisis organizes a variety of forms of political labor, ranging from biopolitical state efforts to regulate black motherhood, to black mothers advocating for health care that ensures their survival; from "baby friendly" hospital initiatives designed to promote breastfeeding, to women of color (WOC) birth workers organized around birth justice. Black mothers have been transformed (or perhaps have transformed themselves) into objects of "attention, compassion, analysis, and sometimes reparation" that echo earlier forms of more retributive state discipline, but here with a seemingly "compassionate" difference (Berlant 2007b, 761). While I critically interrogate the crisis discourse that surrounds black maternal bodies, my intention is not to discount the racial disparities in health care that have deadly consequences for black women and their children.[2] My desire, instead, is to understand how black women seem to only come into political view through their proximity to death.

In the midst of the "crisis," birth workers—particularly birth doulas—have become increasingly visible agents of birth justice as doula-assisted pregnancies have been imagined as successful not only in transforming birthers' perinatal experiences, but also in improving the health of mothers and infants (see Gruber, Cupito, and Dobson 2013). Doulas, particularly WOC doulas, are imagined to play their most politically and ethically significant role in the birthing experiences of black mothers who labor in a milieu marked by stark racial disparities and often deathly outcomes. In this article, I turn attention to WOC doulas who have become foot soldiers in a birth-justice movement rooted in black feminist praxis and increasingly supported by state actors invested in eradicating—or at least mitigating—the crisis. Put differently, I observe a moment where WOC doulas' efforts have been taken up—incorporated—by the state as a crisis-mediation tactic rather than as an oppositional stance that makes visible and interrupts the relentless tethering of black female flesh generally, and black maternal flesh specifically, to crisis. This process of incorporation is not, however, one of cooptation, but one where WOC doulas are increasingly working within state bureaucracies in the service of crisis mitigation. This is a movement which recognizes the endless threats against black life as beginning in utero, and which draws connections among state violence, environmental racism, nutrition, quality schools, and access to transportation, to craft a broad conception of the conditions necessary for black life to thrive. Under the auspices of reproductive justice, WOC doulas are increasingly recruited by community-based doula programs to transform the birthing experiences of black women. They disproportionately fill the ranks of pro bono doula programs which provide low-cost or free doula services to vulnerable communities, programs which have been celebrated by the state in the face of "crisis," even as that celebration unfolds with little or no compensation for the doulas whose labor is imagined as integral to preserving black life.[3] WOC doulas are increasingly hailed by the state as medical missionaries whose antimedical ethics and paraprofessional practices are precisely what is required to save the lives of black women and children.

In this article, I treat WOC doulas as actors who have put into practice—and brought into institutional visibility—a set of black feminist frameworks, including allegiances to reproductive justice, a commitment to black life, and an investment in care and love as radical world-making forms of togetherness. In so doing, they have effectively recast the maternal black body not as a medical or embodied category, but as a political one. For doulas, black mothers' bodies are symbolic terrain that reveal the proximity of black maternity to death, both underscoring the utter necessity of doulas' life-affirming labor and placing doulas' rhetoric surprisingly close to the state's rhetoric: for both, black maternal bodies are the paradigmatic site of crisis. This article argues that WOC doulas guide the production of the birthing black maternal body as a political category through a methodology of "togetherness"—the placement of the doula body in the birth room alongside the birthing body—as an imagined form of crisis mitigation. Here, the presence of another body in the birth room—a doula, an advocate, a trusted guide—is envisioned as something that can produce more equitable outcomes, particularly for black women and their children, transforming the birthing room from a space of death into a scene of life affirmation. Yet that same "togetherness" often shores up the black reproductive body as a site of both profound political desires and intense struggle, and helps to produce the temporality of crisis that doulas also attempt to ameliorate. This paper traces three tensions that undergird contemporary doula practice: questions about training and professionalization; questions about the meanings of medicalization; and questions about the exceptionality of birthing. These three tensions reveal how doulas' collective labor to "resolve" or mitigate the crisis black mothers face often secures the notion of black maternal bodies as in need of remediation and repair.

Laboring and the Politics of Professionalization

My analysis in this portion of the paper draws on twenty-three interviews I conducted in 2018 with birth doulas working in the Chicago metropolitan area. These doulas performed their work in a moment when Illinois was increasingly attentive to maternal and infant mortality rates, particularly in light of the state's Maternal Morbidity and Mortality Report (2018) which found that since 2008, more than 650 women had died of pregnancy-associated deaths in the state, and that black mothers were six times more likely than their white counterparts in the state to die from pregnancy-related complications (see also Bowen 2018a, 2018b). In 2018 a collective of state representatives and senators introduced the Mothers and Offspring Mortality and Morbidity Awareness Act (MOMMA Act) to collect data on infant and maternal mortality, and to establish statewide protocols for obstetric emergencies. That same year the state's Maternal Morbidity Report recommended expanded state engagement with pregnant and postpartum bodies, including universal home visits to all mothers within three weeks of birth, home-visiting programs for "high-risk" mothers, and state-funded doula programs for "high-risk" mothers. Then-governor Bruce Rauner applauded the efforts of the Illinois Maternal Mortality Review Committee, noting:

The work of the Illinois Maternal Mortality Review Committee is essential for reducing maternal deaths and improving the health of all women. I am proud that Illinois has prioritized this issue and, along with CDC, is setting national standards for reviewing and ultimately preventing these deaths. (Rauner qtd. in Illinois Department of Public Health, 2018)

In that same moment, Illinois invested in an array of efforts to ameliorate the maternal mortality crisis, including Illinois's Maternal Infant and Early Childhood Home Visiting Program, which supports doula programs in Illinois, and the Chicago Doula Project (run by the Illinois Bureau of Maternal and Infant Health and focused on providing doulas to pregnant adolescents). The state also supports nonprofit efforts like Health Connect One's community-based doula program (which has been replicated nationwide) and Ounce of Prevention Fund's doula-training program. Illinois, like a number of other states including Oregon and New York, has also recently seen proposed legislation for Medicaid to cover doula services. In short, this is an era where maternal and infant mortality has placed maternal health generally, and black maternal health specifically, squarely on the political agenda.

Despite the rhetorical investment in black infant and maternal health, it remains the case—both in Illinois and nationwide—that few state resources have been devoted to WOC doulas, the very subjects who are charged with saving black women's lives. New York City and Baltimore, for example, have begun recruiting and training doulas to work as a stopgap for dealing with the black maternal health crisis. New York's doula program—which was designed as a state response to staggering black maternal mortality rates—expands Medicaid coverage to include doulas, while Baltimore's program trains doulas to become "independent contractors" committed to ending racial disparities in infant mortality and maternal health, and as key symbols of a state investment in black maternal health, even as the state reminds doulas that they are performing a community service, and will be unlikely to earn a living as a doula.[4]

Though my interlocutors all identified as birth doulas, they labored under vastly different conditions: one works full-time as a doula in an agency she runs with two business partners; two work full-time through a combination of solo practice and agency work; and the remainder are engaged in part-time birth work and other full-time work, generally in feminized fields like childcare. All of the doulas I interviewed had worked—for varied amounts of time, and with different levels of commitment—in the city's volunteer doula program. The doulas performing birth work part-time specifically noted that they found it unlikely they could perform birth work full-time, noting that the biggest economic challenge of the work is that solo practice requires financial reserves to offset the sporadic nature of business. Moreover, the number of births they had attended and the amount of training they had completed varied significantly, and they had radically different relationships to the feminist birthing industry, a term I use to describe the array of trainings, techniques, and certifications that have proliferated under the auspices of maximizing birthing women's birthing autonomy and freedom.

I take this variation in experience as evidence of the paraprofessionalism of doula work, and I argue that the paraprofessionalism of the work—its capacity to evade and even refuse standardization—is precisely what allows many doulas to describe their labor as both radical and invaluable. When I use the term paraprofessional, I do not mean it as a devaluation of the tremendous physical, emotional, and spiritual work that doulas perform as advocates. Instead, I mean it to describe the lack of regulation and organization of a birthing profession that is increasingly hailed as the birthing innovation that will save black women and children's lives. Paraprofessionalism describes the "low-tech, high-touch" nature of doulas' work which emphasizes togetherness as a radical birth practice and as a practice of black survival. Paraprofessionalism also captures the fact that, while doulas emphasize that they are not medical practitioners, and often define themselves against conventional medical institutions, they perform the majority of their labor in medicalized spaces alongside workers whose professions are highly professionalized, including midwives, lactation consultants, nurses, and doctors. It is doulas' capacities to reside in medical spaces while maintaining minimal (if any) medical training that can make murky the relationship between birth work and medical care, a murkiness that is perhaps most profound—and potentially most dangerous—for birthing mothers.

All of the doulas I interviewed had participated in a two- or three-day intensive training, though the content of that training varied tremendously. Some trainings are led by formal organizations like Doulas of North America (DONA) or ProDoula, while others are led by community organizations or campus initiatives specifically designed to train WOC doulas. Most of the doulas I interviewed identified strongly with their training institution, particularly those that had elected community-based doula trainings or WOC doula-training initiatives, which were often imagined to index a commitment to WOC birthing bodies. For most doulas, the training was an experience of self-actualization, community building, and solidarity, more than it was an orientation to the physiology of labor, or the physical experience of birth. It was, then, an intensive introduction to togetherness as a central birth-work ethic. Faith, for example, a doula who labors as a solo practitioner while working full-time as a therapist, described her training as organized around "spiritual and emotional connection," and noted that it transformed a group of strangers into "doula sisters," women she still texts every day to discuss challenging births, to share "doula stories," and to exchange "affirming messages" (pers. comm., 2018). She noted, "You can read every book, but it's really just learning about compassion. I think you have to have it in you. You can read anything on doula work you want, but it's about having compassion." In many ways, Faith suggested that a robust doula training should not focus on "book learning," but should instead center ethics of witnessing and empathy, even as she paradoxically noted that a doula's most important trait—compassion—cannot be learned. Samantha, a WOC graduate student who had completed her doula training and understood the work as a "calling," also described the communal aspects of her training. "We began," she said, "by talking about how we were called to the work. Sometimes the calling comes in your dreams" (Samantha, pers. comm., 2018). Her training ended with newly minted doulas washing each other's feet, a profound symbol of birth work as a commitment to service. Like Faith's conception of training as a site of compassion, Samantha's training emphasized the ethics of doula work: a commitment to service, solidarity, and friendship.

Perhaps most controversial was the question of how much training should focus on the business of birth work. A number of doulas mentioned that one of the profession's main organizations—for-profit ProDoula—had become too focused on encouraging doulas to organize efficient businesses, and had lost sight of the compassionate ethics at the heart of birth work.[5] ProDoula's mission to help doulas become "entrepreneurs" and to "turn passion into a paycheck," distinguishes itself from other doula-certification programs by its heavy emphasis on professionalization and its member benefits, which include discounted printing, liability insurance, and networking events. In its emphasis on making doulas entrepreneurs, the organization is often cast as transforming birth work from a feminist intervention into a neoliberal business endeavor. Moreover, ProDoula's emphasis on doulas as *workers* often led its founder, Randy Patterson, to critique volunteer doula initiatives—the pro bono initiatives most closely associated with birth justice, and most often staffed by WOC—as undermining the economic viability of the profession by discounting birth workers' labor. While ProDoula's capitalist underpinnings were staunchly critiqued by many of my interlocutors, the National Black Doula Association's Training and Business Academy, which also trains doulas on how to advertise, draft contracts, and price their services, often evaded critical interrogation, perhaps because it explicitly sought to "empower" black doulas.

Despite WOC doulas' critiques of corporate logics entering birth work, some doulas noted the importance of professionalization to make possible the togetherness that doulas promise. Jasmine, a recently certified WOC doula who worked full-time as a massage therapist, described DONA's certification process as a "bit of a process," but felt it was ultimately appealing because "I want to be accessible to multiple moms and partners. The credentials look nice, you put the abbreviation next to your name" (pers. comm., 2018). For Jasmine, the "abbreviations" were imagined as something that would appeal to a wider clientele, and might even allow her to make birth work a viable profession. Similarly, Jasmine insisted that the DONA certification made her easier to find. While doulas often advertise on websites like Doula Match and Sister Midwife, professional organizations maintain searchable databases that allow clients to find local doulas with ease.

Community-based doula trainers—disproportionately WOC—often set their "community" orientation against the imagined corporate logics of organizations like ProDoula. Miriam, who works at a nationally recognized community-based doula training program, described community-based trainings as powerful because they "come from the people who will benefit from the learning" (pers. comm., 2018). While community-based programs are often cast as more radical than their "corporate" counterparts, it is worth noting that they are often far more demanding (Miriam's program required twenty three-hour sessions as opposed to the fourteen to sixteen hours of training required by many of the professional organizations). This particular community-based program emphasized its desire to train doulas to work in their own communities, yet emphasized—in much the same vein as bemoaned corporate models—that doulas are not volunteers. Miriam said:

> One of our central components is that the community-based doulas are employed, and preferably they are employed with a salaried living wage, not an hourly wage, not a per contact or a per birth wage, but with an ongoing, dependable, every two weeks or every month, the same amount you can depend on to live with, wage. We're not looking for people to be entrepreneurs or volunteers. (pers. comm., 2018)

Ultimately, the fight over professionalization was imagined as an index of a birth worker's politics: Is birth work simply a job, or is it an opportunity to be a guide on a mother's spiritual journey, to practice togetherness in the space of medicalized violence? If, as many doulas—particularly WOC doulas—indicated, one is "called" to birth work, then what is the place of a doula's desire for a wage in relationship to this "calling"? And how does a doula reconcile a desire to serve vulnerable populations who might not be able to afford birth work with her own need to survive?

If professionalization debates constituted a battle over the ethics of the work itself, doulas also debated the lack of standardization in the field. Doulas are outliers in the larger field of birth work. Midwives and lactation consultants, for example, require substantial training, certification, and licensure, and many doulas noted the costs associated with meeting credentializing mandates have made those professions largely unavailable to WOC. Miriam, who began her career as a lactation consultant, noted the "impossibility" of finding a black lactation consultant in Illinois because of the heavy cost of certification, demands which she felt had been imposed only to the benefit of the field's credentializing bodies. She noted, "Lactation consultants have a monopoly to the exclusion of other lactation support. Even so, it's peer counselors who are more effective. We actually got better outcomes with less credentials" (Miriam, pers. comm., 2018). Despite the efficacy of peer counseling, lactation consultants are privileged in the breastfeeding-consultant sphere because of their elaborate and expensive credentializing. Indeed, for some doulas, the growing visibility of doula work, including state efforts to imagine doulas as the frontline of black maternal health care, led to anxieties that standardization would be imposed. Miriam suggested that any push toward standardization would simply serve the field's professional organizations, not birthing mothers, and especially not birthing black mothers. She noted, "What happens with standardization is the one who can make the most money is the one who ends up on top. . . . Making everybody ascribe to one standard is oftentimes the enemy of true equity" (Miriam, pers. comm., 2018). Here, the threat of standardization is its erosion of "equity" and its exclusivity. Standardization undermines the field's paraprofessionalism, which for the doulas I described, constitutes the radical promise of the field, its capacity to labor in medical spaces while subverting medical logics, its insistence that physical pain can be responded to with pressure points, rebozos, and breathing together. For others, standardization threatened to undermine the historical and ongoing labor of WOC doulas who had performed their work as a community service and a spiritual "calling." As Harriet, a licensed social worker with two years of formal experience as a doula, indicated,

> I don't believe that certification means that you're qualified. A lot of people are doulas and they don't even realize they're being doulas. Your auntie could be a doula, as long as she's providing, somebody who is catering to you and not taking that power away from you in your birth moment, that's a doula. (pers. comm., 2018)

For those doulas who view birth work as a calling, the field's "radical" paraprofessionalism affords them the opportunity to select clients who match their ethics, namely those who are imagined as most vulnerable to forms of birth violence. Many WOC doulas articulated a preference for working with WOC clients, or described their "pro-black" orientation—a term Brianna used—as part of how they imagine their practice. Samantha, for example, noted that she had not worked with a white female client, and emphatically stated, "I don't feel safe with white women" (pers. comm., 2018). Sydney, a recent college graduate pursuing birth work for a few years before applying to medical school, suggested that WOC and white clients come to birth work with different agendas and aspirations, and that her practice aligned with the priorities of her WOC clients. She noted, "Women of color and queer birthers *need* a doula for birth justice. White birthers use doulas because they want boutique birthing experiences" (Sydney, pers. comm., 2018). And Imani—who splits her work between her solo practice and laboring for a birth-work agency—described her dislike of the agency's primarily affluent white clients, even as she appreciated the steadiness of the work. She noted:

[The owner] has completely catered to people in Laketown. She has catered to that demographic, that socioeconomic status. Those are the clients. Those are the attitudes about who I am, and what I am there to do.
It's especially for postpartum clients. It tends to be, like, I am there for
servitude. . . . With my own clients, I have only once had my client where
we have not become friends. (Imani, pers. comm., 2018)

Other WOC doulas indicated that the benefit of agency work was both
the steady income and a potential respite from the emotional demands of
birth work, even as multiple doulas described agency clients as the antithesis of who they had been "called" to serve. Harriet described her agency
clients as

the more anxious client, the more need to be in control of that situation and not wanting to relinquish that control. Whereas when I worked
alone—it's more personal. It's not client and a doula, it's like a friend. It's
more personal. At the agency, it wasn't personal, and that's what I missed.
I wasn't connecting in the same way I wanted to connect with clients. And
it just wasn't as fulfilling for me in the moment. . . . It got to the point where
I didn't even want to show up to work. (pers. comm., 2018)

One of the benefits of solo WOC doula practice, then, is the ability
to eschew professional (and medical) norms of distance and to embrace
the political potential of friendship with clients. Indeed, all of the WOC
doulas I talked to described birthing together as the beginning of an intimate bond, and for many, the friendships borne through birth constitute
the possibility of doula work to fundamentally remake black mothers *and*
black communities. Imani noted:

I see it as building that community. . . . A doula becomes your friend, your
midwife becomes your friend, then you have this vast network of people
who are constantly looking out and supporting you. . . . If you can have a
sister come with you every time you go to the doctor, things are very different. (pers. comm., 2018)

For Imani, the capacity to select black clients allows her to perform
birth work in the ways she deems most politically promising: granting
black mothers access to a nurturing and caring "community." What the

paraprofessional nature of doula work makes possible—even if not always economically viable—is a selectivity about clients that allows WOC doulas to work with birthing mothers in the service of community building and radical care work.

Ultimately, at the heart of the complex politics of doulas' paraprofessionalism is the elevation of doulas to medical missionaries in the face of "crisis." The state has increasingly latched on to doulas as the solution to the problem of black maternal and infant death. Yet it is worth interrogating why the state has outsourced black maternal and infant health care to underpaid and often minimally trained workers who are governed by their own hierarchical system—highly paid doulas laboring in white agencies are often able to sustain full-time doula work, and black solo practitioners generally must seek other employment to do the work they want. In posing these questions, I am not at all critical of doulas who engage in demanding physical and affective labor out of a genuine belief in care, togetherness, and witnessing as politically powerful, particularly for black mothers and children. Instead, it is worth us rigorously interrogating how doulas have become rhetorical devices for the state to gesture to a desire to ameliorate the crisis, all the while refusing to devote any substantial resources to safeguarding black life.

The Political Aesthetics of Birth

In this section, I move from the paraprofessionalization of the field and its relationship to doulas' social justice projects to doulas' collective productions of "good" birthing experiences. While I focus here on doulas' preoccupations with unmedicated births, it is worth noting that the feminist birthing industry has produced an elaborate taxonomy of "good" births, including the highly celebrated vaginal birth after cesarean (VBAC), unmedicated births, and "slow birthing," while the C-section is cast as the paradigmatic "bad birthing" experience, often because C-sections are presumed by doulas to be unwanted.[6] Unmedicated births are often imagined as the touchstone of doula-led birthing, even if not all doula-facilitated births are unmedicated. While most doulas used the terms "medicated" and "unmedicated" to describe birthing experiences, a few still used the term "natural" interchangeably with "unmedicated," capturing a collectively held perception that unmedicated births are the hallmark of the body's "natural" state. Indeed, all doulas emphasized a desire to treat pregnancy not as a time of unwellness that warrants medical intervention, but instead as a "natural" life process, one that should be treated with minimal medical intervention, and with a deep respect for the body's inherent knowledge and self-determination. While unmedicated births were the preference of every doula I interviewed, the rationale undergirding this preference varied. For some, an antimedicalization politic unfolded as a critique of medical capitalism that grounds itself in an insistence on granting birthers complete autonomy over the birthing process. Here, the violence of medical temporality inflicts itself on maternal flesh in the forms of epidurals and compulsory C-sections, and by a refusal to simply let bodies birth in their own time. At other times, the preference for unmedicated birth was rooted in a desire for the spiritual transformation of black mothers, and thus black communities, one that was imagined to only be made possible through "natural" birthing methods. In these cases, the preference for unmedicated births couched as a political commitment to togetherness—to a radical patience with the time required to let maternal bodies labor without intervention—actually contained an aesthetic preference as well. "Natural" birthing was imagined to produce more authentic and more "natural" forms of motherhood rooted in deep affection for black communities.

WOC doulas often cast the medicalization of pregnancy and labor as a particular kind of obstetric violence that disciplines black women's reproductivity. Brianna described how her doula practice is shaped by her own traumatic birthing experiences. She said,

> The midwife kept asking the same question. I got to wondering: Do you ask *all* of them that? About birth control, about a hysterectomy, about permanent birth control? I told you no, and you keep asking me. I told her I'm getting offended because you keep asking me and I keep telling you no. Do you ask white women that all the time? I'm only on baby number two. (Brianna, pers. comm., 2018)

For Brianna, it is the institutionalization of medical authority that allows medical staff—including midwives and nurses, medical practitioners who are often imagined to be feminist in their approaches to the birthing process—to encourage women of color to seek "permanent" birth control, that permits doctors to police what she termed "my plus-size, black woman body." Brianna's "pro-black" stance *requires* an antimedicalization stance since it is medicine that is the site of antiblack misogynist violence, the space that seeks to curtail black women's reproductive freedom. For other WOC doulas, critiques of medicalized births are also critiques of the violence imagined to be inherent medicalized spaces. Imani noted that she encouraged WOC clients to "seriously consider" birthing at home, and described how her own decision to birth at home was shaped by experiences of medical racism:

> I just started to play back every experience I've had at a doctor's office. It was never good. They made assumptions about me, maybe because I look so young: You don't know anything. Also, you're black. I was just, like, with all of that *plus* everything I had researched about infant and maternal mortality in the black population, I thought I don't want to chance it. . . . What's risky is for me to go in a place where I know I won't be respected. (pers. comm., 2018)

For Imani, home is cast as a site of black women's safety and control, and the hospital as a space of risk, a death world where black mothers have to guard their yet-unborn children and their own bodies' health.

For other WOC doulas, an antimedicalization stance constitutes a critique of medical temporalities. Sydney described conventional medicine as undergirded by an attempt to place all births on a normative timeline. She noted, "Doctors and nurses—with the exception of midwives—just think of all the things that can go wrong, and they preemptively treat it versus letting things happen naturally in their own time. . . . Physicians have time limits, they are taught that birth has to happen this particular way in a particular time frame" (Sydney, pers. comm., 2018). Here, medical time is imagined as a structure of discipline that seeks to align birthing bodies with dominant conceptions of time. Moreover, some doulas suggested that the hypermedicalization of birth allows doctors (and insurance companies) to earn money. Brianna noted that her own birthing experience taught her to see "dollar signs everywhere," with each pill and procedure wearing a price tag that she would ultimately bear (pers. comm., 2018). That many doulas also charge money for their labor is, of course, another tension undergirding birth work's antimedicalization worldview as doulas never cast their own needs for an income as part of "medical capitalism."

Doulas' critiques of medicalization also often unfolded as spiritual ones, analyses of unmedicated birth as a rich opportunity for self-discovery. For some doulas, medicated pregnancies rob mothers of an experience to recognize unknown strength. Imani said:

> If you have an unmedicated birth, or a birth without a lot of interventions, you get to see probably for the first time how your body can come through for you. Sometimes people compare it to running a marathon.... It builds this level of trust in something that's unseen and something you can't touch. (pers. comm., 2018)

Here, medicalization forecloses an important opportunity for mothers to recognize their bodies' inherent strength, to develop a kind of faith in "something that's unseen." This potential for self-actualization through pain is even more important for black mothers, since, as Imani noted,

> if you can birth your baby ... you feel like everything this baby needs, I got. I can do it. That changes the way you parent, it changes your family structure, it changes the way people's children grow up. It's for the mom, it's for the baby, it's for the community to be fully empowered. (pers. comm., 2018)

Unmedicated births empower black mothers to parent differently, with a fundamental sense of their own capacity and autonomy. They refuse logics of pregnancy as a time of unwellness and debilitation, and thus act as a larger catalyst for urgent forms of togetherness waged in the face of anti-black violence that threatens black life.

Unmedicated births, then, serve various kinds of aesthetic and political work for WOC doulas. The preference for unmedicated births is often articulated as saving black women from the "violence" of medical intervention, yet these births are also often hailed because of their imagined capacity to remake black mothers and black communities. Unmedicated births are a gateway into a different kind of sociality, the beginning of practices of togetherness rooted in perseverance. Unmedicated birth, then, is a training ground for cultivating a faith in what "can't be seen," precisely the kind of faith that black mothering in the midst of crisis requires. In this regard, unmedicated birth is both a crucial preparation for black motherhood, *and* a central metaphor for black mothering in crisis.

A Birth Like No Other Birth

If birth is a moment of intense self-discovery, many doulas advocated that their clients prepare for birth by imagining their ideal "birthing experiences." They noted that these desires vary—sometimes they are explicitly medical decisions (e.g., decisions about pain medication, when to cut the umbilical cord, if the baby should receive antibiotic eye treatment), and sometimes they are preferences that seem aesthetic (e.g., preferred birthing music, preferred lighting). The increasing expectation that mothers enter labor with a detailed "birth plan," a plan that takes on a particular urgency for mothers who seek to have unmedicated births, underscores just how much birth has been reconstituted as a space where mothers articulate their individuality. Even as doulas emphasize that birth plans are merely a statement of desires, and not a binding medical contract, the elaborateness of the template birth plans that doulas often provide clients suggests the detailed ways in which mothers are encouraged to "imagine" the birth they want. Crucially, then, doulas are instrumental in treating birth as a space that mothers *design*, in making explicit birth as a site of dense meaning making onto which mothers project—and hopefully realize—their aesthetic, physical, and political desires.

The conception of birth as deeply personal and politically significant means that doulas often emphasize how every birth is distinctive, particular, and unique, even as this exceptionality is described differently. For example, Camille, a doula with a thriving birth-work agency located in an affluent suburb, noted, "Every birth is different. I learn something from every birth. We're never just going to the same hospital and dealing with the same care team. The care looks different depending on where you give birth. It looks so different depending on where you go" (pers. comm., 2018). For Camille, the distinctiveness of each birth is rooted both in how each birth presents its own challenges and in the variety of forms institutionalized care can take. Camille uses extensive prepartum meetings to offer strategies for birth customization, for navigating birth's medicalization through a practice of personalization that does justice to the particularities of each birther's experience. She described how her investment in personalization was shaped by her first pregnancy:

> We were living in Millbrook and found out we were pregnant. We had no support and didn't have any family around. I was going in to my appointment with my provider feeling like, Why doesn't anyone want to know

anything about me? This is the most intimate experience of my life and no one seems to care what I want. (Camille, pers. comm., 2018)

The notion of her birth as "the most intimate experience" of her life shaped her commitment to asking clients "intimate questions" including "if they have planned their pregnancy, how they met their partner, and then getting into the birth stuff . . . especially if they experienced something in their past that might impact their birth experience" (Camille, pers. comm., 2018). For Camille, the intimacy of birth requires a close relationship between doula and mother, a commitment to "care [about] what clients want." In this light, the doula critique of medicalization that I described in the previous section is an indictment of normative medicine's refusal to recognize the particularity of maternal bodies and desired birth experiences. The labor of the doula, then, becomes to ensure the particularity of every labor, and to insist that what has become a medical process has stripped the "transformative" from labor. The doula's task, then, is to personalize labor, to craft a particular experience—in fact, Jasmine described a doula's key role in "producing good memories of birth; happy, personal memories a mom can look back on" (pers. comm., 2018). Here, the "boutique experience" that Sydney attributed to white mothers is transformed into a form of anti-racist justice that ensures that all birthers—particularly black mothers—are recognized as distinct birthing subjects.

While many doulas emphasized the particularity of each birth, for many WOC doulas, birth work underscores the deep "togetherness" of all birthing bodies, interrupting a narrative of the exceptionality of birthing experiences. Imani noted, "The way that I see birth . . . is very spiritual. When I'm working with mothers I try my best to remind them that yes, every birth is unique, but we are a part of this larger universe just like the plants, the other mammals, we are just doing our job in the chain of life" (pers. comm., 2018). For Imani, birthing's power comes from its capacity to upset narratives of our exceptionalism, to situate mothers in a larger "chain of life." Imani also emphasized that the power of birth is that it ushers black women into the collective experience of motherhood, one that is marked by the "seriousness" of dedicating one's emotional, affective, spiritual, and financial resources toward someone else. In this account, it is the ordinariness of birth that produces its radical capacity, and the labor of doulas is to urge birthing mothers to recognize birth as an ordinary moment when they are ushered into deep communion with other birthing bodies. This notion of birth as both ordinary and exceptional is a tension that WOC doulas were always navigating as they labored on behalf of black mothers, insisting on demedicalizing and deexceptionalizing black women's birthing experiences while also arguing for the fundamentally transformative nature of birth for black women and black communities.

Birthing Black Women's Bodies

This article argues that WOC doulas' labor interrupts the "crisis" facing black maternal bodies by using togetherness—the proximity of maternal and doula bodies—as a strategy of solidarity that exposes and remedies obstetric violence. And yet, WOC doulas' advocacy of togetherness often reproduces the ongoing cultural tendency to yoke black women's bodies to suffering in the service of uplifting and aiding them, shoring up the notion of black maternal bodies *as* the scene of the crisis. Here, doulas make "black mother" into a *political* category that stands in for woundedness, much as the state presumes "black mothers" (and black women more generally) are injured subjects, with the wound becoming the only way that black women generally, and black mothers specifically, come into political view. The labor of doulas, then, is not merely to aid in birthing, but to make visible black mothers' suffering, a suffering which also makes apparent the utter necessity of WOC doulas' labor. Put differently, WOC doulas make the case that black mothers need "bodyguards" in the space of the hospital as a tool of crisis mitigation. WOC doulas' important care work, then, can secure the idea of black women's bodies as in need of reform, rather than radically rejecting the myriad ways black women's bodies are called upon to symbolize and meaning-make, including in this moment where black maternal bodies are rhetorically gestured to as evidence of the unmattering of black life. In naming these paradoxes, my effort is not to critique the labor of doulas—I understand their work as rooted in fundamental desires to offer more equitable birthing experiences—but instead to map the contours of the present moment and the challenges it poses for black feminist theory as we contend with the materiality of medical racism and with feminism's institutional politics. My critical ambivalence about the present moment is marked not by a desire to disavow doulas' labor on behalf of black mothers, including their partnerships with the state in the service of protecting black maternal life. Instead, I argue that it is crucial that feminists interrogate how doulas are called upon *by the state* even as they are uncompensated by the state, as evidence of a state effort to ameliorate medical apartheid. Indeed, many of my interlocutors noted that the landscape of birth work had changed dramatically since Black Lives Matter, since the increased attention to black maternal and infant mortality, with Harriet noting, "It always takes a tragedy for anything to change" (pers. comm., 2018). And yet, her sense of the "change" was both positive (more WOC doulas serving more WOC birthing bodies) and anxious (a wide number of WOC doulas who could not earn a livable wage performing birth work, even as they were called upon to serve their communities). In other words, we must grapple with a moment where black women—both mothers and doulas—continue to perform symbolic labor for the state, allowing the state to gesture to a commitment to ameliorating the "crisis" while the conditions of the present persist. It is equally crucial that feminists grapple with how the state has invested in paraprofessional WOC birth-worker labor, rather than a wholesale reimagination of institutionalized medical practice, as the solution to black maternal and infant mortality. Despite the rhetoric of crisis and the state's symbolic efforts on behalf of black women, the struggle for black children and mothers to quite literally live is still exclusively and entirely in our own (underpaid or unpaid, largely untrained) hands. Indeed, the only bodies mobilized to care for black women's lives are other women of color, and that care is increasingly described not as work but as a "community service," as a labor of love, and thus as something that need not be compensated. The ongoing task of contending with the hospital, the doctor, or the insurance system, as *the* crisis—and not black women's bodies as the crisis—remains the site where feminist intervention is most urgent.

Acknowledgments

The Sexualities Project and the Faculty Research Grant at Northwestern University supported my research. Thanks to Samantha Pinto and Emily Owens, as always, for their careful reading of this work.

Jennifer C. Nash is associate professor of African American studies and gender and sexuality studies at Northwestern University. She is the author of *The Black Body in Ecstasy: Reading Race, Reading Pornography* and *Black Feminism Reimagined: After Intersectionality*. She can be reached at jennifer.nash@northwestern.edu.

Notes

1. My impulse is not to conflate "birther" and "mother," or to negate that various kinds of bodies both mother and engage in childbirth, but instead to think in specific ways about how the rhetoric of "crisis" and the feminist birthing industry each construct black women's maternal bodies.
2. For some examples of popular coverage of the racism that black mothers face, see McClain 2017 and Randall and Vembar 2018.
3. A number of metropolitan areas house pro bono doula projects, including the Chicago Volunteer Doulas, New York's the Doula Project, the Baltimore Doula Project, and the Minnesota Prison Doula Project.
4. Two states, Minnesota and Oregon, include birth doula services in Medicaid coverage. In spring 2018, New York Governor Andrew Cuomo piloted a program to expand Medicaid coverage for doulas in New York. In his public statement broadcast on New York news stations and transcribed on the Governor's website, Cuomo noted, "Maternal mortality should not be a fear anyone in New York should have to face in the twenty-first century. We are taking aggressive action to break down barriers that prevent women from getting the prenatal care and information they need." As of the writing of this article, the New York State Department of Health still has not begun its doula program.
5. For more information on ProDoula, a for-profit doula company, see Baker 2017.
6. Birth-justice advocates have treated C-sections as a crucial site in the reproduction of medical apartheid, as black women have the highest C-section rates in the United States. In 2010 *Time* magazine reported that "in 2008, black women had more C-sections than any other group—34.5% delivered via cesarean in contrast to 32% of whites and 31% of Hispanics," and found that there was no medical reason for the racially disparate C-section rates (Rochman 2010). There have been recent popular attempts to make visible desired C-sections. See, for example, Mae 2014; Jones 2018; and Prentis 2016, 2017.

Works Cited

Baker, Katie J. M. 2017. "This Controversial Company Wants to Disrupt the Birth World." *BuzzFeed*, January 4, 2017. https://www.buzzfeednews.com/article/katiejmbaker/doula-drama.

Berlant, Lauren. 2007a. "Slow Death (Sovereignty, Obesity, Lateral Agency)." *Critical Inquiry* 33, no. 4: 754–80.

———. 2007b. *Cruel Optimism*. Durham, NC: Duke University Press.

Bowen, Alison. 2018a. "Too Many New Moms are Dying. Illinois Health Officials Are Trying to Understand Why." *Chicago Tribune*, August 7, 2018. https://www.chicagotribune.com/lifestyles/ct-hlth-maternal-mortality-mothers-dying-illinois-20180727-story.html.

———. 2018b. "Black Moms in Illinois 6 Times More Likely to Die from Pregnancy Related Conditions," *Chicago Tribune*, October 19, 2018. https://www.chicagotribune.com/lifestyles/ct-life-black-women-mortality-childbirth-20181018-story.html.

Editorial Board. 2018. "Easing the Dangers of Childbirth for Black Women." *New York Times*, April 20, 2018. https://www.nytimes.com/2018/04/20/opinion/childbirth-black-women-mortality.html.

Gruber, Kenneth J., Susan H. Cupito, and Christina F. Dobson. 2013. "Impact of Doulas on Healthy Birth Outcomes." *Journal of Perinatal Education* 22, no. 1: 49–58.

Illinois Department of Public Health. 2018. "Maternal Morbidity and Mortality Report." http://dph.illinois.gov/sites/default/files/publications/publicationsowhmaternalmorbiditymortalityreport112018.pdf.

Jones, Honor. 2018. "Not Every C-Section Is a Bad Birth Story." *New York Times*, October 27, 2018. https://www.nytimes.com/2018/10/27/opinion/sunday/c-section-risks-rates.html.

Lane, Sandra D. 2008. *Why Are Our Babies Dying? Pregnancy, Birth, and Death in America*. New York: Routledge.

Mae, Kristin. 2014. "Why I'd Rather Give Birth Via C-Section." *HuffPost Life*, November 6, 2018. https://www.huffpost.com/entry/why-id-rather-give-birth-via-c-section_b_6104136?ncid=fcbklnkushpmg00000037.

McClain, Dani. 2017. "What It's Like to Be Black and Pregnant When You Know How Dangerous That Could Be." *The Nation*, March 8, 2017. https://www.thenation.com/article/what-its-like-to-be-black-and-pregnant-when-you-know-how-dangerous-that-can-be/.

Prentis, Nicola. 2016. "Why I Fought So Hard to Have a C-Section." *Cosmopolitan*, August 4, 2016. https://www.cosmopolitan.com/health-fitness/a62338/maternal-request-c-section/.

———. 2017. "I Gave Birth the 'Lazy' Way—& Why Wouldn't I?" *Refinery 29*, September 13, 2017. https://www.refinery29.com/en-us/2017/09/172050/elective-c-section-procedure-birth-story.

Randall, Kayla, and Kaarin Vembar. 2018. "Women in DC Face Obstacles at Every Step of Pregnancy and Childbirth." *Washington City Paper*, August 30, 2018. https://www.washingtoncitypaper.com/news/article/21020181/women-in-dc-face-obstacles-at-every-step-of-pregnancy-and-childbirth.

Rochman, Bonnie. 2010. "C-Sections on the Rise, Especially for Black Moms."

Time, December 20, 2010. http://healthland.time.com/2010/12/20/c-sections-on-the-rise-especially-for-black-moms/.

Villarosa, Linda. 2018. "Why America's Black Mothers and Babies Are in a Life-or-Death Crisis." *New York Times*, April 11, 2018. https://www.nytimes.com/2018/04/11/magazine/black-mothers-babies-death-maternal-mortality.html.

Unhomely Alliances:
The Coalitional Possibility of Migrant Homes

Renu Pariyadath

Abstract: Feminist scholars have argued that contesting the unity of the discourse of "home" is the foundation for building non-identity-based community. For many migrants, home is often a space one cannot return to, making it a generative site to study alliance-building practices that are not attached to similarity, such as a common nation or identity. Migrants and the multiple metaphorical and material homes they occupy allow for disruptions in imagining home as a space of stability and comfort. This paper focuses on an ethnographic case study of a diasporic organization to illustrate how the conscious and collective practice of questioning "home" allows for nontraditional alliances. **Keywords:** diaspora, discourses of home, privilege, discomfort, space, identity, coalition building, ethnography

On Memorial Day weekend in May 2012, over one hundred diasporic Indians from all over the United States converged in San Francisco for a two-day conference held annually by the Association for India's Development (AID), a nonprofit diaspora organization. The conference was winding down with "AID and Me," a humorous sketch featuring two fictional volunteers Evvar Reddy (Ever Ready) and Nevvar Reddy (Never Ready), who reflect on the question: "What can we do for India from the U.S.?" Nevvar and Evvar joke about a longtime volunteer who had returned to India and was having trouble engaging in campaigns and political issues that he had easily followed and participated in from the United States. He was instead entangled in everyday middle-class Indian concerns, and the dream of being more involved on the ground had gone sour.

The sketch, a conference staple, led to a lively discussion about the

WSQ: Women's Studies Quarterly 47: 3 & 4 (Fall/Winter 2019) © 2019 by Renu Pariyadath.

dilemma of not being able to engage in social justice issues while living a middle-class Indian life. An AID volunteer brought up the distance and disconnect between the "real" India and middle-class existence when one was on vacation in India, even for a short holiday. The volunteer related her recent experience at a project "site visit,"[1] during which she traveled to many locations in rural India in a comfortable, air-conditioned car. The car afforded her the opportunity to move swiftly in rural terrain within the limited time frame she had. This allowed her to grasp, firsthand, how grassroots projects that received AID funding worked on the ground. But it also made obvious her privilege, and structured the interactions she had with local project coordinators and the communities they served. A senior volunteer who was visibly upset by this dilemma added that cozy, air-conditioned vehicles had made it difficult for the middle classes in India to empathize with the ordinary Indian toiling in the heat outside. Through these observations, the volunteers suggested that privilege, for members of the diaspora and urban India, was located within the spaces they called home and felt comfortable in. These spaces, such as gated communities, were enclaves of privilege that enabled and also restricted practices of relating to Others, sustaining the power structure between the privileged and the marginalized.

Transnational feminism and postcolonial theory offer similar discussions about spaces of privilege and the relations they enable. In these scholarly discussions, "home" is often identified as a physical and metaphorical space of privilege that functions to permit as well as to barricade alliances within and between communities. This scholarship has often eschewed community that is based on essential identity, assumed similarities, or resistance against a common "ahistorical power structure" (Martin and Mohanty 2003, 20), pointing to the home as a space where the struggle of consolidated identities is evident (Grewal 1996).

Home is a similarly powerful concept in Indian diaspora studies. Within the Indian diaspora, many have documented an obsession with the cultural reproduction of home as a material and metaphorical space. Home has multiple connotations as a private space, as nation, and as an imaginary location that traffics differently in colonial and anti-colonial nationalistic narratives (George 1999). It also "represents multiple concepts for people whose consciousnesses are shaped by migration," experienced as the patriarchal home, the South Asian community, and the nation, thus complicating Western feminists' understanding of "home," "outside home," and state, as well as notions of "private" and "public" (Bhattacharjee 2006, 338).

This project points to the coalitional possibilities that arise when communities collectively inhabit the dis/comfort of categories that don't quite capture the lived experience of home. Using the case study of the Indian diaspora organization AID, I argue that home functions both as a space of comfort and struggle for AID members, and the collective recognition of and response to "home" as an unstable and fictional construction becomes the foundation for building more inclusive spaces and restructuring alliances. Specifically, I examine AID's responses to the torture and sexual assault of Soni Sori in 2012 and also the notorious Delhi rape case and mass protests in 2012 and 2013 to indicate the shifts these events precipitated in AID's conceptions of nation, community, and the patriarchal home, altering home-building practices in the United States. While Soni Sori's torture by law enforcement signaled to AID volunteers that the nation was not a space of comfort for all women, the Nirbhaya case in Delhi permitted a critical inquiry into how volunteers themselves inhabited multiple homes, foregrounding previously unexamined spaces and home-building practices. I show in this paper how both cases, and the publicity they afforded to the unsustainability of the Indian nation as a safe home for women, allowed AID as an organization to reimagine and reconstruct the spaces it had been creating for diaspora members in the United States.

Diaspora Home Building in the United States and in India
Gayatri Spivak (2000) distinguishes between the "old" Indian diaspora that emerged from the British imperial movement of labor to colonies and the "new" migration of people from independent India to the rest of the world. The old, "exclusive" diaspora and the new "border" diaspora are radically different in that, while the former transplanted cultural symbols and created "little Indias," the newer diasporas—with considerable support from the Indian state—continued to maintain networks of relationships with kin in India. Old diasporas, Spivak argues, were formed through "religious oppression and war, slavery and indenturing, trade and conquest, and intra-European economic migration," and new diasporas of transnationalism are formed through immigration and migration (2000, 4).

Although there has been Indian migrant presence in the United States since the 1800s, the 1965 Immigration and Naturalization Act lifted the system of quota and restrictions on immigrants of non-Western origin, provided these immigrants possessed the immediate technical and/or scientific expertise necessary to enhance the U.S. nation's labor needs. This significantly increased the numbers of the Indian community in the United States. Historian Vijay Prashad (2000) argues that the successful interpellation of Indians in the United States into a transcendental, essential spirituality worked alongside the group's "model minority" positioning to limit solidarities with other racial minorities. Bakirathi Mani (2012) adds nuance to the model minority discussion in her observation that Indians self-identifying as South Asian often buy into the framework of multiculturalism to better assimilate *as* Americans. Amid attempts to belong, the patriarchal home becomes a gendered space where women are burdened with upholding tradition and Indianness as opposed to Americanness. Im/migrants' cultural reproduction of an ideal India has sometimes, unwittingly, severed non-kin relationships in the United States, in the interest of occupying a position of relative legitimacy in the racialized host nation.

Critical development studies scholarship has also inculpated the diaspora's need to belong in the homeland and the consequential displacement of non-kin communities in India. Pablo Bose (2008) discusses the construct of the "Mythic Global Indian" that appears in government policies as well as real estate advertisements for luxury condominiums in Kolkata aimed at elite audiences in India and abroad. This discursive construction acts to mobilize both people in the Bengali-Indian diaspora and those in urban elite India who aspire to be like the diaspora. The two groups materially shape prime real estate in the global city while concealing the displacement of populations that used to occupy these spaces. Bose's work indicates that, fueled by the need to belong, sections of the Indian diaspora that migrated to the United States after 1965 recover their "loss of homes" by buying property in the homeland. Thus, we see that diasporic privilege is complicit in and hinges on the exclusion and marginalization of particular nondiasporic groups.

Comparing the privileged migration of the Indian diaspora abroad with subaltern displacements due to development, Spivak notes that some "groups . . . subsist in transnationality without escaping into diaspora" (2000, 4). She defines "groups that cannot become diasporic" as those who have stayed in place for more than thirty thousand years (Spivak

2000, 4). Spivak, of course, does not mean that anyone who migrates from the "Third World" falls under the rubric of "groups that cannot become diasporic" (2000, 7). Women and other disenfranchised groups have never been full subjects in civil society, and Spivak maintains that this continues in the transnationalization of global capital and the concurrent lack of a transnational civil society. The privilege of the Indian diaspora in the United States, its practices of cultural reproduction, and how these practices determine whom the diaspora allies with both at home and abroad may also be understood through discussions about the politics of home within transnational feminism and postcolonial theory.

Diasporic Privilege and the Politics of Home

In the essay "What's Home Got to Do with It?" Martin and Mohanty (2003) argue that within feminist inquiry, conventional and unexamined reproductions of home, family, and nation have led to a severely restricted notion of community. Martin and Mohanty submit Minnie Bruce Pratt's essay "Identity: Skin Blood Heart" as a fine exemplar of feminist writing that addresses the concept of home as a space of comfort and the alliances fostered by such a space. Pratt's essay questions the validity of a "coherent, historically continuous, stable identity" by politicizing the "geography, demography and architecture" of the many communities we consider home (Martin and Mohanty 2003, 89). They suggest that home, in Pratt's text, functions as a material space as well as a metaphor for familiarity, safety, and stability. When Pratt discovers "local histories of exploitation and struggle" associated with places she called home, she realizes that she had shared these home spaces with invisible others who, unlike her, did not take for granted the safety and stability of these spaces (Martin and Mohanty 2003, 89).

Rosemary George's examination of the changing meanings of home and nation in postcolonial literature engages Martin's and Mohanty's analysis to include discussions of the home-country—a space of exclusion in which "some persons were/are/will be 'at home'" (1999, 11). George suggests that one's sense of "feeling at home" is conscripted into nationalist discourses to construct the fiction of safe homes, whereas in times of political turmoil home becomes a project of self-preservation. While nationalist discourses translate all invocations of home into nostalgia for the nation, George reads global English literatures to argue for moving beyond and rejecting such a singular construction of "safe homes." Pratt's essay offers some insight into how safe homes may be taken down—by intentionally recounting instances where "threats and protections" were used "to consolidate home, identity, community and privilege," thus exposing the process through which a coherent identity is produced (Martin and Mohanty 2003, 98). Similarly, George's (1998) earlier work discusses the significance of dismantling "the domestic" and of responsibly recycling domesticity by attending to the histories of its foundations and making visible all of its social arrangements.

Diaspora studies suggests that for diasporic people, constructing a coherent narrative of home is near impossible to accomplish. "Home" is a category that is continually built and rebuilt through efforts to approximate the everyday rituals one performs in the country of origin and/or the place of settlement. The everyday production of the unity of home is disrupted in the diasporic individual's traveling back and forth between homes, forcing the diasporic subject to attend to what Martin and Mohanty call "the exclusions, the denials, [and] the blindnesses" in constructing the fictional unity of home as nation (2003, 101). For people whose consciousnesses have been shaped by migration, home functions in multiple ways—as the nation, community, and the patriarchal home (Bhattacharjee 2006)—complicating Martin and Mohanty's notion of a movement outside home to repair the relational practices that homes structure. Being doubly or even multiply conscious of home as a place of terror/safety, dis/comfort, and un/belonging, for diasporic peoples, disrupting home would involve the continual destabilization of the many homes that migrants inhabit.

In the following pages, I discuss how the Soni Sori torture case in 2012 and the Delhi rape case and mass protests of 2012 and 2013 occasioned new alliances among gendered subjects in diaspora and also between diasporic communities and the Indian nation-state. I first offer a background of AID and its members to help contextualize the organization's position within the Indian diaspora in the United States.

Engaging Home as a Place of Dis/comfort

AID was set up in 1991 by Indian graduate students at University of Maryland, envisioned primarily as an organization to raise funds for development projects in India. Later, informed by interactions with partners in India, AID arrived at a critique of the hegemonic discourse of development. Currently, there are over one thousand AID volunteers across about thirty-five chapters. Of these, roughly half are located on university campuses, populated with graduate students from India. The remaining chapters are based in large cities, where the volunteer base is comprised of mostly working and salaried professionals.

At the central level, the organization has a board of directors (BOD) and an elected executive board (EB) that meet weekly on matters pertaining to the organization as a whole. Members of the board are responsible for leading and coordinating projects and campaigns, managing the treasury and fundraising efforts, crafting publications, and governing AID's chapters and volunteers. Hierarchy is flat across the organization, and central-level teams only lead the group with respect to their roles. AID had no paid employees until 2011, when it hired the first of its two development coordinators.

AID sees volunteer involvement as a three-fold engagement in *Sangharsh* or struggle, *Seva* or service, and *Nirman* or creation. While sangharsh involves supporting advocacy campaigns such as the *Narmada Bachao Andolan* and the International Campaign for Justice in Bhopal, nirman involves sustaining community-led alternative development projects. A majority of the project proposals seeking funding from AID are received through the group's network in India, sustained by five *jeevan-saathis*.[2] These are former volunteers now based in India and working on social issues full-time, supported by an annual AID fellowship. Seva includes a broad range of service related to fundraising. Chapters are expected to meet at least once a month for a Community Service Hour (CSH), which includes sangharsh, seva, and nirman activities.

I was an "active volunteer" with AID from 2011 to 2016, first at the chapter level and then as the organization's chapters and volunteers coordinator, an elected position on the EB. In 2011, after receiving permission from the organization for my multi-sited ethnographic research, I followed "connections, associations, and putative relationships" (Marcus 1995, 97) to map how AID *does* development and soon found myself *doing* development AID's way. I employed participant observation and qualitative interviewing of over forty members, and took detailed field notes across chapters and conference sites in the United States. I also drew from publicly available documents on the group's website, proceedings of annual conferences, and email listservs. I traveled to and gathered field notes at four annual AID conferences held between 2012 and 2015 in San Francisco, Charlotte, Boulder, and Austin.

As my fieldwork progressed, I took on more responsibilities at AID, which gave me nuanced insight into what volunteering with AID was about, and what was considered desirable citizenship, both within the organization and between volunteers and partner organizations in India. At conferences, I especially tuned in to the way keynote speakers from India would address the group with respect to its role and responsibility as members of the diaspora. In these moments, I noticed volunteers inserting themselves into the vision of India's development as "members of civil society" rather than as residents of the United States. When activist keynote speakers from India suggested that AID engage with South Asian and minority communities in the United States, volunteers would clarify that their mission involved contributing to India, rather than engaging in social change in the United States. Much research on Indian diaspora advocacy and community organizing focuses on groups and their identification as South Asians and immigrants, and their rights-claiming practices as U.S. residents and citizens (see Rudrappa 2004; Das Gupta 2006). However, in this paper I center an organization that, regardless of its members' country of citizenship, constitutes itself as an enclave of privileged Indians in the United States, with a responsibility to contribute to inclusive development in India.[3] To illustrate the coalitional possibility of engaging home as a place of dis/comfort, I first analyze the campaign against human rights violations that AID initiated on the occasion of Republic Day in 2012.

The Soni Sori Protests

In 2012, as India's Republic Day drew near, AID volunteers and other human rights activists from India expressed reasons for not celebrating the occasion. These volunteers and activists were outraged by the human rights and constitutional violations that had occurred in 2011. They were concerned about the central and state government's treatment of *adivasis* (indigenous communities) in the state of Chhattisgarh. Since 2005, three districts in this state, including Bijapur, Dantewada, and Bastar had internally displaced thousands of adivasis. These districts had become conflict zones with the Indian government's security forces, Maoist rebels, and state supported anti-Maoist vigilante groups wreaking violence on adivasis. Activists in India and AID volunteers in the United States were especially troubled by the Indian government's announcement of the 2012 Republic Day Gallantry Awards and the inclusion of Ankit Garg, a police officer from the state of Chhattisgarh, as an awardee. Garg was facing a Supreme Court lawsuit for torturing in custody an adivasi human rights defender named Soni Sori. A schoolteacher from Dantewada, Sori was arrested in October 2011 on charges of having associations with Maoist rebels, and was sexually assaulted and tortured in police custody by Garg and his subordinates. The Supreme Court was to examine Sori's case on January 25, the day before India's Republic Day, but did not.

A frustrated AID volunteer emailed the group to inform them about what happened:

> Soni Sori's petition did not come up for hearing today. Despite the last order on Dec 2nd . . . stating that it should be listed among the first three items scheduled to be heard today, it got listed as item 14. Tomorrow, the 26th is a holiday, of course, to congratulate ourselves on the Constitution. (pers. comm., 2012)

Through his email, the volunteer was calling to attention the glaring gaps between the fictional narrative of the nation constructed by the state and the lived experience of the millions whom the nation was unable to protect.

As a first step to protest the Gallantry Awards, AID volunteers across chapters petitioned the Prime Minister of India, the President of India, and the Chief Minister of Chhattisgarh with the demand: "Uphold the Indian Constitution! Defend Human Rights Defenders in India! Free Soni Sori!" The statement was endorsed by international organizations such as Amnesty International and about seven hundred individuals from around the world. In San Francisco, the AID–Bay Area chapter organized a protest and displayed on its website a call for volunteers to participate. However, volunteers did not undermine what the day symbolized for the Indians everywhere. Instructions accordingly requested that protesters follow decorum that suited the occasion:

> It would be good to keep the tone of the demonstration positive, since it's the anniversary of India adopting a constitution. We are campaigning to uphold rights of every citizen as ensured by the constitution. (pers. comm., 2012)

Thus, volunteers emphasized what the day symbolized—the adoption of the Indian constitution—making visible the ways in which the lived experience of violated communities exceeded the state's coherent and celebratory narrative of home.

On the twenty-sixth, a handful of AID demonstrators protested on the sidewalk by San Francisco's Palace of Fine Arts, where Republic Day celebrations were taking place, in solidarity with the cause of Soni Sori and other human rights defenders. They held signs such as "Torture is Illegal Unconstitutional and Wrong," "Life Liberty and Due Process, Article 21—Constitution of India," and sang "We Shall Overcome" and its Hindi translation, "*Hum Honge Kaamyaab.*" As several formally attired members of the Indian diaspora made their way to a celebratory event, AID members stopped them, related Soni Sori's and other human rights defenders' stories, and asked for help in petitioning the government to uphold the constitution. While protests were directed at the celebrations and members of the diaspora attending the event, a video of these events were uploaded to YouTube, inviting broader global audiences to see the apparent disconnect between the celebrations and the inability of the Indian state to uphold the constitution.

A few days later, on January 30, Martyr's Day, AID chapters in twelve cities held public protests, candlelight vigils, and information sessions to protest human rights violations in India. Protests identified recently instituted repressive laws, such as the law against sedition, the Armed Forces (Special Powers) Act (AFPSA), Chhattisgarh Special Public Security Act (CSPSA), and Unlawful Activities (Prevention) Act (UAPA), which were being used to silence dissent in India. Volunteers from AID-Boston, for instance, gathered in a public place for a teach-in and protest against Soni Sori's unlawful detention. Protesters chanted slogans against silencing dissent in a democracy, reminding the public that "Corporations are not People, People are People," and also read aloud a poem that Soni Sori had written from prison. The teach-in constantly reminded onlookers and the viewers of the YouTube video that Gandhi, a martyr, had stressed the importance of dissent in a democracy. They listed the recent repressive laws that had been introduced in India to book dissenters for sedition. In this way, the protest pointed to the discord between the ideals on which the nation was founded and the lived experiences of people living on the margins. Again, the protests inhabited the tension between reality and the fiction of the Indian Republic.

Another notable celebratory event that AID volunteers picked for their protests was International Women's Day in 2012. In early February, AID members received an email calling for volunteers:

> The idea is to put together two videos (in English and Hindi) of different people reading out one of the letters that Soni wrote from prison . . . and release the videos on March 8th, which marks five months since Soni was tortured . . . is around when SP Garg will be awarded his medal, and is also observed worldwide as International Women's Day. (pers. comm., 2012)

On March 8, after recruiting volunteers from across chapters, AID released a video montage of men and women reading Soni Sori's letters from prison in Hindi and English on YouTube (Peaceandjustice 2010). The letters were a graphic, first-person account of Sori's torture and sexual assault by Garg and his subordinates in the Chhattisgarh police force.

These various ways in which AID disrupted days of celebration exemplify how the category of home as nation is destabilized. Volunteers pointed to the discrepancy in the national narrative and in the nation's inability to protect human rights defenders. By renarrating the nation as a space of terror for adivasis, particularly adivasi women, and for human rights defenders, AID volunteers invited the broader diasporic community to consider the discord in the unquestioned fiction of the national home as a place of security, comfort, and belonging. However, in their effort to recalibrate the narrative of home, AID locates privilege squarely within and across elite urban India and the diaspora. Below, I analyze AID's responses to the Delhi rape case and mass protests in 2013 to illustrate that multiple homes and their shifting valences present opportunities for collective reflection. Witnessing the unraveling of home as a monolithic space of comfort for all citizens and inhabitants compelled AID volunteers to rethink the process of imagining and constructing home and community.

The Nirbhaya Case and Its Impact on AID

As 2012 drew to a close, media reports about the gang rape of a young woman from Delhi shocked the world. When the woman, who became known as Nirbhaya—or, fearless—died later from her injuries, thousands of protesters in cities throughout India took to the streets demanding stronger laws for rape deterrence and violence against women. Protests at multiple locations in the nation's capital turned ugly, as police teargassed, water cannoned, and beat agitators outside the parliament with batons.

The incident arguably gave rise to one of the nation's first organic people's movements across power divides. Middle-class Indians who had often held candlelight vigils to protest injustices that affected their own class organized around the pain and outrage of the violated working-class woman and her family, temporarily lifting a particularly opaque class curtain. The protests that followed gave privileged members of Indian society a glimpse into the terror an ordinary citizen endures in her everyday relation to the state.

Several diasporic cultural organizations across the Indian diaspora joined in the state's celebration of Republic Day in 2013, barely a month after the mass protests. AID, meanwhile, marked the occasion by holding vigils and discussions on gender violence and discrimination across its chapters. An AID volunteer wrote to the group's volunteer mailing list, proposing a day for coordinated actions in solidarity with the rape victim and protesters in India: "Jan 26th would be symbolically important because the Constitution is supposed to guarantee right to life and dignity regardless of gender, caste, class or race" (pers. comm., 2012). In 2012 AID had used days of celebration to focus on the national home as a safe space for privileged citizens, arguing that marginalized adivasi women like Soni Sori experienced the everyday terror of the same space. The Nirbhaya case, however, challenged this argument that located privilege and safety for women within the diaspora and in urban Indian cities. Although AID did not label actions planned for Republic Day as a "boycott," in 2013, it used the holiday and celebration to question the viability of the nation as a safe space for *all* women.

The Nirbhaya case and the mass protests in India also prompted women volunteers to question the safety of AID, their communal home in the United States. These volunteers began to express anxieties about being a community that sheltered similarity, shutting out difference within the diaspora. Their anxieties were reflected in the proceedings of the AID conference in 2013, with plenary sessions on caste, indigeneity, and women's rights. While diversity had been an ongoing concern at numerous conferences, the Nirbhaya case brought to bear a certain urgency, resulting in the initiation of changes and introspective exercises within AID's volunteer body. Below, I examine how the Nirbhaya case sparked a period of introspection within AID, leading to differently imagined homes and alliances among its gendered subjects and also between AID and the Indian nation-state.

Gender Equity as an Exercise in Remaking Home

In January 2013, I heard that a gender survey would soon be circulated among all AID members and expressed interest in observing conversations around this survey for my research. I was then invited to be part of the group that would design and analyze the survey. The survey group determined that the study would have two main purposes. The first was to examine AID chapters, meetings, events, conference calls, conferences, or any other forums where volunteers communicated, as gendered spaces. In particular, every volunteer was to report on who held power in these spaces, how much freedom male and female volunteers had to express themselves in these spaces, and steps that could be taken to make these spaces more inclusive. Secondly, the survey would serve as a tool for introspection for those volunteers who had never considered gender as an axis of power in their everyday life. The survey was anonymous and only required volunteers to identify themselves by gender (male, female, transgender, or other) and by how many years they had volunteered with AID. Following the theme of the Nirbhaya case, questions engaged volunteers on sexual assault, bystander roles, rape culture, gender role expectations in society and in intimate relationships, and gender role performance within AID. There were many apparent concerns undergirding the need for a survey, and the foremost among these was: If AID is a space of comfort, *for whom* is it such a space? In some ways, the survey was a tool to interrogate "the exclusions, the denials, the blindnesses" (Martin and Mohanty 2003, 101) that structured relations within the organization. Results from the survey were published in the February issue of AID's volunteer newsletter KoolAID and were discussed by individual chapters in their CSHs and at the AID conference that year. Gender equity became an issue of priority at that year's conference, where one of the keynote speakers Dr. Ilina Sen, a prominent gender studies scholar in India, spoke on the status of adivasi women.

Later that day, the Nirbhaya theme continued in a skit named "December Revolution," depicting the life of a typical middle-class family in India, scripted and performed by volunteers. In the skit, a family of five—two parents and three children—watched the evening news report about protests over the Nirbhaya case. The two older children were girls and the youngest a boy. The older daughter and her father got into an argument about the protests and how they could (or could not) be instruments for change, and more generally about the role and rights of women in society.

A guest, who had never visited before, arrived at the home. Ostensibly dressed in a lawyer's attire, the guest remarked to the father that he knew the youngest child would be a boy when he had first heard there were three children. The remark set off a tense situation and once the guest left, the mother disclosed to the family that she had had multiple abortions to ensure that her third child was a boy.

The remaining part of the skit engaged the issue of male child preference in India and tied it to the rape culture that had led to the nationwide protests supporting Nirbhaya, arguing for systemic changes through activism and introspection. To drive the point home, the women in the skit and other women in the audience joined together for a call-and-response protest song, demanding change not only in the district of Bastar in India (where Soni Sori was tortured) but also at "home." The skit and the song illustrated Martin and Mohanty's (2003) proposal to move outward to rebuild community, prompted by relational practices that had structured the patriarchal home in the past. At the same time, in this case, it is not an individual movement but a collective one, where everyone inhabiting the space of home, whether as a space of comfort or discomfort, came together to reflect on the communal home. The song at the end indicated that while changes were needed, and occurring, in India, it was also necessary to change current relational practices within AID and the Indian diaspora.

Immediately following the skit and song, the survey team debriefed the audience on the AID gender survey. During the Q&A session, a volunteer shared that her family back in India was seeking a dowry from her future sister-in-law. Arguing with her family about this had led to them excluding her from all communication about the wedding. Many volunteers sympathized with the volunteer and commended her for her brave decision to confront her family. This organically led to a call for the renewal of the anti-dowry pledge that AID had drafted and adopted in 2002, and all men in the room stood up, extended their fisted right hands, and pledged to never give or receive dowry. Another volunteer requested that we also pledge to oppose all kinds of discrimination and everyone rose to participate in this pledge. The message from coinhabitants of the communal diasporic home was that the structures upholding the patriarchal home in India had to be reflected on and dismantled, to make space for the (heterosexual) women inhabitants within home in the diaspora.

Finally, as the 2013 conference drew to a close, it was time for "AID and Me," the much-anticipated comedy sketch performed every year since the 2003 conference. The sketch predictably unfolded as a conversation between the two male volunteers Evvar Reddy and Nevvar Reddy. As always, Nevvar and Evvar roasted various AID volunteers and carried on their banter, but eight minutes into the sketch, Nevvar Reddy left the stage and a brand-new character, Newer Reddy, came on. Newer Reddy was a highly motivated volunteer but much younger than Nevvar and Evvar—and a woman. Evvar engaged Newer in a conversation about young volunteers who were always on social media and had different conceptions about development than did senior volunteers. Newer explained to Evvar that "many of us" grew up in a different time than "establishment" AIDers. Evvar demanded to know who was being referred to as "establishment folks." Newer described them as:

> . . . usually thirty- or fortysomethings, wearing long kurtas, attending more AID conferences than chapter meetings . . . and of course, overwhelmingly male. And whenever anybody brings up a new idea during a [Community Service Hour] or in an informal setting, these establishment crazies unfailingly offer an opinion on the idea. (pers. comm., 2013)

To this, Evvar countered that older volunteers were influenced by AID's founding members and reeled off a list of five jeevansaathis who always "had an opinion on everything." Newer was quick to point out to Evvar that all the jeevansaathis he had listed were male. AID also had three female jeevansaathis, Newer observed, two of whom were activists in the states of Madhya Pradesh and Bihar, and one who had revolutionized parenting techniques within AID by promoting breastfeeding, cloth diapering, and attachment parenting. Next, Newer made a metadiscursive move, drawing attention to the sketch "AID and Me." The two-person sketch, considered a primetime conference offering, had been a tradition for ten years, but 2013 was the first time a woman (Newer) was featured.

Newer: Evvar, you tell me how long it has taken to feature a woman in "AID and Me" . . . If I didn't know better I would have thought it's all about "AID and *YOU*"—the male AIDer. No, seriously, tell me. When you developed "AID and Me" for the first time, why were they both male and what assumptions did you make while bringing them to life?

Evvar: Maybe it's because only two guys would sit around pontificating

forever without doing anything. I think girls are far more practical
and deal with dilemmas in a much more practical way.

Newer: Nice try, Evvar. But look, all I'm saying is that even progressive
thinkers tend to have their blind spots . . . if we can introspect on our
blind spots we might find we have some in AID too.

Evvar: For example?

Newer: You know, simple things but significant, like, how many times
do you hear [about] a female volunteer's marital status in the chapter? Or suggestions about how [women] should cook more at pot-
lucks as they're better cooks? Or that [meetings] become more
interesting, when a new female volunteer joins?

Evvar: Never thought about it so deeply but I think you might have
something there. (unpublished transcript, 2013)

When Newer pointed out that "AID and Me" was written from a male
perspective, we see Evvar attempting to downplay the significance of her
observation by attributing to women the essential characteristics of dealing with dilemmas practically. Newer did not take Evvar's excuse for an
answer, and continued to press for introspection within AID and the need
to be reflexive about the subtle practices of sexism that permeated the everyday experience of being an AID volunteer.

Responding to the Nirbhaya incident, the 2013 conference was punc-
tuated with attempts to disrupt an AID volunteer's everyday participation
in systemic and systematic discourses of gender within its communal
home. The conference critically examined patriarchal practices within adivasi and also urban communities in India, had members in the diaspora
dissociate from the illegal custom of dowry, and urged AIDers to be reflexive about their practices within and outside the organization, all in order
to make AID a more inclusive space for women.

However, there still was room for improvement in how AID volunteers
conceptualized gender and a certain discomfort about discussing sexual
harassment. For instance, many of the attempts to interrogate and inter-
rupt continued to assume that the typical fe/male AID volunteer was heterosexual (e.g., not taking or receiving a dowry, when same-sex marriage
is still not legal in India). Aravinda, a Development Coordinator with AID
and a former jeevansaathi, spoke to me about the Freedom from Sexual
Harassment policy that women volunteers had proposed in 2010. The EB
had asked chapters to read, discuss, and comment on the proposed policy
but it was not at the top of anybody's agenda, Aravinda noted. In its final

version, which was voted on and passed at the 2013 conference, the word "sexual" was dropped and AID adopted the Freedom from Harassment Policy to cover "all forms of harassment." There was a lot of work to accomplish at AID with respect to making it a safe space for women. Being a vocal women's rights activist in India and within AID, Aravinda had heard volunteers sometimes refer to her as the "gender police." For many years, few women were elected to the EB, and even now there are fewer women on the BOD than men.

Conclusion

I have used this paper to grapple with the multiplicities of home engaged by the diaspora organization AID, and the relational practices that home, as a space of dis/comfort, enables. The special relationships diaspora has with home, defined variously as the home nation, the community, and the patriarchal home, is well-documented within migration studies. Orientations to these various homes have given migrant and diasporic groups purchase as citizens, forged new identities, and offered the promise of belonging. Much critical work on im/migrant communities has identified the preoccupation with nurturing a particular imagining of the homeland, suggesting that in assimilating to Americanness, the diasporic home becomes a space that sustains and reproduces gender hierarchies. While this scholarship offers a bleak outlook on diaspora's engagements with marginalized communities in the home and host nation, I use AID's case to demonstrate how diasporic communities also work to reconfigure traditional and restrictive narratives of homes and homelands. Several scholars have argued that privilege is made visible by interrogating the erasures that help produce the mythical unity of the patriarchal home as a space of comfort. This interrogation reveals home as a repressive space and also makes visible the political stakes inherent in and nurtured by it.

An im/migrant community is an exemplar, constantly at work in home building. Multiple im/migrant homes—the patriarchal home, community, and the nation—allow for multiple and differently situated consciousnesses about home as a space of comfort, to be constantly interrogated and refashioned. Soni Sori's torture by the state did not register a sizable national or international protest, arguably because of Sori's marginalized adivasi identity. AID seized this opportunity to argue against the fictional narrative of the Republic of India as a safe space for all women. At this stage, the implicit logic driving volunteer protests was: "For whom is India a space of comfort?" Volunteers did not initially consider the middle-class Indian woman as a particularly vulnerable kind of citizen. For women in India, the Nirbhaya incident offered the opportunity to rethink narratives about home, and protest the everyday terror experienced within and outside the patriarchal home. The incident and the mass protests called forth a political moment for AID and triggered a series of "introspective" exercises within the organization. Following the protests in India, AID began to focus on the question: "For whom is AID a space of comfort?" The gender survey and conference sessions helped identify the patriarchal home, the nation, and AID (i.e. the diasporic communal home) as spaces of comfort for some while violently excluding other gendered subjects.

What AID's case demonstrates is that not every interrogation of home necessarily responds to histories or to current disruptions by "moving outward" and rearticulating home. Rather than a movement between home and not home, Aimee Carrillo Rowe (2008) has suggested that the interstitial space between privilege and the margins is generative for building alliances. Through collective reflection, AID volunteers recognize their many homes as interstitial spaces. The impossibility of both nostalgia and an optimistic future presented by this diminishing interstitial space leads its inhabitants to see home as a fictional, constructed space that can be refashioned to be more inclusive. To put it another way, home here functions as the quilt and its patchwork in Gopinath's (1998) reading of Ismat Chugthai's short story "Lihaaf" ("The Quilt"), representing not a space of fixities but a space where multiple, alternative narratives and significations are possible.

AID's case also illustrates that not every interrogation of home requires meditating on repressive *histories*. Rather, witnessing changes in narratives of home as these changes unfold in present time could also trigger a reexamination of these spaces of comfort. Finally, while individual ruminations on the patriarchal home, nation, and community may well enable one to reimagine and reconfigure alliances predicated on comfort, the original constructions of home and their restrictive sense of community remain intact for Others inhabiting those spaces of comfort. Ultimately, AID's case illuminates that productively engaging the dis/comfort of home is a collective exercise, undertaken by every body that inhabits this home. We see then how spaces of comfort and exclusivity are not only constructed collectively but also collectively dismantled.

Acknowledgments

I thank Kundai Chirindo, Jeffrey Bennett, Jiyeon Kang, Meena Khandelwal, and Aimee Carrillo Rowe for their thoughtful comments and suggestions on earlier drafts of this paper. I also acknowledge the Office of Sponsored Awards and Research Support at the University of South Carolina Upstate for, partial funding toward the completion of this article.

Renu Pariyadath is an assistant professor of communication at University of South Carolina Upstate, researching social/environmental justice organizational strategies to resist restructuring in the Global South. She has a PhD in communication studies from the University of Iowa. She can be reached at renup@uscupstate.edu.

Notes

1. During the "site visit," a volunteer personally visits an AID-funded project in India and brings back a comprehensive report, which is used to review the project and make future funding decisions.
2. Jeevansaathi literally translates as "life partner."
3. Even though AID buys into the mainstream portrayal of the group as a homogenous enclave of privilege, there is considerable scholarship that challenges this narrative, such as Mathew's (2008) work on the New York Taxi Workers' Union and Das Gupta's (2006) study of labor activism among queer and lesbian South Asians.

Works Cited

Bhattacharjee, Anannya. 2006. "The Public/Private Mirage: Mapping Homes and Undomesticating Violence Work in the South Asian Immigrant Community." In *The Anthropology of the State: A Reader*, edited by Aradhana Sharma and Akhil Gupta, 337–55. Malden, MA: Blackwell Publishers.

Bose, Pablo Shiladitya. 2008. "Home and Away: Diasporas, Developments and Displacements in a Globalising World." *Journal of Intercultural Studies* 29, no. 1: 111–31.

Carrillo Rowe, Aimee. 2009. *Power Lines: On the Subject of Feminist Alliances.* Durham, NC: Duke University Press.

Das Gupta, Monisha. 2006. *Unruly Immigrants: Rights, Activism, and Transnational South Asian Politics in the United States.* Durham, NC: Duke University Press.

George, Rosemary Marangoly. 1998. "Recycling: Long Routes to and from

Domestic Fixes." In *Burning Down the House: Recycling Domesticity*, edited by Rosemary Marangoly George, 1–20. Boulder, CO: Westview Press.

———. 1999. *The Politics of Home: Postcolonial Relocations and Twentieth-Century Fiction*. Berkeley: University of California Press.

Gopinath, Gayatri. 1998. "Homo-Economics: Queer Sexualities in a Transnational Frame." In *Burning Down the House: Recycling Domesticity*, edited by Rosemary Marangoly George, 102–24. Boulder, CO: Westview Press.

Grewal, Inderpal. 1996. *Home and Harem: Nation, Gender, Empire, and the Cultures of Travel*. Durham, NC: Duke University Press.

Mani, Bakirathi. 2012. *Aspiring to Home: South Asians in America*. Palo Alto, CA: Stanford University Press.

Marcus, George. 1995. "Ethnography in/of the World System: The Emergence of Multi-Sited Ethnography." *Annual Review of Anthropology* 24: 95–117.

Martin, Biddy, and Chandra Talpade Mohanty. 2003. "What's Home Got to Do with It?" In *Feminism without Borders: Decolonizing Theory, Practicing Solidarity*, 85–105. Durham, NC: Duke University Press.

Mathew, Biju. 2008. *Taxi!: Cabs and Capitalism in New York City*. Ithaca, NY: ILR Press.

Peaceandjustice2010. "Reading Soni Sori's Letters from Prison: An International Women's Day Video Montage." YouTube video, 7:08, March 7, 2012. https://www.youtube.com/watch?v=UWnCrB1qwE4.

Prashad, Vijay. 2000. *The Karma of Brown Folk*. Minneapolis: University of Minnesota Press.

Rudrappa, Sharmila. 2004. *Ethnic Routes to Becoming American: Indian Immigrants and the Cultures of Citizenship*. New Brunswick, NJ: Rutgers University Press.

Spivak, Gayatri Chakraborty. 2000. "Diasporas Old and New: Women in the Transnational World." In *Revolutionary Pedagogies: Cultural Politics, Instituting Education, and the Discourse of Theory*, edited by Peter Pericles Trifonas, 3–29. New York: Routledge.

Colonial Loops of Displacement in the United States and Israel: The Case of Rasmea Odeh

Eman Ghanayem

Abstract: This article analyzes the legal journey of Rasmea Odeh, a Palestinian American woman found guilty of immigration fraud in a U.S. federal court in 2014 and eventually deported in 2017. In a previous life, Odeh was embroiled in the bombing of a supermarket in Israel, sexually tortured while under investigation, placed in Israeli prison for ten years, and deported from the West Bank in 1979. Using a comparative analytical approach, I argue that these two legal experiences subjected Odeh to a colonial loop of displacement—a global cycle of removals that implicate the United States and Israel as active and interconnected settler colonies. **Keywords:** settler colonialism, race, gender, displacement, Palestine/Israel

On November 10, 2014, Rasmea Odeh, a sixty-seven-year-old Palestinian American woman, was found guilty of immigration fraud in the United States District Court of Detroit in Michigan. Odeh was the associate director of the Arab American Action Network (AAAN), the founder of the AAAN's Arab Women's Committee (AWC), and had been living and working in Chicago since 2004. On October 22, 2013, the Department of Homeland Security arrested Odeh in her house and filed a case against her under allegations of fraud. She was accused of failing to disclose a past conviction of terrorism and a ten-year imprisonment by the Israeli government upon her entrance to the United States in 1995 and on her naturalization forms in 2004. The verdict issued on November 10, 2014—almost twenty years after Odeh's immigration to the United States—led to a one-month imprisonment and subsequent denaturalization and deportation in 2017.

Rasmea Odeh was an active and longtime champion of immigrant,

WSQ: Women's Studies Quarterly 47: 3 & 4 (Fall/Winter 2019) © 2019 by Eman Ghanayem.

women's, and Palestinian rights, and so her legal conviction shook many in these communities. Spearheaded by the United States Palestinian Community Network, the Committee to Stop FBI Repression, and the Coalition to Protect People's Rights, hundreds of Odeh's community members and supporters in Chicago and elsewhere started the Justice4Rasmea campaign and a nationwide call for action.[1] They signed petitions, organized rallies, and started a legal fund for Odeh's defense. They demanded her immediate exoneration and an acknowledgment of the harms inflicted on Odeh and, by extension, targeted minorities including Arabs, Muslims, immigrants, and African Americans. The campaign garnered the support of organizations like the Chicago Alliance Against Racist and Political Repression, Black Lives Matter, BYP100, We Charge Genocide, Survived and Punished, INCITE!, Jewish Voice for Peace, Code Pink, Voces de la Frontera, and National Students for Justice in Palestine, among others.

Odeh herself continuously noted these connections and reaffirmed how her experience brought her closer to these groups, specifically to women of color, with whom she shared a prolonged subjugation to state-sanctioned injustice. On March 25, 2015, Odeh gave the opening plenary at the INCITE! Color of Violence 4 conference. At the podium, she insightfully wove together her one-month imprisonment in 2014 with her prison experience in Israel in the 1970s. Odeh (2015) explained how these experiences are designed to instill despair:

> My incarceration [in Michigan] forced me to relive my experience in Israel prisons. While in custody, they tried to control every aspect of my life, my physical body, my mind, and it reached a point where I would not sleep, because I did not want to put myself in a position where I was weak and could be controlled. The whole system of incarceration is designed to destroy people's humanity and make them feel hopeless and in despair. I saw with my own eyes how the other prisoner women were driven to extremes, like screaming and shouting, just to feel like they were still human and still alive. Humans are social; to be in isolation not only cuts you off from other people, it also cuts you off from yourself. It destroys you emotionally, psychologically, and spiritually, and makes you feel as if you are no longer whole. This is the deadliest thing.

Odeh's words resonate with the pains of incarceration in the United States and Israel, and elucidate how in both contexts, she was forced into an isolation that overwhelmed her immensely. In a broader sense, Odeh is also suggesting that social separation and separatist thinking are outcomes, if not directed strategies, of the two settler nation-states that convicted her. Accepting them as normal, she tells us, is the "deadliest thing."

In this essay, I build upon Odeh's relational and political commitment to examine the connections between her criminalization in the United States and Israel.[2] I ask: What might these two legal cases—charges of terrorism in Israel and immigration fraud in the United States—reveal about the nature of exclusionary regimes? From this comparison, what insights can we draw about colonial displacement and its global manifestations? By way of answering these questions, I argue that Odeh's case represents what I describe as a colonial loop of displacement, a framework that conceives the United States and Israel as comparable and interconnected settler nation-states that rely on displacement—understood here as a range of practices that includes expulsions, removals, enclosure, imprisonment, and similar immobilizing tactics written as policy.[3] Both the United States and Israel were created by settlement, land theft, genocide, and a continued contestation of indigenous presence. They both practice legalities that have historically disenfranchised Indigenous populations and unwanted racial others. I refer to the United States and Israel as "exclusionary regimes" because as settler nation-states, they are built on obtaining and bounding land by all means necessary, establishing a nationalism that reaffirms itself in that practice, and criminalizing and denaturalizing those they perceive to be a threat to their existence.

Rasmea Odeh, as someone who was displaced by the two countries, can help us better understand the similarity of their biases and the recyclability of their brand of persecution that decides who comes in, who stays, and who is always to remain away—and to understand all as foundational to contemporary colonialisms. In addition, Odeh's grueling battle with U.S. immigration law proves her to be what scholar Mae Ngai (2004) calls "an impossible subject" in her examination of U.S. legal constructions of unwanted immigrants—those marked for deportation—whose humanity and citizenship are simultaneously disputed. Ngai's model reveals the problematic normalization of exclusionary policies, coded as "positive," that build on what the state construes to be "illegal" immigration (2004, 6). This state-mandated process of making people into noncitizens does not proclaim itself racist, dehumanizing, or biased. Rather, it structures itself on the principles of a proper citizenship whose safety and consistency is the moral end to all possible means. It is in that vein that we should approach Odeh's immigration case with great caution and with a suspended belief in what normally might be accepted as legal. As a Palestinian woman who stands at the intersection of settler colonialism, immigration, prison torture, sexual assault, and the global "War on Terror," Odeh offers a closer look at the multilayered nature of settler state violence, its reliance on a constructed legality, and its usual targets. To that end, this essay does not reinscribe the legal terminology used against Odeh, nor does it wish to make the case for her innocence. Rather, it intends to show why she was assumed guilty regardless of all possible vindication and the type of gaze that produced her as a terrorist, a prisoner, and a deportee in that order and twice in her life.

Rasmea Odeh's Story

To a large extent, Odeh's political status derives from her national background. She was born in Lifta on the outskirts of Jerusalem in 1948, a year on which nearly seven hundred thousand Palestinians were expelled from their homes so that the foundation of the State of Israel could occur. Odeh's family fled to Ramallah, a city in the West Bank, when she was one month old. Like other refugees, her family of seven lived in a small tent, then one room. At an early age, Odeh was politically oriented and involved in Leftist activism. It was out of that context that she was later assumed to be involved with the Popular Front for the Liberation of Palestine (PFLP), a Marxist party that was listed by the United States Department of State as a "Foreign Terrorist Organization" in 1997.

On February 21, 1969, the PFLP was accused of planting bombs in a SuperSol supermarket in Jerusalem that killed two Hebrew University students, Leon Kanner and Eddie Joffe, and wounded nine others. The young Odeh was implicated in that incident, as well as a bombing that took place in the British Consulate four days later. Odeh was arrested and placed in jail for forty-five days. Describing how she was taken from her house without an arrest warrant late at night and forced into intensive investigation, Odeh narrates,

> They asked me at once, "[D]id you put the bomb in the supermarket?" I said I knew nothing. They wouldn't let me dress so I just put a coat over my nightgown as it was raining. As soon as we got into the car they started slapping and punching me . . . Then they blindfolded and handcuffed me

and took me to a place that I thought [was] very far, because we drove for so long, but I learned later that it was the Moscobiya, the torture factory. (Miller 2013)

Moscobiya, an interrogation center in Jerusalem, is known for its unchecked, extreme use of torture. Odeh details her experience with the brutality at Moscobiya:

The first time they stripped me and threw me on the floor, the room was full of men—civilians and soldiers. They laughed at my nakedness and kicked me, beat me with sticks, pinched me all over, especially on the breasts; my body was covered with bruises. Then they got a wooden stick, not a smooth one, and pushed it into me to break the hymen. They brought my father and fiancé to see me. I lost consciousness and when I woke I was in another room, lying on the floor with a blanket over my legs but my body still naked. (Miller 2013)

The interrogation eventually reached a breaking point. According to one report of the events, Charlotte Silver (2014) writes, "Odeh's father was brought into a room where she was lying naked on the floor, and ordered to have sex with her. It was this threat that Odeh says finally coerced her to signing a confession." On January 22, 1970, Odeh was convicted for the two bombings and her alleged involvement with the PFLP. Odeh was sentenced to life in prison although she maintained throughout the trial that she was not guilty of these charges. In 1979, Odeh was part of a prisoner exchange deal between the Palestinians and the Israelis. She was released and removed to Jordan.

Decades later, this case would haunt Odeh, and she would find herself in 2014 pleading guilty of immigration fraud in the U.S. District Court of Detroit for failing to disclose this past conviction as procedurally expected in the United States. Her lawyers argued that Odeh's omission on her immigration forms was induced by the post-traumatic stress disorder (PTSD) that she struggled with since experiencing intensive torture and sexual assault. Odeh and her legal team demanded that they bring an expert psychologist to the stand to examine and evaluate Odeh, a request that was continually rejected by the court, until it eventually agreed to a new trial to take place in May 2017. Odeh and her legal team intended this psychological evaluation to take place not only to foreground her experience with PTSD but also to emphasize Israeli violence and its effects on her as a Palestinian woman. To circumvent Odeh's PTSD defense, the United States government filed new charges in December 2016, accusing her of being affiliated with a "designated terrorist organization," in reference to her past PFLP involvement allegations. Putting this legal journey to an end, Odeh decided on March 23, 2017, to accept a plea agreement that would protect her from going to prison on these new charges of terrorism and, in return, she was to be stripped of her U.S. citizenship. Her lawyer, Michael Deutsch, explained, "[The] government took a run of the mill immigration violation case and they made it into a terrorism case. . . . We knew that given the climate and given all the things the government was prepared to do, she was not going to get a fair trial around these charges" (Palestine Legal 2017). On September 19, 2017, Odeh was deported to Jordan after hundreds of her supporters from a myriad of communities and organizations bade her farewell.

A "Terrorist" Again: Odeh in Colonial Discourse

There is much to analyze about Odeh's story and the mistreatment she received throughout her life. I am particularly interested in how the language used against her manifest the constructs of race, gender, culture, and religion that her opponents used as identifiers of a perpetual (i.e., timeless) and boundless (i.e., including more than one country; global) Palestinian Arab Muslim criminality. In this section, I examine the dominant U.S. discourse that circulated following Odeh's arrest. Between 2013 and 2017, news coverage about Odeh's case totals approximately two hundred articles. Two surges in coverage occurred upon her conviction of immigration fraud in 2014 and the addition of terrorism charges in 2016, with the majority of analytical pieces circulating in news sources outside of corporate mainstream media, and next to nothing in papers such as the New York Times and the Washington Post. The majority of articles divided as follows: proponents of social justice causes who have not been afraid to publicly critique Israeli policy, and who largely published in outlets that have not censored Palestinian narratives like most U.S. news outlets such as Electronic Intifada, Mondoweiss, and the Chicago Monitor; and opponents of Odeh whose views align with attacks on Palestinian social justice and self-determination, and who tended to publish in journalistic organizations that exhibit ardent support for Israel and a bias against Palestinians, such as Legal Insurrection, the Daily Caller, and the

Times of Israel. The clear distinction between the two—and the explicit polarity of their language—provide ample material by which to study the discourse surrounding Odeh's criminalization. Opponents of Odeh devalued her community activism, refugee background, and experience with torture—which was highlighted in many reports—and instead opted for the nomenclature "terrorist," her alleged connection to the PFLP, and the bombing of SuperSol in 1969 as primary identifiers. Their overall patterns reflect how critics of Odeh could not but see her U.S. immigration case in relation to her political clash with Israel, and how they wanted that past to cast a shadow over her 2014 trial and preemptively instigate a renewed conviction of terrorism, or at least, lead the public into mistrusting her character and discrediting the story she tells.

To begin with one major example, in an article titled "Spinning a Terrorist into a Victim - Part 1 - Who is Rasmieh [sic] Odeh?," which was cited by many opponents, Odeh is described as "a Palestinian woman who slipped through the cracks" and who "has a bloody, dark side that she has kept hidden all these years" (IPT News 2014). The article initially featured a picture of Odeh, the black hood of her jacket covering most of her hair and her face showing signs of seriousness and aloofness.[4] Written by the Investigative Project on Terrorism (IPT), and incorporating the first of a five-part video series on Odeh, the article called her a "convicted terrorist" and described the Justice4Rasmea campaign as "aggressive" despite the lack of any recorded evidence to that end—though one can argue that, with or without evidence, aggression was assumed by the architects of this "investigative project" as either self-evident or as a potential threat equally steeped in Islamophobia. The video-makers stage a historical trajectory of Odeh's history of "terror." They select footage of various rallies which include, curiously enough, not only the Justice4Rasmea campaign, but also what they call the "Pro-Gaza" protests, which were organized to voice a U.S.-based support for Palestinians in the wake of Israel's 2014 attack on Gaza that resulted in the death of nearly 2,200 Palestinians. After showing footage of Odeh at one of the "Pro-Gaza" Chicago rallies, the viewer is told of her alleged immigration fraud and the campaign calling for her legal clearance. Juxtaposed with the high-toned, angry, and mostly brown supporters at the rallies are the calm and collected voices of the two brothers of Edward Joffe, one of the two Israeli students who were killed at the 1969 supermarket bombing. Joffe's two brothers speak of Odeh's inclinations to terror and claim that her supporters are "misguided" and delusional in their support. Their views are presented as unbiased and reasonable.

Alongside the peculiar choice of Odeh's photograph, the video carefully selects footage to reproduce a specific criminalizing gaze. Odeh's visual representation as it relates to the word "terrorist" in the title, as well as its repeated usage in the article and video, ushers readers and viewers into a possible misreading: Odeh's tired face, as contextually attributed to her arrest and week-long court proceedings, becomes an expression of hostility and aversion. Additionally, her partially covered hair fits the stereotypical image of the Muslim, Arab woman veiled and clad in black. This figure of purported religious extremism is commonly projected onto Middle Eastern womanhood in mainstream media. (Odeh does not wear the hijab in her daily life but looks like she does in the picture.) It comes as no surprise, then, that the video portrays supporters of Gaza and Odeh as one and the same, and predominantly as veiled brown women and bearded brown men. They are also presented as single-minded, aggressive, angry-looking, and loud in contrast to the performed civility and calmness of Harold and Basil Joffe, the unquestioned white Israeli settlers and designated victims, who are supposed to see Odeh and her presumed hostile character impartially.

Using popular stereotypes of Palestinians as aggressive, dubious, and perpetually foreign, articles in support of Odeh's indictment in the United States strongly connected these charges to her past criminalization in Israel. For instance, in "Detroit: Middle Eastern Jihadist Bomber Found Guilty of Immigration Fraud" (2014), Brenda Walker describes Odeh as "another reminder of how inept the feds are at barring the entrance of dangerous people into America." Using the same picture of Odeh with her hair covered, Walker criticizes what she sees as lax immigration laws that allow "Syrians with limited terror ties [to] be admitted." Her usage of "Syrian" here recalls a late nineteenth-century policy that used the orientalist misnomer "Syrian" to conflate immigrants of various Middle Eastern backgrounds under one national banner. Additionally, she further implicates contemporary Syrians, who are currently caught in one of the world's worst refugee crises, and who have been used in the United States to propagate the fear of hostile immigrants. Walker's article continues to illustrate a deeply rooted Islamophobic stance that puts Odeh, who immigrated six years before 9/11, in the context of the ongoing "War on Terror," and which necessitates seeing Middle Eastern subjects in and outside the United States as suspect. This simple equation implies that Odeh committed fraud because she is a terrorist, and that she is a terrorist because she is Middle Eastern. Throughout, the logic that enabled such association to become self-explanatory remains unquestioned.

Similarly, the article "Rasmea Odeh Gets Justice" with the subtitle "A Palestinian terrorist—and former Obamacare navigator—is caught for immigration fraud," Odeh's "evasion" of immigration laws, and her ability to briefly occupy a government job under the Obama administration, are seen as further proof of what writer Jillian Kay Melchior (2014) presumes to be Odeh's capacity to murder two Israeli students. Her certification as an "Obamacare navigator" is used as additional attire in the threatening depiction of Odeh. At one point, Melchior postulates, "It's not clear what would have happened if, for example, an Israeli American had gone to her seeking help with signing up for Obamacare, but imagine the possibilities" (2014). In this open-ended statement, Melchior is toying with the implication that Odeh would, in an unspecified way, threaten the livelihood of an Israeli American person. She is employing for herself and her readers an imagination that can freely authorize unchecked speculation: She might not help them? She might be irresponsible? She might harm them? The statement, though an offhand comment in what is rather structured as a journalistic exposé, reflects a discursive practice through which Melchior, and similarly the IPT and Walker, can freely omit colonial violence—whether in the fact of the Israeli Occupation, the horridness of sexual assault and prison torture, or the institutionalized racism embedded in the American legal system. What remains in their narration is selective evidence and biased conjecture built on the safekeeping of American and Israeli nationalisms and, even further, their intersection in the Israeli American figure that Melchior conjures as a potential victim of Odeh. It is no wonder, then, that the majority of Odeh's critics wrote within and through conservative media—the armored knight of nationalist culture and the vehicle that could freely propagate a fear of immigrants, Palestinians, and Muslims.

Gender, Race, and Colonial Loops of Displacement

To understand the colonial loop of displacement, one must recognize how the criminalizing discourse it recycles depends on the racialized and gendered nature of settler colonial management. When considering the language of the previous articles, I am thinking through interdisciplinary scholarship that intertwines an examination of racist language alongside critiques of empire and colonial violence, thus exposing the ways through which religious and national subjects such as Muslims and Palestinians, and Muslim Palestinians, are racialized and made inferior. As contended by the contributors in the 2018 essay collection *With Stones in Our Hands: Writings on Muslims, Racism, and Empire* and its editors Sohail Daulatzai and Junaid Rana, the global making of Muslim terrorism operates in the languages and practices of white supremacy, settler- and neocolonialism, and a persistent orientalism that demands an "unmodern" other or enemy to rehearse its modernity. Framing their collection as a political and intellectual dissent that metaphorically simulates the Palestinian act of throwing stones at Israeli soldiers, bulldozers, and watchtowers, the editors contend, "Regardless of the overwhelming imperial relationship that works to submerge the memory and presence of Muslims in the Americas, the history of anti-Muslim racism has seeped into the forefront of the American imagination to foment systematic forms of racism, sexism, xenophobia, and homophobia" (2018, xiii–xvi). Subsequently, the collection frames anti-Muslim racism as an overarching and historical phenomenon, while recognizing its origination in complex prejudice that involves non-Muslim others. Such approach participates in the growing scholarly commitment to global thinking, to a more comprehensive investigation of the intersectionality of harm, and to an informed demand for what one of the contributors, Rabab Abdulhadi, calls "the indivisibility of justice" (2018).

Echoing this move, I triangulate my approach to Odeh's case by putting into conversation the scholarship of Angela Davis, Lisa Cacho, and Shaista Patel. These scholars are an appropriate fit for this approach because they each discuss social devaluation in relationship to what the nation-state in its Global North formation prescribes as political dissent, deviance, and madness, as respectively addressed in their writings. As I later show, their scholarship assists in attending to the nuances of Odeh's narrative in comparative and global ways that can adequately incorporate Palestinian experiences within the wider implications of colonial discourse, particularly as a far-reaching tool that continues to overwhelm and transform the lives of multiple peoples around the world. It is important here to acknowledge that by seeking these different vantage points, I am inspired by Arab American women scholars who have made possible comparative discussions of Palestinian affairs within academic and activist circles in the United States, and in relation to racial struggles domestically and internationally. Seminal collections like *Food for Our Grandmothers: Writings by Arab-American and Arab-Canadian Feminists* (1994) edited by Joanna Kadi and *Arab & Arab American Feminisms: Gender, Violence, & Belonging* (2011) from editors Rabab Abdulhadi, Evelyn Alsultany, and Nadine Naber have confronted anti-Arab, anti-Palestinian, and anti-Muslim language within critical theories both before and after its proliferation around 9/11. Critiquing both American and Israeli discourse on Palestine, Arab women scholars and activists have highlighted "Arab American women's invisibility within progressive and feminist circles in the United States" (Naber et al. 2016, 107). These circles often shroud these women in a hypocritical gaze that sees them both as helpless victims of the men in their cultures, and as transgressors of American and Israeli civil orders when resorting to anti-colonial resistance and critique.

Taking all that into consideration, in order to understand the journalistic discourse that criminalized Odeh, it is pertinent to recognize its place in a larger network that would necessarily include questionable feminist writings on Palestinian women. In many ways, the representations of Odeh in media reports are strikingly similar to unchecked misreadings of Palestinian womanhood that circulate in some contemporary academic writings, and which equally coconstitute the larger context of racial bias that perpetuates the depiction of Odeh as a threat. For example, in "Martyrs or Murderers? Victims or Victimizers? The Voices of Would-be Female Suicide Bombers" (2007), scholars Anat Berko and Edna Erez attempt to analyze the "culture" that produces female suicide bombers. Berko, who is trained in criminology and currently a Likud member in the Knesset (the Israeli Parliament) and a research fellow at the International Institute for Counterterrorism, and Edna Erez, a professor in the Department of Criminology, Law, and Justice at the University of Illinois at Chicago, rely on a speculative methodology that sees innate and potential violence in a particular type of culture. Berko and Erez are writing within what Amal Amireh (2011) describes as an "ambivalence" around Palestinian women and the kind of motivation that drives them to a path of suicide bombing and, more generally, armed resistance. Though such motivation is directly articulated by Palestinian women as national and anti-colonial, Amireh contends that these women are usually painted as "[sometimes] veiled, sometimes in 'Western dress,' [their] body moves away from home, crosses borders, and infiltrates the others' territory. It is a protean body in motion and, therefore, needs a translation" (2011, 32).

The "translation" work that Berko and Erez undertake is ripe with problematic language. To begin, Berko and Erez's approach in investigating subjects they call "would-be female suicide bombers" relies on popular tropes around gender and family in Arab cultures, while refuting scholarly claims that suicide bombings constitute a form of resistance that consciously responds to colonial violence. Instead, these scholars blur the implications of the Israeli Occupation in the making of the suicide bomber, and instead locate their reasoning in Palestinian patriarchy and social ills:

> [Reasons] include the need to fight political subjugation, the wish to retaliate for the loss of a loved one, or they comprise responses to events that have touched people's lives as members of the Palestinian community. Resisting gender oppression is another reason that brings Palestinian women to suicide bombing. In a society where women are rigorously controlled and monitored, suicide becomes a way to remove gender-based shackles, or loosen their grip. Suicide is used to get back at uncompromising disciplinarian male family members, or as a way to relieve boredom, escape a monotonous life, and have excitement and thrills that young women in restrictive Muslim society are precluded from experiencing. (Berko and Erez 2007, 159–60)

Reading through Berko and Erez's conclusions, their discursive choices stand out as questionable and their consideration of violence reflects active omission. For instance, the "political subjugation" they speak of hints at the Israeli Occupation of the West Bank, but it does not name it. Rather, the authors leave that open for speculation and misidentification. Later in their article, these scholars use the word "colonization," yet they do not identify or critique it. Instead, they locate the problem in Palestinian society, presented here as fully agentive in its self-making. Ironically enough, the passive voice used to describe these women as "controlled" and "monitored" reproduces the subjugation these writers critique: they are subjugated to male control, and they are subjugated to the biased "translation" of these writers. In other words, these women, the "would-be female suicide bombers," are passive, even when they are spoken of as producers of violent action, and even by two women scholars whose essay starts with the promise of a feminist critique.

Berko and Erez's approach to armed resistance resonates with popular perspectives in the United States that dub political dissent as violent and anti-national, particularly in its physical forms. As prison abolitionist and scholar Angela Davis observes in her support of Palestinian rights, Odeh's case compares to "Assata Shakur's 2013 naming [on] the FBI's Most Wanted Terrorist List, US political prisoners who still remain incarcerated such as Black Panther Party member Mumia Abu Jamal and American Indian Movement activist Leonard Peltier, as well as the recently-released Cuban Five" (Davis Bailey 2015). Davis perceives state violence as the cause and origin, not the outcome, of public unrest. This approach aptly reflects the overarching argument that similarly binds critiques of police violence in the United States, of the Israeli Occupation, of the "War on Terror," and of colonial violence, past and present. In that context, the "resistance" aspect of armed struggle, often corrupted or misunderstood in Israeli and American settings, demands an answer to a question adjacent to Davis's well-known "Are prisons obsolete?": Is violence absolute? More specifically, what are the structures that push political dissenters, "uncivil" disrupters of state order like Odeh and Davis, into the path of armed resistance? Evidently enough, the essays on Odeh discussed thus far in their state-nationalist impulse disengage from answering such questions or approaching cultures of resistance through the eyes of their actors, not their persecutors. Erez and Berko offer no exception to that pattern.

Berko and Erez's perspective makes female suicide bombers a natural and inevitable occurrence, even as they, and the Israeli court system, maintain that the act itself is voluntary and, hence, prosecutable without dispute. Once these acts of armed resistance are emptied of their settler colonial context, all kinds of stretched speculations circulate without restraint. In an algorithm where the colonized subject is given inherent immorality and violence, any explanation, even one that sees that Palestinian women kill Israelis and themselves because they desire romancing Palestinian men (Berko and Erez 2007, 160), becomes plausible. More importantly, that algorithm entails that the native body, even when unnamed as such, is violent prior to and despite any colonial violence committed against it because of its assumed ontological rejection of civil order and its willingness to terrorize others. Under that colonial logic, there is no distinction between "female suicide bombers" and "would-be female suicide bombers." They are made to be one and the same.

To a large extent, the discourse of the "would-be female suicide bombers" recalls Lisa Cacho's (2011) insights in "Racialized Hauntings of the Devalued Dead" about the criminalizing gaze that predetermines the nature and worth of certain people. As she writes of the inscription of biopolitical value, and the efforts of the "dehumanized" to make themselves worthy of the nation-state's inclusion, Cacho writes, "Ascribing (readily recognizable) value to the racialized devalued requires recuperating what registers as deviant and disreputable to reinterpret those devalued beliefs, behaviors, and bodies as misrecognized versions of normativity who deserve so much better" (2011, 26). Cacho puts into question the normative (read: heteronormative) power structures that grant value based on the compliance of the human subjects to definitions of normalcy. In Cacho's framework, not only is that power structure violent in its projections, but the value that it ascribes and the logic it employs should be disregarded altogether. In settler colonial orders, such as those of the United States and Israel, the measure of deviance unquestionably and unapologetically implicates race, gender, and religion (among other identifiers), as they mark nonconforming bodies that exist below, and subsequently outside, measures of civility, humanity, and value.

Reflecting on the death and criminalization of her cousin Brandon Jesse Martinez, who died of a car accident at the age of nineteen and who was accused of mischief and coded by those around him as a "bad kid," Cacho gestures toward the larger historical context of criminalized Latino and nonwhite bodies in U.S. settler colonial space. Brandon represents one victim among many in the unmitigated dehumanization of racialized, gendered, and queer bodies and the pathologization of their difference. One can see a similar historical discourse around Odeh, as well as Palestinian Muslim women and Muslim and Arab Americans at large, who are implicated in acts of violence and psychologized as always terrorists. Returning here to Walker's article, her seeming misplacement of Odeh's "immigration fraud" in the context of post-9/11 and the U.S. "War on Terror" is no coincidence. Rather, this misplacement replicates the strong connections between the image of the "Palestinian suicide bomber" and that of the "Muslim terrorist," and their shared grounding in a racialized and gendered inheritance of deviance and incivility.

The process of criminalizing and devaluing Odeh in legal and popular contexts is meant to undermine her refugee narrative and humanity. In that context, the trauma that she has accumulated over the years remains outside the colonial boundaries of legible experience. The only psychological reading her critics and persecutors project onto her is the one that sees her through a racialized and gendered pathologization of violence. In her essay, "Racing Madness: The Terrorizing Madness of the Post-9/11

Terrorist Body," Shaista Patel (2014) traces the genealogies behind the creation of the "mad Muslim terrorist" in the Global North and its appearance in mainstream media, as well as what she calls the "racial logic" that pathologizes brown and black bodies and deems them inherently mad. She writes, "Race and disability have worked closely in the extermination of millions seen as bearing human otherness" (2014, 202). Approximating Muslims into racialized identification, and "[d]rawing upon nineteenth-century discourses of racist scientific categorization of the Self and Other, the West constructed Muslims into a distinct race, which allowed the Orientalists to make essentialist statements about the way Muslims necessarily 'think and behave'" (Patel 2014, 203). In that respect, their "madness" becomes a physical, understood as racial, property. Because of their "otherness," these "Muslims" exist outside the borders of respectability and sanity.

In the historical context of the U.S. "War on Terror" and the subsequent creation of the Guantánamo Bay Detention Camp in 2002, the "Muslim," because of their historical inscription as mad, becomes a "suspect of terror," and both are used interchangeably. In that sense, the colonial violence that continually marks people and women of color for incarceration, persists in ascribing human value even after their death, and projects a presumably scientific unfitness—according to Davis, Cacho, and Patel—is never publicly recognized as violence at all. The complications faced by Odeh's legal team connote the impossibility of comprehending Odeh's story and trauma within the American legal system. As Davis, Cacho, and Patel prove, violence, deviance, madness, and overall unfitness have always already been projected on people such as Odeh, consequently creating a prison of words and prejudgments that made her actual incarceration and continued immobilization possible.

The Loop Persists: Displacement in a Global Context

As scholars of settler colonialism and indigenous politics have argued, Israel is comparable to the United States, and evidently so in the discursive motifs of their national cultures (Warrior 1996; Salaita 2006; Salaita and Cheyfitz 2014). In order for their national myths to provide a pseudolegal grounding for settlement, the American Indian in the United States had to be forced into a narrative of extinction and absence. In similar ways, the Palestinian was rendered "nonexistent," as early Zionists announced to prospective Jewish immigrants that Palestine was "a land without people for a people without land."[5] The tropes of the dead Indian and the nonexistent Palestinian continue to inform the modern dominant rhetoric in the United States and Israel. For settlers in both spaces, the native was pushed outside the boundaries of legibility and sight. This is what Ojibwe historian Jean O'Brien (2010) has called "firsting and lasting" in her examination of how the settlers of New England were only able to see themselves as the native and rightful inhabitants of the land after they discursively, through formal and popular language, made American Indians "disappear." Here, this loop of erasing and replacing becomes a built-in process through which Israeli and American settler nationalisms reproduce themselves, the forced invisibility of those who constitute a threat to that order, and a penal regime whereby any escaped visibility is met with punishment and removal.

Odeh's story of displacement from her Palestinian home is neither new nor exceptional. Her transition from being native, to becoming a refugee, to then being named a terrorist in the Israeli legal system is also neither new nor exceptional. The view of Palestinians' inclination to violence and self-sacrifice has always been a staple of Israeli social and political discourse. Odeh's indictment for acts of terrorism by false association and her subjugation to torture to force a confession are commonplace in the Israeli judicial system. Her later exile through a prisoner exchange deal is in line with multiple expulsions that happened and continue to happen in a land where nearly half of its Palestinian population live in the diaspora. What stands out in Odeh's narrative, however, is the salience of the colonial loop of displacement. That is, her arrival to the United States warranted a similar process of displacement as that of her earlier life. Her migration to the United States in search for asylum, then her naturalization as a citizen, did not guarantee her protection. Upon detection of her political activity as an Arab community leader in Chicago who spoke against U.S.-supported violence in Gaza, Odeh was yet again labeled a terrorist, again put in jail, and again deported.

Understanding Odeh's experience through a colonial loop highlights displacement as a global condition cosigned, in this particular example, by Israel and the United States, but more importantly, by what these two exemplify: modern nation-states that depend on exclusion to validate their territorial and legal jurisdiction. That continued exclusion is part and parcel of their foundation, their present, and most likely, their future.

Understanding Odeh's experience in isolation or avoiding theoretical paradigms that could implicate the United States and Israel in transactional relations obscures that loop, and subsequently, the ways in which criminalization vis-à-vis racialization represents a global phenomenon. Here, Odeh's story exemplifies that structural operation. She brings into light the patterns involved in the making of settler states and their jurisdiction, and how much of that jurisdiction is predicated upon the ability to settle certain people and unsettle others, the right to remove people under pretenses of their possible threat, and to justify all of these actions as essential for the making of a safe home for its proper citizens. For that reason, Odeh exists as the improper subject, body, and narrative that is and will always be denied entry into the real and imagined spaces of settler homeliness.

In fact, in her most recent clash with national borders, Odeh was deported from Germany and her visa revoked after she was invited to speak at an event in Berlin on March 15, 2019. Organized by Samidoun: Palestinian Prisoner Solidarity Network, the event was meant to mark International Women's Day and introduce Odeh to Palestine and Boycott, Divestment, and Sanctions (BDS) supporters in Germany. Pressured by the Israeli Strategic Affairs Minister Gilad Erdan and the Israeli ambassador in Germany, the German government contended that Odeh's visit "could endanger Germany's relationship with Israel and threaten peaceful coexistence" (Hylton 2019b). Odeh herself has stated that the government's twenty-five-page report that justified her deportation contained "copied and pasted" parts of the news articles that smeared her character, including those from the United States (Hylton 2019a). This incident confirms the circularity of Odeh's displacement, but more so, it reveals the outreach and contagiousness of displacement policy and how it is continuously fueled by nationalist strategy and prejudice. In addition, criminalizing language remains in full force throughout these loops and their multiple geographies. For these reasons, an approach to that type of language in ways that consider indigenous narratives, settler colonial violence, the global formation of the modern nation-state, and the intersection of race, gender, and culture is of utmost urgency.

Odeh Talks Back

I return here to Odeh's (2015) words with which I began this essay: "The whole system of incarceration is designed to destroy people's humanity and make them feel hopeless and in despair.... It destroys you emotionally, psychologically, and spiritually, and makes you feel as if you are no longer whole." To feel no longer whole is a product of a continuous displacement that inhibits one's freedom and sense of fulfillment. The questions to ask here are how that kind of experience is created and how it continues to be a reality for many people. Odeh's story is one of many that unsettle the boundaries between migration in its legal definition and migration as a process of state-making that creates refugees and undesired peoples. Through the legal systems of settler states and their cyclical affinities, Odeh is locked in an infinite loop of displacement, just like multiple-time refugees, political prisoners, global terrorism suspects in Guantánamo Bay, undesired migrants in detention centers, and asylum seekers in constant transit across Europe—all suspended in a temporality that makes them movable and immovable simultaneously and as the state wishes.

It is, however, of equal importance to remember Odeh's active use of her intricate life to create a community committed to bringing together multiple narratives of oppression. Later in her INCITE! Color of Violence 4 Conference speech, Odeh describes how her imprisonment in Michigan helped her see the connections she had with the other women in jail (2015). Odeh's realization of how her experience intertwines with others under the U.S. judicial system highlights a decolonial perspective that aims to break loose from colonial loops and their alienating impact. Even as the United States and Israel imprison her within a spectrum of racial and colonial figurations and confined spaces, Odeh's humanist approach toward contact and dialogue and her embodiment of the true potential of collective solidarity have kept her afloat. When we understand Odeh's story in relation to nationalist regimes of displacement and their violent making of discursive and material boundaries, we can truly grasp the importance of investigating the circulation of identity, criminality, and belonging under continuing settler policies. As Odeh, her supporters, and critics of empire prove to us, the response to colonial loops of displacement, of racism, of global bias is informed solidarity. Only when we all come together can we become the force that breaks colonial loops and sets them straight.

Eman Ghanayem is a PhD Candidate in English at the University of Illinois at Urbana-Champaign. Her research examines Palestinian and American Indian literatures, and the larger context of global indigenous and refugee narratives, through a framework of interconnected settler colonialisms and comparative indigeneities. Eman can be reached at e.ghanayem@gmail.com.

Notes

1. A list of the organizations that were involved with the campaign and its inception can be found on justice4rasmea.org.
2. I borrow relationality as Indigenous conceptualization of solidarity and intercultural affinities from Jodi Byrd (2011, xvi), and Glen Coulthard and Leanne Betasamosake Simpson (2016, 254).
3. Most current research that critiques the United States and Israel, whether separately or comparatively, as settler colonial states is done in the fields of American Indian and Indigenous studies, settler colonial studies, and Palestine studies. On Israel and the United States as existing, yet loosely similar, settler colonialisms, the writings of Patrick Wolfe and Lorenzo Veracini remain the most widely cited. For analyses that see Israel and the United States as similar and interconnected settler colonialisms, the scholarship of Steven Salaita is particularly useful, as well as his collection of essays and responses with Eric Cheyfitz in the fall 2014 issue of *Native American and Indigenous Studies*. Outside of academic research, and especially within activist movements in North America and Palestine, the last ten years have witnessed an exponential growth in the use of the term "settler colonialism" when discussing American and Israeli politics together.
4. The article removed the image shortly after its publication (the exact date and reason are unclear).
5. A phrase popularized by advocates of Zionism, or Jewish statist nationalism, in the late nineteenth century. It is largely attributed to British author Israel Zangwill.

Works Cited

Abdulhadi, Rabab Ibrahim. 2018. "Palestinian Resistance and the Indivisibility of Justice." In *With Stones in Our Hands: Writings on Muslims, Racism, and Empire*, edited by Sohail Daulatzai and Junaid Rana, 56–72. Minneapolis: University of Minnesota Press.

Abdulhadi, Rabab Ibrahim, Evelyn Alsultany, and Nadine Naber. 2011. *Arab & Arab American Feminisms: Gender, Violence, & Belonging*. Syracuse, NY: Syracuse University Press.

Amireh, Amal. 2011. "Palestinian Women's Disappearing Act: The Suicide Bomber Through Western Feminist Eyes." In *Arab & Arab American Feminisms: Gender, Violence, & Belonging*, edited by Rabab Ibrahim Abdulhadi, Evelyn Alsultany, and Nadine Naber, 29–45. Syracuse, NY: Syracuse University Press.

Berko, Anat, and Edna Erez. 2007. "Martyrs or Murderers? Victims or Victimizers? The Voices of Would-be Palestinian Female Suicide Bombers."

In *Female Terrorism and Militancy: Agency, Utility, and Organization*, edited by Cindy D. Ness, 146–66. New York: Routledge.

Byrd, Jodi. 2011. *The Transit of Empire: Indigenous Critiques of Colonialism*. Minneapolis: University of Minnesota Press.

Cacho, Lisa Marie. 2011. "Racialized Hauntings of the Devalued Dead." In *Strange Affinities: The Gender and Sexual Politics of Comparative Racialization*, edited by Grace Kyungwon Hong and Roderick A. Ferguson, 25–52. Durham, NC: Duke University Press.

Coulthard, Glen, and Leanne Betasamosake Simpson. 2016. "Grounded Normativity/Place-Based Solidarity." *American Quarterly* 68, no. 2: 249–55.

Daulatzai, Sohail, and Junaid Rana, eds. 2018. *With Stones in Our Hands: Writings on Muslims, Racism, and Empire*. Minneapolis: University of Minnesota Press.

Davis, Angela Y. 2003. *Are Prisons Obsolete?* New York: Seven Stories Press.

Davis Bailey, Kristian. 2015. "Angela Davis & Rasmea Odeh: Connecting Palestine, Prisons & Police." *Ebony*, July 13, 2015. https://www.ebony.com/news/angela-davis-rasmea-odeh-connecting-palestine-prisons-police-495/.

Hylton, Riri. 2019a. "German Expulsion Based on Media Smears, Says Rasmea Odeh." *Electronic Intifada*, April 2, 2019. https://electronicintifada.net/blogs/riri-hylton/german-expulsion-based-media-smears-says-rasmea-odeh.

———. 2019b. "Under Israeli Pressure, Germany Revokes Rasmea Odeh Visa." *Electronic Intifada*, March 19, 2019. https://electronicintifada.net/blogs/riri-hylton/under-israeli-pressure-germany-revokes-rasmea-odeh-visa.

IPT News. 2014. "Spinning a Terrorist Into a Victim - Part 1 - Who Is Rasmieh Odeh?" Investigative Project on Terrorism, October 27, 2014. https://www.investigativeproject.org/4627/spinning-a-terrorist-into-a-victim.

Kadi, Joanna, ed. 1994. *Food for Our Grandmothers: Writings by Arab-American and Arab-Canadian Feminists*. Boston: South End Press.

Melchior, Jillian Kay. 2014. "Rasmieh Gets Justice." *National Review*, November 11, 2014. http://www.nationalreview.com/article/392513/rasmieh-gets-justice-jillian-kay-melchior.

Miller, Anna Lekas. 2013. "Prominent Palestinian-American Community Activist Arrested." *Daily Beast*, November 1, 2013. https://www.thedailybeast.com/prominent-palestinian-american-community-activist-arrested.

Naber, Nadine, Eman Desouky, and Lina Baroudi. 2016. "The Forgotten '-ism': An Arab American Women's Perspective on Zionism, Racism, and Sexism." In *Color of Violence: The INCITE! Anthology*, edited by INCITE! Women of Color Against Violence, 97–112. Durham, NC: Duke University Press.

Ngai, Mae M. 2004. *Impossible Subjects: Illegal Aliens and the Making of Modern America*. Princeton, NJ: Princeton University Press.

O'Brien, Jean M. 2010. *Firsting and Lasting: Writing Indians Out of Existence in New England*. Minneapolis: University of Minnesota Press.

Odeh, Rasmea. 2015. "Rasmea Odeh Speech to the Opening Plenary of the INCITE! Color of Violence 4 Conference." Justice4Rasmea, March 26, 2015. https://justice4rasmea.org/news/2015/03/26/rasmea-odeh-speaks-at-INCITE/.

Palestine Legal. 2017. "Rasmea Odeh: Community Leader Prosecuted." *Palestine Legal*, October 3, 2017. https://palestinelegal.org/case-studies/2015/3/10/rasmea-odeh-prosecuted.

Patel, Shaista. 2014. "Racing Madness: The Terrorizing Madness of the Post-9/11 Terrorist Body." In *Disability Incarcerated: Imprisonment and Disability in the United States and Canada*, edited by Liat Ben-Moshe, Chris Chapman, and Allison C. Carey, 201–16. New York: Palgrave Macmillan.

Salaita, Steven. 2006. *The Holy Land in Transit: Colonialism and the Quest for Canaan*. Syracuse, NY: Syracuse University Press.

Salaita, Steven, and Eric Cheyfitz. 2014. "Perspectives on the Israeli-Palestinian Conflict from Indigenous Studies." Introduced by Jean M. O'Brien and Robert Warrior. *Native American and Indigenous Studies* 1, no. 2: 105–48.

Silver, Charlotte. 2014. "Court Motion Details Palestinian American Rasmea Odeh's Torture by Israeli Jailers." *Electronic Intifada*, February 11, 2014. https://electronicintifada.net/blogs/charlotte-silver/court-motion-details-palestinian-american-rasmea-odehs-torture-israeli.

Walker, Brenda. 2014. "Detroit: Middle Eastern Jihadist Bomber Found Guilty of Immigration Fraud." VDARE, November 11, 2014. http://www.vdare.com/posts/detroit-middle-eastern-jihadist-bomber-found-guilty-of-immigration-fraud.

Warrior, Robert Allen. 1996. "Canaanites, Cowboys, and Indians: Deliverance, Conquest, and Liberation Theology Today." In *Native and Christian: Indigenous Voices on Religious Identity in the United States and Canada*, edited by James Treat, 93–104. New York: Routledge.

Reproduction, Technology, and Neoliberal Entanglement

Jennifer M. Denbow's *Governed Through Choice: Autonomy, Technology, and the Politics of Reproduction*, New York: NYU Press, 2015

Daisy Deomampo's *Transnational Reproduction: Race, Kinship, and Commercial Surrogacy in India*, New York: NYU Press, 2016

Rajani Bhatia's *Gender Before Birth: Sex Selection in a Transnational Context*, Seattle: University of Washington Press, 2018

Juli Grigsby

We are now living in a time when an aborted fetus can be assigned legal representation in the United States (Alabama Secretary of State 2018), and in early 2019, Ryan Magers has done just that, by initiating a wrongful death suit against the clinic where his ex-girlfriend received an abortion (Dickson 2019). This litigation is in part made possible by advances in ultrasound technology and the rise of personhood legislation that seeks to naturalize gendered behaviors. Legislation, policy, and political debate in the United States and abroad continue to be informed by advances in reproductive technology impact policy, as well as discourses around bodily autonomy, the social construction of motherhood, and the stratification of reproduction. Activist scholars invested in reproductive justice are called upon to develop nuanced research agendas to contend with the ways technology expands the biomedicalization of reproduction, which at times reifies discourses of gender, racialization, and motherhood. The scholarship of Jennifer M. Denbow, Daisy Deomampo, and Rajani Bhatia, when read together, presents a conversation on the ways that assisted reproductive technologies (ARTs), neoliberal ideology, juridical discourse, and racial formation converge within international discourses of reproduction.

Combining interviews with technicians, clients, physicians, and clinic observations, Bhatia's interdisciplinary text *Gender Before Birth* accessibly maps the scientific development, reproductive market integration, and commercial popularity of sex selective MicroSort™ technology within Fertility Inc. The author presents the compelling development of sperm separation, which was initially FDA-approved for female bovine cultivation

WSQ: Women's Studies Quarterly **47**: 3 & 4 (Fall/Winter 2019)

in the mid-1980s. Yet this technology soon advanced to medicalize reproductive procedures to aid individuals experiencing infertility where the preemptive sort would mark genetically "defective sperm," lessening the risk of failure. According to Bhatia, by employing preimplantation genetic diagnosis, physicians worked to distance medical sex selection from abortion discussions (2018, 86). The author then turns the analysis to the ways competing discourses of ethical sex selection within the medical profession was both unregulated and "ultimately depended on the 'comfort level' of the individual physician providers" (91). In this case, physicians that provide MicroSort™ technology become brokers of family creation and arbiters of ethical responsibility. Moreover, scientific advancements in successful in vitro fertilization (IVF) treatments and other ARTs meant that clients seeking fertilization were employing a combination of medical diagnostic procedures that drew no clear ethical boundary between medical and nonmedical sex selection of sperm and fertilized embryos (94).

Bhatia then expertly turns the book's argument to the ways that nonmedical sex selection required the deployment of a "family balancing" framing, the use of international capital, and orientalist heterogendered discourses to produce a neoliberal self-interested consumer who, as a "global citizen subject," has a right to a reproductive market. Bhatia argues, "Family balancing not only provided a means to expand the market for MicroSort™ but also a way to keep it alive as a potentially viable commercial product" (80). Bhatia explains the ways transnational capital, neoliberal consumer markets, and gendered heteronormativity are key to the popularization of "Lifestyle Sex Selection," which requires a gendered-specific imagined family made complete by parenting boy and girl children. Bhatia writes, "Within the figuration of the gender dreamer, it follows that the market is driven to meet her desire for a particular imagined life" (102). Bhatia takes this a step further by detailing the intricacies of cross-border travel to laboratories, then asserts the necessity of extended research on reproductive travelers by exploring the constellation of transactions between clinics, laboratories, providers, and clients. She suggests transnational exchanges can circumvent state stipulations on sex selections, ultimately arguing that reproductive justice advocates must develop a more complex analysis of sex selection as more than a practice engaged in "other countries" (191).

In *Governed Through Choice*, Denbow produces a close read of juridical discourses of autonomy as they apply to abortion, informed consent, and sterilization. Denbow argues that the commonly accepted deployment of "autonomy" necessitates a rational self-governing individual that adheres to the social morals and values of society. Given this, the author reiterates that the paternalism of autonomy has always already excluded women as rational political subjects and, for this reason, it is in the interest of the state to prohibit abortion for the protection of women. Here Denbow's analysis of informed consent laws produces the book's clearest read of the biomedicalization of abortion as the site where cis women's natural desire for motherhood should be surveilled and controlled through sonogram technology. She states, "In requiring ultrasounds, the state is violating a [cis] woman's bodily autonomy and using her body to produce the state's message" (2015, 115). The state uses reproductive technology to institute control over women's bodies while relying on gendered tropes of natural "mothering instincts" to deter cis women from obtaining abortions. When women seek out abortions, it is the very same neoliberal market-driven self-interest valorized in autonomous cis men that pathologizes women who do not wish to remain pregnant as deviant, selfish, or anti-family (147). Therefore, Denbow explains how legal discourses present women as unable to make rational choices that secure their reproductive futurity.

However, Denbow challenges this and argues that "the significance of the right to abortion is not limited to individual control over one's repro- ductive processes, but also includes the right's potential to play a role in opening up new cultural understandings of womanhood and reproduc- tion" (61). To reconceptualize autonomy Denbow suggests moving to- ward transformative autonomy where reproductive choice requires the juridical and medical discourses of the state to decouple motherhood from womanhood to make way for the eccentric, autonomous, childfree indi- vidual. The author builds on John Stuart Mill's discussion of the eccentric individual as the purveyor of transgression against social norms which can reflect autonomous behavior. According to Denbow, the eccentric individ- ual's behavior "prompt[s] reflection and critique in others," forcing social transformation that eventually leads to juridical change (55). The author's argument is the most salient in this conversation of childfree women and the need to reconfigure self-interest where voluntary sterilization may be an opportunity to decouple cis womanhood from motherhood so the ec- centric individual can transform the norm of the autonomous rationale. To further the argument, Denbow asserts that the conversation of voluntary sterilization must be analyzed in tandem with historical and contemporary forced sterilization as a means to reveal binaries of fit and unfit mother-ing. Employing a sustained analytic of race as well as an engagement of work by scholars such as Laura Nixon (2013), Laura Mamo (2007), and Laura Mamo and Eli Alston-Stepnitz (2015) who engage the subject of trans bodily autonomy and queer family formation through reproductive justice frameworks would strengthen Denbow's argument. Specifically, Mamo and Alston-Stepnitz detail the pursuit of queer and trans families that are often preceded by forced sterilization and exclusionary practices. This would have provided a nuanced example of parenthood decoupled from cisgender women as a move toward transformational autonomy.

Deomampo's *Transnational Reproduction* is a mesmerizing ethnograph-ic read of global racial formation, assisted reproductive technologies, and the impact surrogacy has on ideological discourses of kinship, ethnicity, gender, and nation. The author employs the terms "reproductive therapeu-tic landscape," "racial reproductive imaginaries," and "stratified reproduc-tion" as theoretical frameworks to analyze the ways that multiple actors are embedded in social, political, and economic contexts that contribute to transitional reproductive travelers' racialized subjectivities. Deomam-po's fieldwork took place in 2010 before the 2013 and 2015 restrictions regulated surrogacy in India. As such, this text documents a time when international surrogacy in India soared and shifting discourses of racial-ization emerged.

Deomampo's intent to "view surrogacy as a technology of race is to highlight the process of racialization that occurs through a specific set of practices. It is to understand surrogacy as more than simply reflecting forms of racial categorization but as a complex site of racialization—a place from which actors 'make' race in particular ways" (2016, 226). While this seems an ambitious task, Deomampo's commitment to nuance is deft-ly handled throughout the text; each set of interlocutors have a dedicated chapter with acute attention paid to race, gender, class, kinship, and the transnational aspects of racial formation. Chapter 3 details the stories of the providers who categorize egg donors by caste, skin color, and educa-tion. Chapter 2 discusses prospective parents' deployment of essentialized notions of race and ethnicity to achieve perceived genetic sameness or ex-otic otherness. In Chapter 7, Deomampo analyzes surrogates' perceptions of the intended parents and their quest to assert financial agency when possible. Deomampo reveals the prevalence of racial tropes and state ra-cial projects that produce bureaucracy, which converges with neoliberal reproductive markets in an attempt to keep up with shifting discourses of citizenship across nations. Further, the author details the lived experiences of surrogates negotiating health care while also experiencing the medicalization of reproduction through the rise in cesarean sections, multiple births, and fear of litigation from clients that disrupt their health and families.

The three books under review present a triangulation of how global reproductive technologies impact legal discourse in the United States, the entanglements of neoliberalism in international markets, and the impact on local actors' imagined reproductive possibilities as well as material realities. All authors employ a reproductive justice framework that not only interrogates the legal implications but also explores the root of reproductive oppression by moving past binary discourses.

Juli Grigsby is an assistant professor of anthropology at Haverford College. Her research explores violence, social inequity, and Black women's political subjectivities in reproductive justice organizing. She can be reached at jgrigsby@haverford.edu.

Works Cited

Alabama Secretary of State. 2018. "Statewide Ballot Measures | Alabama Secretary of State." Accessed March 14, 2019, https://www.sos.alabama.gov/alabama-votes/voter/ballot-measures/statewide.

Dickson, E. J. 2019. "Alabama Court Awards Aborted Fetus the Right to Sue Abortion Clinic." *Rolling Stone*, March 6, 2019. https://www.rollingstone.com/culture/culture-news/abortion-court-sue-fetus-rights-alabama-804213/.

Mamo, Laura. 2007. *Queering Reproduction: Achieving Pregnancy in the Age of Technoscience*. Durham, NC: Duke University Press.

Mamo, Laura, and Eli Alston-Stepnitz. 2015. "Queer Intimacies and Structural Inequalities: New Directions in Stratified Reproduction." *Journal of Family Issues* 36, no. 3: 519–40.

Nixon, Laura. 2013. "The Right to (Trans)Parent: A Reproductive Justice Approach to Reproductive Rights, Fertility, and Family-Building Issues Facing Transgender People." *William & Mary Journal of Women and the Law* 20, no. 1: 73–103.

PART II. **BORDER CROSSINGS**

Migrating Like a Queen:
Visuality and Performance in the Trans Gay Caravan

Ruben Zecena

Abstract: Focusing on the 2017 Trans Gay Caravan as a form of perfor-mative political intervention, this paper proposes the concept "migrating like a queen" to shed light on how trans women and gay men forge fierce relationalities to survive the gendered and sexual violence of migration. I argue that "migrating like a queen" is a visual and performative strategy that utilizes spectacular femininities as a common ground between trans, gay, Central American, and Mexican migrants. **Keywords:** trans, gay, mi-gration, borders, visuality, performance

"Te amo y yo te veo, ok. Yo los voy a ver."
(I love you and I see you, ok. I will be watching you.)
                                                    —Isa Noyola

I begin with the parting words that Isa Noyola, a trans Latina activist and deputy director of the Transgender Law Center, offered to members of the first Trans Gay Caravan that took place on August 10, 2017, as they en-tered the gates of the Dennis DeConcini Port of Entry in Nogales, Arizona (Nogales TV 2017). The Trans Gay Caravan consists of seventeen trans women and gay men from El Salvador, Guatemala, Honduras, Nicaragua, and Mexico, who traveled to the U.S.-Mexico border together in an effort to flee from gender and sexual violence in their home countries, gain po-litical asylum in the United States, and draw attention to the violence that structures their everyday lives. The significance of Noyola's words lies in the way in which they foreground visuality as a powerful force that can shape the social, and in doing so she extended solidarity and love to car-avan members whose future depended on their ability to gain asylum. At

WSQ: Women's Studies Quarterly 47: 3 & 4 (Fall/Winter 2019) © 2019 by Ruben Zecena. All rights reserved.

the same time, by stating "I see you," she engages in what J. L. Austin has theorized as "performative utterances" (1975, 6). Such utterances are performative in the sense that they have the power to do things in the world. By uttering these words in public, Noyola yields power to the members of the Trans Gay Caravan and posits herself as a witness to their livelihoods. Due to the rampant violence that crossing the U.S.-Mexico border entails, particularly for LGBT migrants, Noyola's assertion of their visibility helps to account for the performative work the caravan's crossing *does*: a contestation of the gendered and sexual violence of nation-state borders and a call for coalition among LGBT migrants, Mexican and Central American alike.

This article analyzes the Trans Gay Caravan's march across Mexico and toward the U.S.-Mexico border as a form of performative political intervention that I call "migrating like a queen." Building on Marcia Ochoa's foundational work on the visual spectacle of beauty and femininity in the context of contemporary transformistas in Venezuela, I argue that the 2017 case of the Trans Gay Caravan offers an important extension of trans, queer, and feminist relationality by forging "queendom" as a common ground. José Esteban Muñoz helps to explicate the nuance of queendom in his analysis of the brown commons, "[which] is not about the production of the individual but instead about a movement, a flow, and an impulse, to move beyond the singular and individualized subjectivities . . . a being with, being alongside" (2018, 395). This approach to queendom as a common ground builds on women of color feminism to think of relational ways of being in the world that work toward social change (Chávez 2013). Moreover, as Martin F. Manalansan IV argues in his text *Global Divas*, the glamorous and exuberant forms of mobility that I map are "not only about the actual physical traversing of national boundaries but also about the traffic of status and hierarchies within and across such boundaries" (2003, 9). These spectacles of excessive femininity, or "fabulousness" as Madison Moore (2018) insightfully proposes, can be seen as points of intervention whereby the power of state violence is challenged. Therefore, my formulation of migrating like a queen draws on visual and performance theory to articulate how caravan members' performance of fierce relationalities embodies the worlds they aim to shape. In these worlds, queens assemble *together* to contest the disciplinary regimes of U.S. immigration control, all the while wearing tiaras in public.

The usage of the term "queen" to describe trans women and gay men is a coalitional gesture that I purposefully employ to move beyond essential-ist notions of identity—and most importantly, to open possibilities for ex-amining how a transphobic and homophobic public sphere engenders the policing of gender and sexuality at the U.S.-Mexico border. I recognize the problems in using the term "queen," particularly as it risks collapsing dif-ferences among trans women and gay men; however, little work in queer and trans studies engages the affinities trans women and gay men share as sexually marked bodies that are prone to violence.[1] Furthermore, I take heed from Andrea Long Chu who asserts that "transness requires that we understand, as we never have before, what it means to be attached to a norm—by desire, by habit, by survival" (2019, 108). These norms do not present an easy recourse to femininity, but instead entail "nonnormative attempts at normativity" that call into question the incessant commitment to antinormativity in queer theory (Chu and Drager 2019, 108). Within this analysis it is crucial to recognize that, as Francisco Galarte reminds us, "queer and transgender need not be mutually antagonistic terms" (2014, 134). This article responds and contributes to these theoretical exchanges by demonstrating that trans and queer migrant crossings are not always explicitly or radically antinormative but elicit the performative power of norms for collective survival.

Drawing from Marita Sturken and Lisa Cartwright's definition of vi-sual culture studies as those "aspects of culture that are manifest in visual form" (2001, 4), I contend that migrating like a queen is a visual practice involved in the production, contestation, and negotiation of meaning. In addition, I am attentive to how a performance studies lens helps to analyze political marches, protests, and crossings *as* performance (Taylor 2003). I employ textual analysis methods to ask: What visual and performative strategies do the members of the Trans Gay Caravan utilize to intervene in the everyday violence of U.S. immigration control? Above all, I con-tend that migrating like a queen illustrates the importance of coming to-gether in political times when migrants are separated from their families, displaced from their homes, and, for trans women in particular, placed in solitary confinement while in detention centers.

To understand how migrating like a queen offers strategies for the creation and sustenance of relationality, I begin with a brief examination of asylum processes for LGBT migrants and trace links between visuali-ty, performance, and surveillance. I then analyze video footage from the Trans Gay Caravan's crossing, which includes testimonios from a press conference and chants from caravan members as they assembled together at the border in Nogales, Sonora. Lastly, I draw on promotional materials for a queer dance party and fundraiser event for members of the caravan. Instead of visualizing an image of a migrant family running away from la migra, as Immigration Control and Enforcement (ICE) is commonly called, the queens cross the U.S.-Mexico border together with an exuberant manner that speaks to the performative and visual power of relationality. Migrating like a queen can be a challenging practice and is not a solution to U.S. immigration control. However, the visual and embodied performance of seventeen trans women and gay men fiercely marching toward the U.S.-Mexico border together serves as point of departure for analyzing the world-making possibilities embedded within this coalitional movement. The bonds, coalitions, and emerging relationalities of the Trans Gay Caravan set a strong precedent for the Central American caravans of 2018, many of which included LGBT factions. With tiaras, heels, and colorful banners, queens deliberately challenge the individuating violence of migration regimes and illuminate the glimmer, hope, and allure of fierce relationalities.

Seeing Surveillance, Seeing Migration

According to the 1951 Asylum Convention, migrants seeking asylum must demonstrate a "well-founded fear of persecution on account of race, religion, nationality, membership in a particular social group, or political opinion" (quoted in Bohmer and Shuman 2007, 605). The process for seeking asylum, however, unevenly marginalizes LGBT migrants through various measures. For instance, Sharita Gruberg (2018) from the Center for American Progress explains that LGBT asylum cases are often denied in the interview stage of the process because applicants must recount traumatic experiences with precision to an asylum officer. Gruberg demonstrates that this requirement is not only an inhumane practice that asks LGBT migrants to relive violence but is also used against migrants' credibility if they provide contradictory information. Given the complexity and challenge of describing previous experiences with violence to a stranger (and authority figure), it is reasonable for migrants to forget or refuse to provide details about these traumatic experiences. In addition, Gruberg shows that for trans women, asylum cases are particularly difficult to win when underground economies, such as sex work, are criminalized and used against their cases. As literature on asylum demonstrates, the "asylum application process uses technologies of surveillance to monitor and contain passage from one zone of social life to another" (Bohmer and Shuman 2007, 605).

Similar to asylum processes, the U.S.-Mexico border functions as a technology of surveillance that has historically excluded lesbian and gay migrants. In her case study on Sara Harb Quiroz, a Mexican migrant who was stopped for questioning by a border patrol agent while crossing the border between El Paso, Texas, and Ciudad Juárez, Mexico, Eithne Luibhéid analyzes how institutions of power construct rigid lines on what homosexuality looks like (2002, 78). This case makes evident that Quiroz was stopped because she "looked" like a lesbian, and Luibhéid turns to the visual as a productive site for analyzing border surveillance. She writes, "The visual, or that which gets seen, is driven by and redeploys particular cultural knowledges and blindnesses" (2002, 83). Thus, she suggests that there is a connection between the institutional and historical policing of women of color sexualities at the border and the officer's visual judgment of Quiroz. The cultural layers of this case prompt Luibhéid to ask: "Was there anything really different about Quiroz to see?" and "What cultural knowledges and blindnesses organized this inspector's regime of seeing, such that he picked out Quiroz for investigation?" (2002, 83–84). These complex and nuanced questions critically reflect on the relationship between the visual and technologies of surveillance, whereby trans and queer bodies of color are rendered deviant and violable. And of keen interest to this essay, Quiroz's case illuminates the potent ways in which sexuality, as an axis of power, shapes the visual registers of border officials as a strategy for nation-building that searches for and excludes deviance.

Such visual judgments are evident in the construction of race (as it intersects with gender and sexuality) through surveillance. Simone Browne's term "racialized surveillance" is particularly useful in the analysis of performative and visual power at the border, as it "signals those moments when enactments of surveillance reify boundaries, borders, and bodies along racial lines, and where the outcome is often discriminatory treatment of those who are negatively racialized by such surveillance" (2015, 16). Her incisive use of this term illuminates the role of race in constructing spaces of surveillance, such as national borders, where physical barriers are built not only to demarcate who is included into the nation but also who is excluded. Racialized surveillance thus works as a "technology of social control" that draws on visual and performative enactments of exclusion (2015, 16). Browne's analysis addresses the role of visual economies as they are embedded within surveillance apparatuses, making sites like the border charged with racial, gendered, and sexed meanings.

Lastly, questions of surveillance as they pertain to the border must be understood through the lens of performance. For instance, Gil Hochberg analyzes checkpoints in occupied territories in Palestine as theatrical "stages" where surveillance apparatuses take hold of the Palestinian body through the gaze of Israeli soldiers and the visual display of military power (2015, 80). She turns to the short video *Chic Point* to locate queer aesthetics that "cal[l] attention to the fact that the exploitative relationship between the gaze and the body . . . is not just about military power . . . but also about fantasy and desire" (2015, 91). According to Hochberg, the forced removal of clothing that Palestinians are subjected to at checkpoints is a form of surveillance that is about humiliation as much as it is about fantasy, desire, and theatrical submission. Similarly, Juana María Rodríguez engages the U.S.-Mexico border as a theatrical stage of social control, particularly in her reading of Xandra Ibarra's show "I'm Your Puppet." For Rodríguez, Ibarra's performance as a Latina migrant who submits to the desires of a border patrol agent exposes the "sanctioned gestures of the state [such as forceful stripping] as the nonconsensual sexualized sadism of border security" (2014, 153). Both Hochberg and Rodríguez shed light on the performative powers of the state and engage surveillance apparatuses (and social actors) as complicit with racialized fantasies of sexual abuse.

In theatrical stages such as checkpoints and international borders, queens refuse the visual and performative power of state surveillance through relationality. For example, as they crossed checkpoints in Mexico, queens were able to deflect the power of the state to ask for identification documents by referencing Article 16 of the Mexican constitution, stating that law enforcement cannot ask for documentation without proof of criminal records (Taracena 2018, 390). When law enforcement persisted, the queens "would start screaming or make a lot of noise" collectively to make a "scene" and managed to pass (2018, 390). These forms of excessive corporeal behavior, even if calling more attention to the queen's racialized, sexualized, and gendered nonnormativities, prove vital for the performance of migrating like a queen. Because surveillance apparatuses demand the performance of submission, what is affirmed through these spectacular femininities is the continued refusal of queens to comply.

Testimonios and Performance at the Border

On August 10, 2017, a group of eleven trans women and six gay men, along with their allies on both sides of the border, traveled from Nogales, Sonora, to the U.S.-Mexico border with the intent of asking for asylum. They constitute the first Trans Gay Caravan to cross the U.S.-Mexico border together and call themselves Arcoíris (Rainbow) 17. They marched for around two hours on Nogales's Calle Internacional, which is a street that neighbors the border. Upon arrival, they presented themselves to border officials at the port of entry in Nogales, Arizona. ICE held the entire Caravan overnight and transferred them to detention facilities in New Mexico.[2] Importantly, activists from Arcoíris 17 communicated with organizations on both sides of the border to obtain free legal aid from pro bono attorneys and rehearsed asylum interview scenarios prior to their arrival at the Nogales port of entry.

This event occurred at a crucial time when the current U.S. presidential administration focused much of its efforts on immigration. As Arcoíris 17 prepared to surrender themselves to ICE, Deferred Action for Childhood Arrivals (DACA) and Temporary Protected Status programs (TPS) were under scrutiny by Congress and pending future termination (Sacchetti and Miroff 2017). Additionally, today's anti-immigrant legislation and proposed policies build on former President Obama's administration through the expansion of deportation practices and rhetorical attacks against migrants' supposed criminality, thus creating violently charged atmospheres for undocumented migrants in the United States. Nevertheless, Arcoíris 17 reached the U.S.-Mexico border, and upon their arrival they marched with a rainbow banner stating, "1ra Caravana Trans Gay Migrante 2017." Rather than displaying fear about their future encounter with ICE, trans women and gay men joyfully put their fists in the air as they marched. Despite the extreme violence that queens endure in their migration journeys, this joy takes part in what the Latina Feminist Group describes as *testimoniando*, a concurrent expression of the "alchemies of erasure and silencing" that Latinas endure as well as their "passions, joys, and celebrations," making possible a relational and transfeminist movement (2001, 20).

Before their actual crossing, Arcoíris 17 held a press conference that I argue is integral to the performance of migrating like a queen. The press conference begins with testimonios from some of the members, where they discuss their desire to live free of violence and explain their reasons for migration. According to the Latina Feminist Group, the genre of testimonio rose out of political movements in Latin America and is often framed as a creative form of expression that contests and narrativizes lived oppression (2001, 13). In their reworking of testimonio as a Latina feminist praxis, they importantly ask, "How can testimonio, a self-construction and contestation of power, help us build a theory of our practice, and the practice of our theory?" (2001, 19). In asking this question the group posits testimonio as a relational practice and tool for theory. If, as Diana Taylor suggests, "every performance enacts a theory, and every theory performs in the public sphere" (2003, 27), the caravan's testimonios, like those of the Latina Feminist Group, perform a theory that challenges the demand for singular stories in asylum processes through relationality.

The press conference begins with a testimonio from Alexandra, who remarks:

> We come seeking the necessary security and protection as human beings who deserve liberty, and who deserve happiness . . . we feel obligated to come here to ask for asylum in our quest for liberty . . . we are talking about a vulnerable group, we are unknown in society and it is because of this that we feel obligated to ask the U.S. government to allow us to leave under paroled detention. (Nogales TV 2017)

By using the first-person plural "we," Alexandra's testimonio draws from a shared knowledge of epistemic violence against trans and gay populations to make a political statement. In engaging the testimonio as relational, I am describing the ways her desire for liberation consciously subverts the individuating powers of asylum processes, those which rely on an individual story for asylum rights and push LGBT detainees into detention centers. She strategically poses LGBT communities as "vulnerable" groups in order to prevent detention and exercise what Judith Butler describes as the "plural and performative right to appear" in public (2015, 11). Because asylum cases can take as long as three years, and detention centers are notorious for placing trans women in solitary confinement, her request for paroled detention is significantly attuned to the powers of U.S. immigration control to separate LGBT migrants from each other and further (in)visibilize their experiences. In the end, the trans women were taken to the privately run Cibola County Detention Center in Albuquerque but were released under parole after a month in detention. This is the same detention center where Roxsana Hernández, a trans Latina migrant from Honduras, died in 2018 from a lack of medical care and the violent conditions of ICE (Gutíerrez and Portillo 2018). While Alexandra's testimonio alone did not prevent detention, she was able to call attention to institutional forms of violence that are constituted through asylum processes. The testimonio is performative because of what it does: it allows Alexandra to request rights from the nation while simultaneously critiquing it.

Expanding on Alexandra's performative strategies, Kimberly, a Honduran trans woman and member of the caravan, begins her testimonio by stating that she will speak about violence against trans women in their countries of origin. Even though caravan members were explicitly prompted to offer their personal testimonios at the press conference, Kimberly also refuses to use "I" when describing her experiences. This decision marks a desire to speak about the collective experiences of the caravan members as mediated through her when she states:

> We come fleeing from our countries of origin, majority of the people do not accept us as trans girls . . . many of us have been abused by gang members, even police officers have treated us badly, raped us, punched us . . . another thing, we have also suffered through our migration here in Mexico. Many of us have been kidnapped, forced into prostitution, we come from our countries fleeing from so much pain and so much suffering to come here to relive in Mexico what we have experienced in our countries. So, we have the option to go to the United States in pursuit of safety . . . our word will matter in the United States, it will not be like in our countries of origin where our word does not matter. Thank you. (Nogales TV 2017)

This testimonio reveals pain and suffering as key factors in the queens' decision to migrate. One way to read Kimberly's testimonio is to critique the ways in which she frames the U.S. as a benevolent nation that offers protection for trans women; thus, ignoring how she strategically draws from the performative power of this genre to ask for the right to migrate. According to Lisa Cacho, "Because the state renders criminalized populations of color ineligible for personhood, and consequently, ineligible for the right to ask for rights, they cannot be incorporated in rights-based politics" (2012, 8). In her testimonio, Kimberly is aware of her inability to ask for rights, so she has to negotiate migrant criminalization by making a claim on the nation. While the testimonio does not challenge rights-based politics, and relies on racist narratives of U.S. exceptionalism, it forces the audience at the press conference to bear witness to violence. Rather than a mere transaction, testimonio offers opportunities to engage the affective experiences of trauma, violence, and displacement. As Kaitlin Murphy lucidly explains, "Testimonio is an act of telling, but one in which the act of *witnessing* is seen as almost equally important" (2019, 42) By thanking her audience, Kimberly is acknowledging the affective experience that was shared, as well as the ethics behind witnessing violence. Clearly, asylum seekers are skilled rhetoricians and performers, so it is important to consider how Kimberly's testimonio engages complicated discourses on LGBT asylum and U.S. exceptionalism.

Following Kimberly's response, journalists asked caravan members questions that highlight performativity as integral to testimonio. Kimberly, who had previously declared that things would be different in the United States, was asked about the caravan's plans if they are denied asylum and what the members make of violence against LGBT populations in the United States. This is a pivotal moment because not only are the journalists seeking to find flaws in the caravan's testimonios but they are also misreading these testimonios as simple truths. Because none of the caravan members used "I" when speaking about violence, it is necessary to address how Arcoíris 17 reworks testimonio for their benefit. Kimberly confidently responded by stating that if they were denied asylum, members would ask for a transitory visa to allow them to travel to Canada and follow the same process. In regard to violence against LGBT populations in the United States, Kimberly reminds audience members that many organizations in the United States already offered support to Arcoíris 17; thus, she demonstrates that their interest in migration emerges not so much from relying on nation-state powers but from the support of activist organizations, such as Mariposas Sin Fronteras, Trans Queer Pueblo, the Transgender Law Center, and Familia: Trans Queer Liberation Movement. Kimberly's testimonio "transcends descriptive discourse to one that is performative," and in doing so she engages audiences to "understand and establish a sense of solidarity as a first step toward social change" (Bernal, Burciaga, and Carmona 2015, 2). Her initial gesture toward the benevolence of the United States should be understood as performative and intentionally using the power of testimonio to obtain asylum rights, as well as an act of transfer that uses embodied behavior to transmit knowledge (Taylor 2003, 2–3). Here the lens of performance studies makes useful interventions by helping us understand that speech is not only about words, but also about corporeal enactments (Butler 2015, 8). While Kimberly does not offer solutions to U.S. immigration control, she reworks the genre of testimonio to encourage transnational solidarity through performance.

Finally, the last testimonio builds on the relational use of "we" by taking it a step further and refusing to provide journalists with the speaker's name. He begins his testimonio with, "I'm going to represent myself as a chico gay of the LGBT community," and reiterates the caravan's two-fold desire for protection and liberation (Nogales TV 2017). His subsequent interaction with one journalist, in particular, merits closer attention. Following the chico gay's testimonio, a journalist asked, "Your name, do you want to tell me your name?" To which the chico gay responded, "I already said that I represent myself as a gay boy from the gay community." At multiple levels, this response is sassy, but it is performative in the sense that he challenges the journalist's power to ask for truth and subject his testimonio to individual experience.

These testimonios demonstrate that for the Arcoíris 17, migration is not an individual journey but collective, relational, and performative. This type of migration is not intimidated by the powers of U.S. immigration control or the political ramifications of asylum. Through the relational and transfeminist practice of testimonio, queens lay claim not so much to the state but to their right to appear in public as a "plural form of performativity" (Butler 2015, 8). Testimonio presents a dynamic performance and strategy for coalitional movements that shifts the focus away from the individual and positions relationality as the locus for liberation.

Queens That Assemble

A potent indicator of the visual and performative dimensions of migrating like a queen is the way in which femininity takes center stage throughout the Arcoíris 17's crossing. In her ethnography on transformistas and beauty queens in Venezuela, Marcia Ochoa proposes spectacularity as a lens to understand how cultural meanings of femininity are produced and made legible in the contexts of beauty pageants and red districts. She writes, "Spectacularity is an important dimension to consider in accounting for how gender is produced in and on the body within discourse. Spectacular femininities, then, are femininities that employ the conventions of spectacularity in their production" (2014, 203). These are the kinds of femininities that the queens of Arcoíris 17 embody. As mentioned early in the essay, "queen" is a useful term for describing trans women and gay men, and Ochoa situates spectacular femininities as a common ground for these subjects when she states that the spectacle "appear[s] time and again among gay men and transgender women in Latin American and other contexts" (2014, 202). Ochoa argues that the spectacular makes discursive conventions available for all kinds of everyday performance. I draw from Ochoa's arguments on spectacular femininities because of a scene in the caravan's performance when they chant: "Que perra, que perra, que perra mi amiga, cruzando las fronteras con todas las culeras." A rough translation of this chant is "My friend is a badass bitch, a badass bitch, crossing borders with all the faggotry." Following Ochoa, this speech act draws on the spectacle to mediate a spectacular femininity, one that exceeds how migration is imaged and imagined.

In alluding to the visual and performative work in Arcoíris 17's crossing, I am particularly attending to how the queens produce, contest, and alter meaning-making practices. For example, the chant "que perra" references a popular song by Dominican singer La Real Lazzy that has gained traction in gay clubs throughout Latin America. According to the singer and writer, the chorus "que perra" is a phrase that she uses with her friends to praise each other at the club but emerges from gay communities (Trujillo 2017). What makes Arcoíris 17's reworking of the phrase full of potential is not so much its origins or popularity among gay men. Rather, the use of "que perra" functions as a disidentification, what José Esteban Muñoz describes as "the survival strategies [that] the minoritarian subject practices in order to negotiate a phobic majoritarian public sphere that continuously elides or punishes the existence of subjects who do not conform to the phantasm of normative citizenship" (1999, 4). In the case of Arcoíris 17, they encountered a phobic majoritarian public sphere that stresses citizenship as a marker of belonging. In order to negotiate how citizenship punishes sexually marked bodies, caravan members disidentified with the original meaning of the song and intensified what is elided and punished in the public sphere: nonnormative genders/sexualities. The visual image of badass bitches crossing nation-state borders among faggots creates a rupture in the public sphere by celebrating sexual perversions; thus, reworking the meaning of the song but also the transphobia and homophobia of the visual. According to Martha Balaguera, cultural anxieties about trans women who migrate from Central America to Mexico are exemplified in migrant shelters when she writes, "Prevalent anxieties about *chicas trans's* sexuality bring about a host of rules and an arbitrary regulation of space that often leads to their isolation" (2018, 652–53). Migrating like a queen runs counter to these systems by establishing a sense of solidarity among trans women and gay men, therefore refusing the violence of isolation and creating avenues for relational movements. Such tactical maneuvers, like disidentification, highlight the ways a phobic majoritarian public sphere monitors and polices the coming together of sexually marked bodies.

In his insightful text *The Land of Open Graves*, Jason De León (2015) describes the U.S.-Mexico border as an abstract killing machine that uses the vast landscape of the desert to (in)visibilize the violent measures of border monitoring. Focusing on Nogales, where Arcoíris 17's performative crossing occurs, De León writes, "The goal is to render invisible the innumerable consequences this sociopolitical phenomenon has for the lives and bodies of undocumented people" (2015, 2). De León's analysis explicitly articulates the power of nation-state borders to inflict violence, but his arguments on Nogales prompt critical reflections on the performative power of queens that assemble in such deadly terrain. In her analysis of the performative work of assembling in public, Butler writes,

> When the bodies of those deemed disposable or "ungrievable" assemble in public view (as happens time and time again when the undocumented arrive in the streets in the United States as part of public demonstrations), they are saying, "we have not slipped quietly into the shadows of public life: we have not become the glaring absence that structures your public life." (2015, 152)

Her observation demonstrates that even when challenged with extreme forms of violence, disposable bodies may assert power in coming together, thus posing a direct challenge to the blinding forces of nation-states and the (il)legibility of violence at the border.

While wearing tiaras in public may seem like a minor or frivolous aspect of Arcoíris 17's crossing, their tiaras function as a spectacle that exceeds the logics of disposability. Rather than becoming a disposable body, these queens insist on carrying rainbow banners, dressing their bodies in accordance with cultural conventions of femininity, and wearing tiaras to shine light on the disturbance that their bodies perform. Writing on frivolity, Ochoa asserts,

> My focus is always on the frivolous: those people most excluded from political possibility because of how ridiculous the idea is that they have

any politics. It is in the lives of *transformistas*, of translatina immigrants to the United States, making their survival out of impossibilities, that I have found the core of political possibility. (2014, 245)

Despite nation-state logics and policies that render migrant trans women and gay men disposable, it is their frivolous bodies and tiaras that make possible a visual and performative redefinition of the political. These are "nonnormative attempts at normativity," like disidentification, that disrupt the logics of disposability through spectacular femininities.

One of the most playful examples of migrating like a queen as a frivolous, and yet powerful, strategy for survival can be gleaned in the queer dance party/fundraiser event called Las Chingonas de la Caravana. This party featured Genesis, Katalea, and Chuleta, three members of Arcoíris 17, with the purpose of raising funds for their asylum cases and celebrating Katalea for being granted asylum. The event was organized by the Tucson-based group Heartbeats, which plans queer dance parties in the Sonoran Desert to raise funds for social justice causes. It occurred on October 13, 2018, and was advertised through flyers and a Facebook event. In her analysis of promotional materials from queer Latina/o/x activist organizations in San Francisco, Juana María Rodríguez draws attention to the "transformative powers of reading and writing language and images as symbolic codes" (2003, 48). In a similar vein, I analyze the visual and textual material from this event as important sites of creativity, frivolity, and relationality.

For instance, the text from the Facebook event captures the significance of frivolous and nonnormative sites of relationality when it states,

> Come out and throw down for these incredible women fighting their asylum cases!!!! There will be music, performances, the calm before the storm, the s t o r m I t s e l f, the perfect language of moving together, snacks and bevs, the installed dreams of everyone who wants you to have the best fucking nite ever, a place to put ur dirty green paper that feels soooo good, 3am mopping and laughing after it's all done. (Heartbeats 2018)

The style and form of this text incites textual, corporeal, and relational movements. As readers, we are invited to "throw down" together and in solidarity with the fierce and fearless members of the caravan. The shortened words and playful tone demonstrate that by assembling together, a

Fig. 1. Heartbeats flyer for the Chingonas de la Caravana queer dance party. 2018. Art created by Genevieve Heron.

space is created for frivolous actions such as dancing, flirting, drinking, or simply laughing. These spaces are vital for the sustenance of bonds and relations among trans and queer communities. Instead of dreaming state legislation, readers are invited to raise funds for caravan members and party alongside these queens. Notably, the violent and deadly effects of the Pulse nightclub shooting, which occurred during "Latin" night and killed forty-nine patrons, serves as an important reminder that literal "heartbeats" cannot be taken for granted in trans and queer of color spaces. In this instance, a frivolous dance party is about having a good time as much as it is about standing in solidarity with the survival of LGBT migrants.

In the flyer that accompanies this text, which was created by artist Genevieve Heron, the queens of Arcoíris 17 pose in front of a disco ball to display their fabulous powers (fig. 1). These include Chuleta's magic wig, Katalea's "destructive" twerking powers, and Genesis with her fierce and dangerous heels. In the context of the violent processes of LGBT asylum, this flyer reimagines the precarious conditions of migrant trans women to highlight their "glittery fabulousness" (Rodríguez 2016). The extravagant use of magenta in the background of the flyer, along with different shades of violet, purple, and pink for the caravan members that are represented, promises a vibrant, energetic, and exciting night filled with desire. Once again, the queens of Arcoíris 17 stand together in an exuberant manner as they confront migration regimes and processes that aim to deport, regulate, and discipline their bodies. At the same time that the flyer provides logistical information about the dance party (and the fundraising efforts), it also redefines what counts as "political" through a frivolous aesthetic. These modes of creative practices "refuse the romance of dissidence and resistance," and instead highlights how LGBT migrants "struggl[e] to create scripts that will enable them to survive" (Manalansan 2003, 121).

The queens on the flyer are, in Rodríguez's words, *divas, atrevidas,* and *entendidas.* As she writes, "*Divas* are a breathing, swishing, eruption of the divine, a way of being in the world, of claiming power as movement, glances, voice, body, and style. *Atrevidas* dare to fulfill desire, challenge assumptions the world has given us. *Entendidas* share a knowledge, understand the significance and nuances of queer subaltern spaces" (2003, 24). Rodríguez's beautiful description helps to illuminate the importance of frivolity in the Trans Gay Caravan. The emphasis on movement, both in the text and the flyer's invocation of dancing, works metaphorically to describe fierce and relational modes of migration, what I call migrating like a queen. In this instance, LGBT asylum practices are shifted from individual and heroic stories to the fabulous assembling of queens in the public sphere and queer subaltern spaces. As such, migrating like a queen offers a platform for queens to come together and transform sites of (im)possibility into relational and coalitional spaces of survival.

Fierce Relationalities

This paper examined migrating like a queen as a relational mode of migration that trans women and gay men employ to challenge the individuating powers of U.S. immigration control, but as my textual analyses demonstrate, this strategy has the ultimate goal of survival. By offering the notion of migrating like a queen, I acknowledged and engaged political strategies that are not recognized as fruitful to the dominant immigrant rights movement or LGBT politics. My employment of a performance studies and visual culture studies lens allowed me to read testimonios as more than simple truths and also helped me navigate complicated questions on frivolity, femininity, and sexuality. However, more research on the intersections between migration, visuality, and performance are necessary, especially when a liberal framework uncritically posits LGBT visibility as a progressive ideal. The visual image of Central American caravans is consistently attacked by conservative media and the presidential administration, therefore alluding to the power of the visual in shaping politics and social relations. Without a doubt, sexual, gendered, and racial anxieties about international migration illustrate the political stakes of migrating like a queen and serve as a point of departure for imagining and imaging migration otherwise.

The relationalities between trans women and gay men from Arcoíris 17 are essential for the sustenance of coalition among migrants and their allies. For instance, as a continuation of their fierce crossing, an LGBT faction of the 2018 Central American migrant caravans employed similar strategies by requesting asylum together and drawing on the support of LGBT organizations. Most recently, a group of drag queens in Texas staged a protest at the border in the Rio Grande Valley to raise funds for LGBT migrants seeking asylum (Leaños 2019). Instead of merely providing visibility, migrating like a queen performatively asserts that trans women and gay men from different geopolitical locations have the power to come together in the public sphere, and in that power rises the promise of fierce relationalities.

Acknowledgments

My full gratitude to Genevieve Heron for allowing her beautiful art to be reprinted. Heartfelt thanks to Kaitlin Murphy, Lizeth Gutierrez, and John Melillo, who provided thoughtful feedback in the early stages of writing. I'm also indebted to the Transfrontera group at the University of Arizona for creating the space to workshop this paper with Frances Aparicio. Lastly, thank you to the fabulous reviewers and special issue editors for seeing promise in this paper.

Ruben Zecena is a PhD candidate in the Department of Gender & Women's Studies at the University of Arizona. He specializes in queer migration studies and his work appears or is forthcoming in *Border-Lines*, *constellations*, and the coedited collection *Queer and Trans Migrations*. He can be reached at rubenz@email.arizona.edu.

Notes

1. In a footnote to their article "Near Life, Queer Death," Eric Stanley argues that it is impossible to make a cut between transphobic violence and homophobic violence since that cut is based on visual judgments against trans subjects and their (in)ability to "pass" (2011, 16). Thanks to Eva Hayward for directing me to Eric Stanley's article.

2. As of today, ten of the trans women were released on parole, enabling them to fight for their asylum cases outside of detention, and one was deported. In the case of the gay men, two gained asylum and the rest were deported (Taracena 2018, 388).

Works Cited

Austin, J. L. 1975. *How to Do Things with Words*. 2nd ed. Cambridge, MA: Harvard University Press.

Balaguera, Martha. 2018. "Trans-migrations: Agency and Confinement at the Limits of Sovereignty." *Signs: Journal of Women in Culture and Society* 43, no. 3: 641–63.

Bernal, Dolores D., Rebecca Burciaga, and Judith F. Carmona. 2015. "Introduction." In *Chicana/Latina Testimonios as Pedagogical, Methodological, and Activist Approaches to Social Justice*, edited by Dolores D. Bernal, Rebecca Burciaga, and Judith F. Carmona, 1–10. New York: Routledge.

Bohmer, Carol, and Amy Schuman. 2007. "Producing Epistemologies of Ignorance in the Political Asylum Process." *Identities: Global Studies in Culture and Power* 14, no. 5: 603–29.

Browne, Simone. 2015. *Dark Matters: On the Surveillance of Blackness*. Durham, NC: Duke University Press.

Butler, Judith. 2015. *Notes Toward a Performative Theory of Assembly*. Cambridge, MA: Harvard University Press.

Cacho, Lisa M. 2012. *Social Death: Racialized Rightlessness and the Criminalization of the Unprotected*. New York: NYU Press.

Chávez, Karma. 2013. *Queer Migration Politics: Activist Rhetoric and Coalitional Possibilities*. Urbana: University of Illinois Press.

Chu, Andrea Long, and Emmet Harsin Drager. 2019. "After Trans Studies." *TSQ: Transgender Studies Quarterly* 6, no. 1: 103–16.

De León, Jason. 2015. *The Land of Open Graves: Living and Dying in the Migrant Trail*. Berkeley: University of California Press.

Galarte, Francisco. 2014. "Transgender Chican@ Poetics: Contesting, Interrogating, and Transforming Chicana/o Studies." *Chicana/Latina Studies* 13, no. 2: 118–39.

Gruberg, Sharita. 2018. "Mass Incarcerations and the Deportation Imperative: How Immigration Enforcement Endangers LGBTQ Immigrants." Keynote address at "No Bans, No Walls, No Detention Cells: A UA Graduate Student Conference on Migration," April 13, 2018. University of Arizona, Tucson, AZ.

Gutíerrez, Jennicet, and Suyapa Portillo. 2018. "Trans(formation) of a Movement." *NACLA Report on the Americas* 50, no. 4: 392–94.

Heartbeats. 2018. "Heartbeats///Baile Queer." Facebook, October 13, 2018. https://www.facebook.com/events/519477508477474/.

Hochberg, Gil. 2015. *Visual Occupations: Violence and Visibility in a Conflict Zone.* Durham, NC: Duke University Press.

Latina Feminist Group. 2001. *Telling to Live: Latina Feminist Testimonios.* Durham, NC: Duke University Press.

Leaños, Reynaldo Jr. 2019. "Drag Queens Protest at the Border Wall to Raise Money for LGBTQ Asylum-seekers." *NBC News*, February 25, 2019. https://www.nbcnews.com/feature/nbc-out/drag-queens-protest-border-wall-raise-money-lgbtq-asylum-seekers-n975666.

Luibhéid, Eithne. 2002. *Entry Denied: Controlling Sexuality at the Border.* Minneapolis: University of Minnesota Press.

Manalansan IV, Martin F. 2003. *Global Divas: Filipino Gay Men in the Diaspora.* Durham, NC: Duke University Press.

Moore, Madison. 2018. *Fabulous: The Rise of the Beautiful Eccentric.* New Haven, CT: Yale University Press.

Muñoz, José Esteban. 1999. *Disidentifications: Queers of Color and the Performance of Politics.* Minneapolis: University of Minnesota Press.

———. 2018. "Preface: Fragment from the *Sense of Brown* Manuscript." *GLQ: A Journal of Gay and Lesbian Studies* 24, no. 4: 395–97.

Murphy, Kaitlin. 2019. *Mapping Memory: Visuality, Affect, and Embodied Politics in the Americas.* New York: Fordham University Press.

Nogales TV. 2017. "Caravana TransGay migrante busca asilo en EUA." YouTube video, 16:46, August 10, 2017. https://www.youtube.com/watch?v=3wOQ48EiGqo.

Ochoa, Marcia. 2014. *Queen for a Day: Transformistas, Beauty Queens, and the Performance of Femininity in Venezuela.* Durham, NC: Duke University Press.

Rodríguez, Juana María. 2003. *Queer Latinidad: Identity Practices, Discursive Spaces.* New York: NYU Press.

———. 2014. *Sexual Futures, Queer Gestures, and Other Latina Longings.* New York: NYU Press.

———. 2016. "Voices: LGBT Clubs Let Us Embrace Queer Latinidad, Let's Affirm This." *NBC News*, June 16, 2016. https://www.nbcnews.com/

storyline/orlando-nightclub-massacre/voices-lgbt-clubs-let-us-embrace-queer-latinidad-let-s-n593191.

Sachetti, Maria, and Nick Miroff. 2017. "How Trump Is Building a Border Wall That No One Can See." *Washington Post*, November 21, 2017. https://www.washingtonpost.com/local/immigration/how-trump-is-building-a-border-wall-no-one-can-see/2017/11/21/83d3b746-cba0-11e7-b0cf-7689a9f2d84e_story.html?noredirect=on&utm_term=.dcbc076e87a5.

Stanley, Eric. 2011. "Near Life, Queer Death: Overkill and Ontological Capture." *Social Text* 29, no. 2: 1–19.

Sturken, Marita, and Lisa Cartwright. 2001. *Practices of Looking: An Introduction to Visual Culture*. New York: Oxford University Press.

Taracena, Maria Inés. 2018. "La Caravana de Resistencia." *NACLA Report on the Americas* 50, no. 4: 386–91.

Taylor, Diana. 2003. *The Archive and the Repertoire: Performing Cultural Memory in the Americas*. Durham, NC: Duke University Press.

Trujillo, Luis. 2017. "La Real Lazzy despeja la incognita de 'Que Perra mi Amiga.'" *dia a dia*, October 30, 2017. https://www.diaadia.com.pa/fama/la-real-lazzy-despeja-la-incognita-de-que-perra-mi-amiga-327462.

Remembrance and Resilience:
Resisting the Violence of the U.S.-Mexico Border

Mizue Aizeki

The fortification of the U.S.-Mexico border dominates the current political landscape. This photo-essay goes back to the mid-1990s, when the deaths of people crossing came to the political forefront. Under the Clinton presidential administration, the U.S. government massively increased the size of the policing apparatus on the U.S.-Mexico border, with a focus on urbanized areas. As a consequence, many communities that had previously been sites of fluid migration were closed off, pushing people to cross in isolated areas with dangerous terrain. This led to a marked increase in migrant fatalities. This photo-essay highlights various responses—including political art protesting border militias and activists leaving vital supplies for migrants who pass through the desert—as well as depictions of border militarization and migrant deaths.

WSQ: Women's Studies Quarterly 47: 3 & 4 (Fall/Winter 2019) © 2019 by Mizue Aizeki. All rights reserved.

Día de los Muertos. Oakland, California, U.S.A., November 2001. Photograph. Courtesy of Mizue Aizeki.

Terrace Park Cemetery. Holtsville, California, November 2001. Photograph. Courtesy of Mizue Aizeki.

Tohono O'odham Nation, June 2004. Photograph. Courtesy of Mizue Aizeki.

Nogales, Sonora, Mexico, October 2005. Photograph. Courtesy of Mizue Aizeki.

Tijuana, Baja California Norte, Mexico, November 2001. Photograph. Courtesy of Mizue Aizeki.

Migrant Trail, Arizona, U.S.A., June 2005. Photograph. Courtesy of Mizue Aizeki.

San Ysidro, California, U.S.A., September 2005. Photograph. Courtesy of Mizue Aizeki.

Mizue Aizeki is a photographer whose work has appeared in *Dying to Live: A Story of U.S. Immigration in an Age of Global Apartheid* and *Policing the Planet: Why the Policing Crisis Led to Black Lives Matter*. She is currently the deputy director at the Immigrant Defense Project, where she focuses on ending injustices at the intersections of the criminal and immigration systems, including criminalization, imprisonment, and exile. She can be reached at mizue@immdefense.org.

Carceral Immigration Reforms and the Joint Project of Abolition

Alexandra Délano Alonso's *From Here and There: Diaspora Policies, Integration, and Social Rights Beyond Borders*, New York: Oxford University Press, 2018

Jenna M. Loyd and Alison Mountz's *Boats, Borders, and Bases: Race, the Cold War, and the Rise of Migration Detention in the United States*, Berkeley: University of California Press, 2018

Marlene Nava Ramos

Jenna M. Loyd and Alison Mountz's *Boats, Borders, and Bases* and Alexandra Délano Alonso's *From Here and There*, two of the most recently published works on the topic of U.S. immigration, build on the now extensive interdisciplinary literature that oscillates between the exclusion of immigrants, on the one hand, and forms of political power and integration, on the other. While they remain within their respective sides of the field, these manuscripts are timely and push the literature empirically and theoretically. Furthermore, these works pair well in order to help readers theorize on the synergism of oppositional forces—"exclusion" versus "inclusion"—affecting U.S. immigrants. In doing so, these works can also guide critical discussions on calls to come "together"—this issue's theme—within the context of mass mobilizations and efforts toward carceral reforms. In their work, Loyd and Mountz ask: How did the largest migrant detention system in the world come about? And now that we are here, Alonso asks: What kinds of counterstrategies exist to support immigrants' political and economic participation and power?

Loyd and Mountz, two geographers with distinct theoretical training, write a metanarrative on the birth and expansion of "migration detention" across onshore and offshore U.S. territories. As in her previous work, *Seeking Asylum*, Mountz uses Giorgio Agamben's philosophies of exceptionalism to study remote, offshore, militarized landscapes, adding to Loyd's perspective on the political economy of prison towns and military bases across the contiguous U.S. and its territories. Lloyd plumbs the archives to understand the broader politics and economies of prison towns holding

***WSQ: Women's Studies Quarterly* 47: 3 & 4 (Fall/Winter 2019)** © 2019 by Marlene Nava Ramos.

federal immigrant detainees in Oakdale, Louisiana, Pinal County, Arizona (Florence and Eloy), and Batavia, New York, challenging the narrative of migrant detention sites as spatially isolated. These chapters are then connected by Mountz's expertise on the use of military bases in remote places such as Guantánamo as well as in the contiguous U.S. (Fort Chaffee, Arkansas) in order to show the plethora and expansion of confinement sites since the late 1970s.

Loyd and Mountz ambitiously unify these case studies under a clever three-part chronology: the federal government's contested but definitive introduction of detention practices as an immigration deterrence strategy in the aftermath of the 1980 Mariel boatlift crisis; the systematic building of prisons throughout the 1980s on military bases and in towns eager to host new facilities; and, finally, the expansion of detention into the "world's largest system"—an accurate proclamation by California prison administrators about California's corrections system (Gilmore 1999; 2007) that also rings true for the federal government's own carceral system.

Their research provides a much needed alternative perspective in the literature about immigration enforcement, which has tended to date the rise of comprehensive enforcement practices to the aftermath of the 1996 anti-immigrant laws and/or post-9/11 responses—these are important moments that expand the breadth and scope of state practices. Loyd and Mountz, however, trace the roots of this phenomenon to the country's prison boom in the aftermath of the Cold War and the shift between what Loyd's academic mentor Ruth Wilson Gilmore (1999) calls Keynesian militarism and post-Keynesian militarism. Loyd and Mountz's joint research maps an extensive onshore and offshore carceral archipelago which should be examined, they argue, from the critical perspective of Cold War refugees and the Caribbean region, challenging the nearly exclusive focus on the U.S.-Mexico borderlands.

Boats, Borders, Bases is a must-read in immigration courses. The authors' ambitious geographic-temporal scope and sophisticated theoretical tools for studying onshore and offshore confinement will need to be contextualized for undergraduate readers to avoid a misreading of temporal and theoretical linkages as undifferentiated forms of confinement. Offshore and onshore confinement, while connected as part of a broader U.S. detention system, also have important differences, highlighted by Loyd and Mountz's vast empirical evidence. Onshore confinement by local, state, and federal agencies, as well as their criminal legal systems, has come to play a much bigger role since the Mariel boatlift. Pairing the book with Gilmore's *Golden Gulag* or Mountz's earlier work would contextualize these empirical differences just as Loyd and Mountz's metanarrative highlights the connective tissues.

Alonso's research questions in *From Here and There*, by contrast, are situated in the "inclusion and integration" subfield. A political scientist by training and granddaughter of a Mexican appointed consul in New York, Alonso writes about the extraordinary efforts of individual consulate offices and diplomats, primarily from México, El Salvador, and Ecuador. Working independently of the U.S. federal government—but often collaboratively with one another and NGOs—they service the Latin American diaspora and their families living in the United States.

As an insider, Alonso's rich ethnographic work captures the country-wide regional networks of consulates that, starting in the 1990s, began linking immigrants and their children to educational, health, and banking services, as well as tools for language acquisition, civic participation, and protections against labor exploitation. Their services include awarding educational scholarships to undocumented youth, helping people gain U.S. citizenship or deferred status, and offering direct onsite health services such as free vaccines and diagnostic exams through partnerships with providers. The variety of these services is extensive and goes well beyond traditional consular responsibilities such as issuing birth certificates.

Her critical analysis will surely cultivate lively discussions in political science or immigration courses on the significance and effectiveness of efforts by Latin American consulate offices to promote economic and political participation despite, or precisely because of, the obvious limitations their constituencies face as undocumented, sometimes criminalized, and exploited populations who are not eligible to vote or hold power in traditional forms. Alonso argues that consulate efforts to protect their constituent populations in the U.S. are in part driven not only by the absence of a national integration policy, but also by the restrictionist turns in U.S. policy and enforcement practices. Her findings will help readers think critically about the forms of power of immigrant communities, especially for those who are on the fringes of the labor market and face detention/deportation under U.S. law.

Although consulate offices' programming and regional collaborations embarrassingly highlight the U.S. government's policy voids, Alonso points out that their efforts can also replicate existing group inequalities from their countries of origin—exclusion or neglect of certain populations in México, for example, is mirrored by consulate practices in the United States. These policies also produce asymmetrical outcomes between destination and origin countries when the member populations that consulate offices service in the United States return to their countries of origin as deportees, and policies there ignore or marginalize them. Alonso also eloquently critiques consulate offices' advocacy limits. Rather than openly lobbying against restrictive U.S. policies, consulate offices intentionally employ "bottom up" strategies by forming coalitions with local agencies and NGOs, as they argue, to empower immigrants to take the lead in advocacy or leadership roles. It is here that Alonso's empirical evidence most closely breaks through the theoretical limitations of the literature's subfield on "inclusion." Her mention of restrictive policies in her analysis thrusts the topic of criminalization and enforcement policies to the fore. She points to the obvious ways these exclusionary regimes, which are otherwise disconcertingly ignored by some in the integration scholarship, actually stymie immigrant integration. Alonso's mention of these forces presents a starting point for much-needed explicit discussions and research on exclusionary mechanisms at work within inclusionary policies.

Reading Alonso's work alongside Loyd and Mountz's research provides a unique opportunity to go beyond the silos of the literature. I close by examining the impact of exclusionary systems on migrant (cis and transgender) women and calls to come "together" through the life and death of Song Yang, a Chinese immigrant who worked in New York City's massage and underground sex industry. In late 2018, Yang plunged to her death from a four-story balcony during a police raid (Barry and Singer 2018). The vice unit that raided Yang's place of work was part of a 2017 criminal legal reform championed by NYC First Lady Chirlane McCray and Police Commissioner James P. O'Neill aimed at diverting *arrested* women from jail time to legal and social services (NYPD News 2017).

Yang's shortened life reveals that the criminalization, policing, and imprisoning of epic numbers of people, whether in prisons, jails, or detention facilities, is predicated on their extrinsic disposability. Moreover, her inclusion into global circuits of capital by way of her exclusion (i.e., sex work and immigration restrictive policies) is in part "reproductive" of existing organizational (and contradictory) forces in racial capitalism. Here, I am referring to the historical and methodological contributions of the late great Cedric Robinson (2000 [1983]), who posits that group differentiation is the very foundation and inner-mechanics of all and renewed forms of capital accumulation. In other words, the country's vast inequality and massive uneven concentration of wealth since the second half of the twentieth century is in part sustained, however insecurely, on the disposability and exclusions of some.

Yang's purported "decriminalization" in the labor market and premature death also reveals the dangers of shortsighted liberal reforms that reconcile and harden systems of exclusion rather than abolish them. Contrary to popular belief, exclusionary systems are not resistant to change, and in fact only survive by their constant transformation. Reforms, sometimes driven by desires to foster inclusion, have in fact built the state's capacity to permanently banish people. Connecting legal and social services to systems of punishment, in this case police and arrest, are reforms that further entrench our reliance on these systems and form part of cornerstone strategies of future forms of exclusion and control. Yang's death calls for coming together under the joint project of abolition of all carceral regimes and the group differentiation which they produce. Abolition calls for laser-sharp analysis and radical forms of solidarity, making the fight against immigration enforcement operations part of the fight against all forms of imprisonment and exclusion.

Marlene Nava Ramos is a PhD student in the Program in Earth and Environmental Sciences (Geography) at the CUNY Graduate Center. Her research is focused on immigration detention in New Jersey county jails from the 1980s to the present. She can be reached at mramos@gradcenter.cuny.edu.

Works Cited

Barry, Dan, and Jeffrey E. Singer. 2018. "The Case of Jane Doe Ponytail: An Epic Tragedy on a Small Block in Queens." *New York Times*, October 16, 2018. http://nytimes.com/interactive/2018/10/11/nyregion/sex-workers-massage-parlor.html.

Gilmore, Ruth Wilson. 1999. "Globalization and U.S. Prison Growth: From Military Keynesianism to Post-Keynesianism." *Race & Class* 40, nos. 2/3: 171–88.

———. 2007. *Golden Gulag: Prison, Surplus, and Crises in Globalizing California.* Berkeley: University of California Press.

Mountz, Alison. 2010. *Seeking Asylum: Human Smuggling and Bureaucracy at the Border.* Minneapolis: University of Minnesota Press.

NYPD News. 2017. "NYPD Announces Expanded Resources to Combat Sex Trafficking." *NYPD News*, February 1, 2017. http://nypdnews. com/2017/02/first-lady-chirlane-mccray-and-police-commissioner-james-p-oneill-announce-expanded-resources-to-combat-sex-trafficking/.

Robinson, Cedric J. 2000 [1983]. *Black Marxism: The Making of the Black Radical Tradition.* Chapel Hill: University of North Carolina Press.

PART III. **REVISITING THE RADICAL POTENTIAL OF THE NATIONAL WELFARE RIGHTS ORGANIZATION**

The Radical Feminist Legacy of the National Welfare Rights Organization

Wilson Sherwin and Frances Fox Piven

Abstract: Relying on archival and firsthand accounts, we argue that existing scholarship on the welfare rights movement has silenced many of the
more radical feminist tendencies and accorded undue emphasis to the way
recipient activists conformed to hegemonic, patriarchal standards. By exploring recipient activists' rejection of waged work, anti-war politics, and
their fight for reproductive justice, we demonstrate how a social movement of primarily poor Black women forged sophisticated arguments for
the importance of guaranteed income as a means of facilitating autonomy
and civic engagement, rather than reifying gendered social roles. **Keywords:** welfare, guaranteed income, feminism, social reproduction, African American

For the propertied bourgeois woman her house is the world. For the
proletarian woman the whole world is her house, the world with its sorrows
and its joy, with its cold cruelty and its brutal size.
> —*Rosa Luxemburg,* The Proletarian Woman

Introduction

In the mid-1960s, welfare recipients, the majority of whom were African
American women, organized in hundreds of local groups across the nation. By 1967 the groups coalesced under the umbrella of the National
Welfare Rights Organization (NWRO), which at its peak represented as
many as one hundred thousand welfare recipients (West 1981). On the
face of it, this development was remarkable, if only because of the multiple degradations which these women endured. But inspired by the larger
Black freedom movement that was transforming southern Jim Crow, and

WSQ: Women's Studies Quarterly 47: 3 & 4 (Fall/Winter 2019) © 2019 by Wilson Sherwin and
Frances Fox Piven. All rights reserved.

propelled by their own experience of exploitative jobs, poverty wages, and paternalistic, intrusive, and stingy public programs, welfare activists took to the streets, welfare centers, and courts alike with the aspiration that women's lives would no longer be dictated by husbands, employers, government bureaucrats, and clerks. In so doing they forged a subversive feminist politics which remains underappreciated and yet is deeply relevant to today's political landscape. In the following article, we reexamine some of the more distinctive features of the movement: their critique of waged work, their prosex attitudes, and their encompassing understanding of social reproduction.

We need to pause to qualify our argument, as we think any argument about the beliefs of a social movement should be qualified. Social scientists often tend to treat the opinions or beliefs they uncover and on which they base their interpretations as *things*, and relatively firm and unchanging things at that. But beliefs are not things. They are rather evanescent and elusive, subject to change or maybe simply to being displaced by one of the other multiple and sometimes contradictory beliefs we also hold in our heads.

Beliefs are perhaps more easily bent or displaced when they fly in the face of dominant or authoritative opinion. Thus there were indeed occasions when NWRO participants invoked the justification of motherhood for their demands, and they were also sometimes responsive to promises of job training, for example. The radical critique that we see in the movement emerged only slowly and irregularly, although it grew stronger as the movement grew. The exhilarating experience of collective action, and defiant collective action, as groups of recipients challenged their caseworkers and welfare officials, occupied welfare centers, spoke out to the press and even to congressional committees, nourished and brought to the surface the subterranean ideas that their experience had generated. It was with the movement at her back that Jeanette Washington, a welfare recipient from New York, could announce to television host David Brinkley, who was taunting her for giving birth to another child: "That money in the White House is mine!" Not very strategic of course, and that is our point.

Against Waged Work, For Motherhood?

The mainstream women's movement was hopeful that the Equal Rights Amendment would finally guarantee women equality in the workplace. By contrast, the NWRO demanded the freedom to *not* work. In 1972, gesturing to their substantive differences with the women's movement, welfare rights activist Johnnie Tillmon proclaimed that the welfare rights movement was the vanguard of women's freedom "because we have so few illusions and because our issues are so important to all women" (Sreenivasan 2009, 671). One of the primary illusions the NWRO militated against was the popular insistence that waged work could offer the solution to the problems of women or people of color (Le Blanc and Yates 2013; Kornbluh 1998; Nadasen 2002; Stein 2016; Sherwin 2019). Participants in the movement developed vigorous critiques of job-training programs, low-wage jobs, and even the broader capitalist institution of waged labor. These criticisms emerged partially in response to new policies at the local and federal levels which sought to curtail rising welfare rolls by imposing work requirements on welfare recipients, as well as from their own extensive experience of often back-breaking and low-wage work. In widely distributed pamphlets, activists rejected the popular argument that waged work would "give them a sense of dignity, self-worth, and confidence," arguing instead that it "institutionalized poverty" (Wiley Papers, box 1952).

In speeches, interviews, newsletters, and more, participants demonstrated a critical stance toward waged work with particularly sophisticated analyses of the intersectional ways their positions as, in one leader's words, fat, Black, middle-aged mothers rendered them particularly vulnerable to exploitation. The culmination of the NWRO's theorization of waged work is most clearly and vociferously articulated in their 1970 proposed alternative to Nixon's welfare reform plan. In Bill HR 7257, also known as the Adequate Income Plan, the NWRO declared:

> The real employment problem is not that people need jobs and jobs need people. It is that employment does not distribute wealth the way its advocates claim it does. As a wealth distribution system employment has never worked well for the poor, especially the black poor. Even if all eligible Americans were employed today, the poverty rate would not be seriously affected. (West Papers, box 25, folder 13)

In the place of "slave jobs" and "forced work," recipients sought a "guaranteed adequate income" for all Americans, similar in many substantive ways to today's calls for Universal Basic Income (UBI).

Many scholars have made sense of this fervent critique of waged work (and the movement's sharp divergence from both the civil rights and women's movements' positions on work) by emphasizing that welfare activists eschewed waged work out of a prioritization of motherhood and care labor. Guida West argues, "Welfare rights women identified themselves primarily as mothers, fought for 'mother power' in the political arena, and argued that mothering was an important job that should be adequately subsidized by the state" (1998, 100). Ellen Reese understands the strategy of demanding income rather than work as "a product of its time. In 1970, only about 30 percent of married women were in the labor force. Like others, the NWRO embraced the family wage system, demanding poor mothers' right to stay at home with their children" (2005, 114). Denton echoes this sentiment, insisting that "welfare recipients focused on mothers' roles as nurturers and providers. . . . Even though many of these women also worked outside the home in low-income jobs, their lives tended to center on home and children" (2012, 217). Premilla Nadasen interprets this aversion to waged work as an expression of Black women's desire to receive benefits, social and material, that maternalists had long granted white, middle-class women. Additionally, Nadasen argues, "Wage work for poor women and most Black women often meant long hours, drudgery, and meager rewards, not a fulfilling career. . . . Given the opportunity, many poor African American women preferred to stay home" (2002, 280).

Although we certainly recognize that the poor Black women who made up the grassroots of the welfare rights movement were long denied the racialized benefits of maternalism, and insisting on those rights challenged some long-standing, discriminatory norms, we believe scholars' interpretation of the movement's objectives, emphasizing as they do "staying home" and lives centered around children, flattens out much of the more vibrant and insightful analyses welfare activists offered. We propose instead that much of the archival record suggests NWRO participants did not uniformly share the presumption that a woman's place should either be at home with their children or at work, but that many fervently challenged these narrow options for women, insisting on a different priority.

These clashing perspectives came to a head when the U.S. Congress Joint Economic Committee held a hearing on Income Maintenance Programs in 1968, where Beulah Sanders, a recipient activist in the NWRO, and Representative Griffiths, the self-anointed "most dedicated feminist we have in Congress," disagreed over the impact work requirements would have on welfare recipients, as well as their understanding of what constituted the life of a welfare recipient. Griffiths argued in favor of attaching work requirements to welfare benefits, claiming that without them, women would be relegated to their homes. By forcing women into the waged workforce Griffiths believed the government would be ensuring "those people [welfare recipients] have a right to participate in the economy of this country" (U.S. Congress 1968, 77). Sanders responded to this argument by asking if she could comment on this claim "woman to woman," therefore challenging Griffith's assertion that she represented the sole voice of feminism:

> One of the things we are concerned about is being forced into these non-existing positions which might be going out and cleaning Mrs. A's kitchen. I am not going to do that because I feel I am more valuable and I can do something else. This is one of those things these people are worrying about, that they are going to be pushed into doing housework when they can be much more valuable doing something else. . . . What they have that is going for them is the nitty-gritty stuff and that is out into the community, mixing with the people, finding out what their problems are, and trying to help solve those problems. (U.S. Congress 1968, 78–79)[1]

Sanders's statement encapsulates a unique position the NWRO developed regarding waged labor, care work, and civic engagement. She challenged the prevalent views that waged work held intrinsic value for women, or that by rebuffing waged work, women would be cloistered in their homes. Instead, Sanders asserts that they had more "valuable"—primarily political—tasks to attend to: going "out into the community, mixing with the people, finding out what their problems are, and trying to help solve those problems" (78–79). Contra many scholarly narratives of the NWRO, Sanders and others often did not appeal to a Black maternalist logic arguing for the importance of care labor provided by mothers, but rather the necessity and relevance of community engagement.

Rather than simply allowing them access to the vaunted but often inaccessible role of housewife and mother, welfare and the welfare rights movement provided recipients with an education in political mobilization, and the means to act on it. This analysis is far from unique to Sanders. In numerous accounts, welfare activists underscore the sense of fulfillment they achieved through their political activism. Jacqueline Pope joined the Brooklyn Welfare Organization (B-WAC) as a recipient and eventually became a national organizer and later, scholar. Her accounts of the movement further affirm that the maternalist discourse deployed at times by recipients and emphasized by scholars was not the entire story. Pope recalled,

> The organizers helped clients face reality about the unlikelihood of obtaining employment that would offer a salary adequate enough to make them self-sufficient and free of the welfare system. Accordingly, B-WAC promoted discussions concerning social or political unsalaried community participation that was as important as salaried work. In essence, people could make contributions to improving the quality of community life regardless of their employment status. Former members agreed that organizers were relatively successful in this effort and that most members were pledged to a continuing civic involvement. (1989, 103)

B-WAC developed an extensive curriculum of leadership classes, which it offered at its Bushwick location to standing-room-only crowds. These offerings included five distinct classes on welfare case law; how to organize welfare rights groups; how to plan and implement actions, particularly direct action related to welfare rights; causes and explanations of the welfare crisis; and understanding the local political landscape. B-WAC was by far the largest welfare rights organization within the NWRO, comprising a third of the national organization's membership, and it's clear their model of education and mutual aid was deeply empowering to participants. More than ten years after the decline of the Brooklyn organization, Ms. Wise, a former participant, reflected on her experience in the movement and the reverberations it had through other civic organizations, saying,

> I learned I am somebody. Welfare Rights meant a right to life—it freed me from emotional slavery. I am a person you can't push aside, I have the right to be. Welfare Rights showed me that my counterparts are all around; knowing this, I no longer felt alone. Welfare Rights lives, I and other people are still active, struggling for a better life. PTAs, school boards, even political clubs have former welfare rights members and we continue pushing the welfare rights agenda. (quoted in Pope 1990, 73)

NWRO members not only sought support and recognition for their community activism, but some recipients expressed irritation with the emphasis on motherhood as patronizing or condescending. Indeed, recipients sometimes became indignant at the emphasis on children as the justification for their benefits. For example, a number of recipients interviewed in George T. Martin's 1972 study of the movement critiqued the insistence on the motherhood framing although their discomfort was often expressed indirectly. "The basic problem with welfare rights in Detroit," one interviewee stated, "is the overbearing influence of X and Y. . . . They have a condescending attitude towards the mothers. They act and talk as if the mothers are incapable of making their own decisions. They refer to recipients as 'the mothers' or 'our mothers' in talking to nonrecipients" (Martin 1972, 143). And another informant: "I don't get along with Y at all. She infantilizes the recipients" (1972, 145). It would be impossible to overlook the fact that motherhood was the condition for all but a very few recipients' benefits, but the fact that the state recognized motherhood as a role which merited some form of recompense—and that it therefore made strategic sense to deploy it at times publicly—does not necessarily mean it was the main way participants ultimately defined themselves or their efforts as worthwhile.

Recipients identified civic engagement as a productive effort, deserving of both respect and remuneration, and movement participants repeatedly challenged the familiar dichotomy between "home or work," and in the process delineated a more innovative form of feminism than is often ascribed to them. Think, for example, of the way they couched their demand for childcare, which they thought should be provided regardless of whether they were working or not. To be sure, lack of childcare was often identified by the NWRO as a reason why it was unjust to expect mothers of young children to work. However, members of the NWRO did not desire childcare solely to facilitate labor market participation: they laid claim to it more generally for the autonomy it would provide. Numerous the NWRO publications argued for opposing Nixon's proposed welfare reforms partially on the basis that childcare provisions were inadequate and overly geared toward enforcing wage labor. They asserted that childcare was "not really designed to help mothers and children; they are designed to rationalize the Family Assistance Plan's onerous forced work requirement—to 'free' mothers so they may labor for slave wages" (Wiley Papers, box 17, folder 5). Other publications highlighting the NWRO's demands emphasized the importance of accessible, high-quality childcare regardless of whether a woman was working or not. "Mothers," they noted, "especially need childcare that will free them for community involvement" (NWRO Archives, box 2179).

The emphasis on motherhood as the justification for welfare support in the existing literature on the NWRO has obscured some of the more nuanced and radical ways recipient activists made sense of their situation and justified themselves not only as productive members of society, but as empowered participants in a democracy. For the NWRO, a woman's place was not exclusively in the office nor the home: it was also, importantly, in the community. This remains a particularly relevant insight today as UBI gains traction. Some feminists have opposed UBI with the belief that it would only further entrench gendered divisions of labor and ensure women would be stuck at home (Bergmann 2004; Robeyns 2008). The history of the NWRO offers an example of feminists who favor a guaranteed income for the increased political engagement it could make possible, not simply so they could "stay home."

Sexual Liberation, Reproductive Justice

It was not just on the question of waged work or motherhood that the NWRO pushed the boundaries of convention. Their trenchant critiques also suggested aspects of a particularly unique, and in many ways avant-garde, feminism that has been either mischaracterized or completely ignored by scholars.[2] As documented in Johnnie Tillmon's 1972 article for *Ms.* magazine, "Welfare Is a Women's Issue," one of the NWRO's major critiques of the welfare system concerned the myriad ways it forced women to "give up control of your own body":

> On A.F.D.C., you're not supposed to have any sex at all. You give up control of your own body. It's a condition of aid. You may even have to agree to get your tubes tied so you can never have more children just to avoid being cut off welfare. (quoted in Nadasen, Mittelstadt, and Chappell 2009, 178)

These constant assaults on recipients' autonomy as women and sexual subjects offered ample ground for criticism and transformation of the existing welfare system, and became the site of some of the movement's most concrete victories.

Establishing bodily autonomy had long been a feminist objective, but the NWRO fought for it in ways that were particularly attentive to the concerns of Black and poor women, offering insights that the mainstream feminist movement did not integrate for generations (Nadasen 2002). Two major legal advancements the movement made in asserting this autonomy included the 1968 Supreme Court case *King v. Smith*, which did away with "man-in-the-house" rules that had permitted midnight raids of women's homes, removing benefits if investigators found any evidence of male presence, romantic or otherwise; and *Relf v. Weinberger* in 1974, which challenged involuntary sterilization as a requirement for welfare (Davis 1995).

These legal gains were important in and of themselves, but the process of achieving them also yielded generative ideological interventions that challenged the moral basis of patriarchal insistence on women's respectability. Intrusions by caseworkers provided an impetus to publicly assert their unabashed right to romantic and sexual lives free from the prying eyes of the state, despite the fact that they were, for the most part, as a virtual condition of welfare eligibility, unwed single mothers. In other words, their heartfelt opposition to man-in-the-house rules entailed defiance of sexual mores.

This insistent and unapologetic approach to women's sexuality is a part of the movement's political analysis, and would in later iterations of feminism come to be known as "prosex." Still, this aspect of the welfare rights movement has been silenced by numerous scholars. Perhaps this is understandable in a society where Black women have often been oversexualized and objectified. To point to their exuberant sexuality might seem to detract from their seriousness as political actors. But in the larger context of the welfare rights movement, it does no such thing; rather, it contributes to an understanding of the profundity of the movement's political vision, a vision we think was predicated on (and uncompromising about) the centrality that pleasure, well-being, and autonomy should hold in a person's life. This conviction animated welfare rights actions around establishing the right to credit (Kornbluh 1997), as well as their right to intrusion-free and shame-free sexuality.

The effort to eliminate man-in-the-house rules was conducted by lawyers allied with the movement, but the undertaking was enthusiastically supported by the movement. In the course of the campaign, the NWRO challenged entrenched and lingering aspects of the respectability politics that cast women's sexuality as an unpolitical and private matter largely relegated to marriage. Seeking the end of these man-in-the-house incursions, which denied them privacy in their most intimate lives, recipients took vocal positions on women's rights to their sexuality. This is particularly notable in transcripts of meetings and offhand comments made by participants, as well as in plans for community-controlled reproductive health centers that the NWRO hoped to develop.

For example, at the organization's 1972 national convention in Miami, Jesse Gray, a leader of the National Tenants Organization, gave one of the conference's plenary speeches. Audio recordings of the speech reveal an extremely engaged crowd, roaring in approval at Gray's characterization of the exploitative nature of rent and the need for tenant control of housing. Simply putting tenants on the board was insufficient, Gray argued; it had to be tenants, who were clearly on the side of residents, and who refused to police recipients' respectability. "You got some people, if you play the numbers, they don't talk to you. . . . If they saw a man slipping through your back door, they won't talk to you. 'You're too old for him!'" (West Papers, audio file wes_012a). The auditorium thundered in approving laughter and applause at this assertion, which clearly resonated with participants' rejection of the surveillance of their sexuality that they had endured, not only by caseworkers but from neighbors who likewise sought to penalize female residents for their sexual or romantic relationships. Gray's added emphasis that nosy neighbors would judge women for having younger lovers played particularly well to a crowd of confident women. Gray's radical, if not downright revolutionary, message that housing is a human right and should be free ("Kill off the private landlord! Kill him off!"; "Lock up a landlord!"; "Free rent is not out of the question!" [West Papers, audio file wes_012a]) was paired with a message about the importance of ensuring women's sexual freedom, to which the audience was extremely receptive.

Frances Fox Piven recalled, in an interview, the excitement at the 1971 annual conference when participants discovered the happy coincidence that the conference was taking place next to a U.S. Navy base, in close proximity to numerous sailors. Participants began planning social events to which they could invite the Navy men. All this was done with a sense of frivolity, she notes. They did not seem concerned with finding husbands; rather, "they treated men just a little like prey, as men had long treated women" (Piven, pers. comm., May 18, 2018).

Recipient activists in the NWRO forged a unique style of feminism that departed from middle-class white feminists, but also attempted to challenge the explicit misogyny of Black nationalism, while not isolating themselves from Black men altogether. Piven recalls, "They liked men, but they didn't want them at their meetings, and they didn't like the men who tried to offer them physical protection, a posture that the rise of the Panthers made fashionable at the time" (pers. comm., May 18, 2018). In this sense the feminism of the NWRO shares commonalities with the

Combahee River Collective who, years later, similarly expressed, "We struggle together with Black men against racism, while we also struggle with Black men about sexism" ([1978] 2014, 274). This seems to be a notable distinction between the NWRO and other feminist organizations of the time whose seriousness as political actors seemed predicated on either distancing themselves from men, as some white feminists advocated, or maintaining an intentional nonsexual outward appearance as many female civil rights activists had (Nadasen 2002).

Importantly, however, the movement was not composed exclusively of bon vivant "man-eaters." A large number of religious recipients were active in the movement, meetings sometimes began with prayers, and churches were some of the largest, most enduring supporters of the organization (West 1981). For them, this "prosex" ethos may not have been ideal. However, in stark contrast to many other movements, feminist and otherwise, which developed contentious fractions over issues such as this, the NWRO maintained a united front and allowed for a true diversity of experiences and values. Although major conflicts certainly arose throughout the organization's life (Martin 1972; West 1981; Nadasen 2005), there does not appear to have been any contention over the struggle for reproductive and sexual autonomy.

Much of the existing scholarship has downplayed this aspect of the movement, overwriting the significance of women's sexual agency and autonomy, and insisting rather that there was "a maternal rationale behind welfare recipients' advocacy of birth control—they believed it would enable them to be better mothers to the children they already had" (Denton 2012, 212). Kornbluh (1998) interprets recipients' desire to end man-in-the-house rules as motivated largely by the desire to be allowed to marry or develop the kinds of relationships with men that would lead to marriage. Kornbluh writes, "Although it is tempting to see this case as an affirmation of women's individual rights to sexual freedom outside marriage, for many welfare recipients it also represented an opportunity to marry" (1998, 73). Of course, mobilization against this invasive and humiliating practice may have been partially motivated by a desire to marry, although the evidence Kornbluh presents for this is sparse.

What we resist, however, is the pattern of silencing evidence of alternative and less "respectable" currents within the movement. By ignoring instances when issues around sexuality emerged within the movement, and by focusing solely on public-facing arguments that appealed to mainstream values (such as the eugenicist argument that better birth control would mean fewer and better-raised children), scholars like Denton and Kornbluh reinscribe onto the NWRO a startlingly patriarchal logic whereby women's sexuality must always be functional.

Social Reproduction Feminism and Anti-war Politics

Not only was the feminism of the welfare rights movement "prosex," but the movement also developed a vision of reproductive politics far in advance of other feminists, one that prefigured what later feminists termed "reproductive justice." In contrast to the narrow focus of "reproductive rights" which often prioritized access to birth control and abortion while ignoring the complex ways different class and racial positions informed access and need for these services, reproductive justice insists that de jure legal access to "choices" about one's body are not truly choices if they are financially untenable (Ross et al. 2017). NWRO participants sought the right to have genuine autonomy over their bodies: to have children if they chose, and to prevent pregnancies if that was their desire. They understood that true reproductive freedom meant not just possessing the negative freedom to decide whether to keep a pregnancy or not, but also the positive freedom to be financially capable of raising a child (Berlin 1969; Nadasen 2002). In doing so, they extended the concept of "reproduction," as many socialist feminists do, to include "social reproduction," which consists not just of the intergenerational reproduction of life but also the daily reproduction of people by providing necessary food, housing, and care (Bhattacharya 2017). The NWRO fought for access to and recognition of those features of reproduction just as much as birth control, abortion, and freedom from forced and coerced sterilizations.

Part and parcel of the social reproduction feminism espoused by the NWRO was an explicitly anti-war stance (West 1981; Kornbluh 2007). The NWRO not only disavowed the Vietnam War, but articulated the inseparability between an unjust war abroad and the struggles they faced at home: "STOP THE WAR IN VIETNAM AND ON THE POOR" was a common refrain throughout campaign materials (Wiley Papers, box 7, folder 8). Indeed, as if they could forget how profoundly intertwined these two "wars" were, Moynihan's notorious 1965 report explicitly justified sending young Black men to fight in Vietnam as a primary solution to the "tangled web of pathology" he ascribed to growing up in Black, female-headed households. Moynihan argued,

> Given the strains of the disorganized and matrifocal family life in which so many Negro youth come of age, the Armed Forces are a dramatic and desperately needed change: a world away from women, a world run by strong men of unquestioned authority, where discipline, if harsh, is nonetheless orderly and predictable, and where rewards, if limited, are granted on the basis of performance. The theme of a current Army recruiting message states it as clearly as can be: "In the U.S. Army you get to know what it means to feel like a man." (1965, 18)

Welfare activists linked their struggles to the Vietnam War in two major ways, denouncing in the first instance the fact that funds were being spent to kill children abroad that could have been used to feed children domestically; and secondly, recognizing that it was their very own children fighting, and often dying at higher rates.

In a booklet intended for children, the NWRO attempted to explain why "many of our brothers and sisters do not have enough to eat or a decent place to live. Do not have nice clothes to wear or enough money to have a pet" (West Archives, box 27, folder 13). Their answer situated war spending at the core of this problem "because America spends too much money killing poor women and children in other lands. And rich people want more than they really need" (West Archives, box 27, folder 13). The NWRO devoted the May 1970 issue of its newspaper, the *Welfare Fighter*, to the theme "Welfare and the War," underscoring how disparate welfare rights groups were linking the two issues around the country:

> There is a close relationship between the way human beings are being treated in Viet Nam and the way human beings are being treated in the United States. WRO members in Ohio have first hand experience in this relationship and therefore join the struggle to end the war. At the November mobilization in Washington DC . . . Ohio's WRO members voice opposition to a system which forces their sons to fight for freedom in Viet Nam when there is a small chance for freedom in this country. A young man is forced to struggle for food, shelter, and clothing for 17 or 18 years because of oppressive social, economic, and political institutions that have oppressed him. Some WRO mothers have suggested that all children of low-income families should be granted amnesty from the draft. It is clear

that WRO members represent a solid opposing force against the war, against the national priorities which subvert rather than subsidize life. (West Papers, box 28, folder 10, p. 12)

The analysis linking domestic poverty and war emphasized the man-made nature of both crises. In the NWRO's view, poverty and the war were the result of unjust use of resources, which could be corrected, rather than a natural course of things. The NWRO underscored this analysis throughout much of their work, repeatedly demanding "welfare not warfare" (also the organization's 1971 national conference theme). For the NWRO, ending the war was the answer to two major problems: the war itself, which they understood to be disproportionately harming their sons; and the issue of how to fund the guaranteed annual income which the NWRO sought.

Implications for Today

Fifty years later, far from having been resolved and resigned to history, the interventions made by NWRO activists remain dispiritingly relevant to the lives of women today. Their perspectives on everything from poverty, reproductive justice, work, and war provide illuminating alternatives for contemporary feminists.

Work has become more onerous and less rewarding for large swaths of the labor force, with many of the worst characteristics of the contemporary labor market—irregular schedules, low wages, and of course sexual harassment—disproportionately affecting women. Nevertheless, too many feminists have continued to insist on "leaning in" at work as the solution to many problems women face.

Although we have challenged the assertions that motherhood was the defining identity for welfare activists, the NWRO certainly understood the problems associated with parenting to be political. Since the 1970s, declining real wages for most working people has forced more and more families to rely on all adults in a household working, sometimes more than full time. Even with two earners, families are often still unable to make ends meet, partially because the cost of childcare has skyrocketed, overtaking even the astronomical increase of rents in many regions.[3] Additionally, given the gendered division in childcare, the lack of paid maternity leave for most mothers, and high rates of Black maternal mortality, the "penalties of motherhood" remain steep. The NWRO's early and expansive analysis of reproductive justice provides a powerful framework for thinking through and fighting for the well-being of women and mothers without relegating them to traditional family roles, while emphasizing at every step that feminist objectives must explicitly include economic security for all. It is unfortunately too rarely asserted, in the era of feminist hawks like Gina Haspel and Hillary Clinton, that a massive reduction in defense spending and a reapportioning of those funds to improving lives, rather than destroying them abroad, should be, without question, one of the foundational elements of contemporary feminist projects.

While many of the NWRO's interventions provide a robust framework for thinking through contemporary feminist concerns (or at least, what we argue, *should* be feminist concerns) they do not directly engage with all of today's questions of political import. How, for example, might they respond to current movements that exclude trans* people from feminism? Or what might they proffer as the solution to the crisis of climate change? We don't have direct statements to turn to on these matters, but we can, however, extrapolate some relevant insights from their broader stances. For example, their deep suspicion of the intrinsic value of waged work, and their concomitant insistence on community-based involvement might lend support for contemporary arguments that less work for all—antiproductivist policies favoring degrowth, shortened work weeks, and more community-based involvement—could be an important component of addressing impending environmental crises caused by greenhouse gas emissions. Welfare rights activists' insistence on bodily autonomy, freedom from intrusion and coercion, and their mobilization for economic freedom might, we hope, provide a historical precedent that contributes to current struggles for trans* self-determination and radical transfeminist critiques of economic injustice. When in doubt we could turn to the powerful words of Beulah Sanders: "Give poor people enough money to live decently, and let us decide how to live our lives" (1969).

Former participants in the NWRO drew on their experience in the welfare rights movement and many remained committed activists throughout their lives. But for many the NWRO would be the last time they situated their political engagement in an explicitly feminist organization. Perhaps this can be explained, as Piven has for herself, by a sense of alienation from the majority of feminist organizations and projects where NWRO-style feminism—prosex, critical of waged work, devoted to working class women's needs, critical of respectability politics with an insistence on a broad vision of reproductive politics and the centrality of economic well-being to achieving any of these other goals—remained all too often silenced.

Even scholars who admire and respect the work of NWRO activists have contributed to this silencing by highlighting aspects of the movement which are congruous with mainstream values and glossing over those we have focused on above. We recognize this impulse as a well-intended one: the intense vilification of welfare mothers in decades following the NWRO's decline has placed those concerned with the rights of welfare recipients in a defensive position. But by insisting on recipients' worthiness in ways that are legible to racist, capitalist, patriarchal society, we lose sight of the militant ways they challenged these social relations and some of the most rousing lessons they leave to guide us forward.

Wilson Sherwin is an educator and activist. She recently received her PhD in sociology from the CUNY Graduate Center. Her dissertation, "Rich in Needs: The Forgotten Radical Politics of the Welfare Rights Movement," was supervised by Dr. Piven. She can be reached at wilsonsherwin@gmail.com.

Frances Fox Piven is distinguished professor of political science and sociology emerita at the CUNY Graduate Center. The books she has authored or coauthored include *Regulating the Poor*, *Poor People's Movements*, *Why Americans Don't Vote*, and *Challenging Authority*. She can be reached at fpiven@hotmail.com.

Notes

1. This passage is also quoted, in part, by Felicia Kornbluh in her book *The Battle for Welfare Rights*, although she leaves out the insight we believe to be especially relevant: "They can be much more valuable doing something else . . . what they have that is going for them is the nitty-gritty stuff and that is out into the community, mixing with the people, finding out what their problems are, and trying to help solve those problems" (U.S. Congress 1968, 78–79). By ignoring the end of Sanders's sentence, Kornbluh concludes that Sanders is articulating a fear that "welfare mothers who wanted to spend most of their time raising their children would be forced to do something else for a living" (2007, 99). We believe this example to be emblematic of the erasure that welfare recipients' distinctive interventions have faced.
2. Nadasen is an exception here; she acknowledges recipients "demanded the right to control their own reproduction, choosing for themselves when and how to take birth control, have an abortion, or be sterilized. And they demanded the right to control their own organizations" (2002, 278).

3. The Economic Policy Institute reports, "Among families with two children (a 4-year-old and an 8-year-old), childcare costs exceed rent in 500 out of 618 family budget areas. For two-child families, childcare costs range from about half as much as rent in San Francisco to nearly three times rent in Binghamton, New York" (Gould and Cooke 2015).

Works Cited

Bergmann, Barbara R. 2004. "A Swedish-Style Welfare State or Basic Income: Which Should Have Priority?" *Politics & Society* 32, no. 1: 107–18.

Berlin, Isaiah. 1969. *Four Essays on Liberty*. Oxford: Oxford University Press.

Bhattacharya, Tithi, ed. 2017. *Social Reproduction Theory: Remapping Class, Recentering Oppression*. London: Pluto Press.

Combahee River Collective. (1978) 2014. "A Black Feminist Statement." *WSQ* 42, nos. 3&4: 271–80. Citations refer to the *WSQ* edition.

Davis, Martha F. 1995. *Brutal Need: Lawyers and the Welfare Rights Movement, 1960–1973*. New Haven, CT: Yale University Press.

Denton, Georgina. 2012. "'Neither Guns nor Bombs – Neither the State nor God – Will Stop Us from Fighting for Our Children': Motherhood and Protest in 1960s and 1970s America." *The Sixties* 5, no. 2: 205–28.

Gould, Elise, and Tanyell Cooke. 2015. "High quality child care is out of reach for working families." Economic Policy Institute, October 6, 2015. https://www.epi.org/publication/child-care-affordability/.

Kornbluh, Felicia. 1997. "To Fulfill Their 'Rightly Needs': Consumerism and the National Welfare Rights Movement." *Radical History Review*, no. 69: 76–113.

———. 1998. "The Goals of the National Welfare Rights Movement: Why We Need Them Thirty Years Later." *Feminist Studies* 24, no. 1: 65–78.

———. 2007. *The Battle for Welfare Rights: Politics and Poverty in Modern America*. Philadelphia: University of Pennsylvania Press.

Le Blanc, Paul, and Michael D. Yates. 2013. *A Freedom Budget for All Americans: Recapturing the Promise of the Civil Rights Movement in the Struggle for Economic Justice Today*. New York: Monthly Review Press.

Martin, George. 1972. *The Emergence and Development of a Social Movement Organization among the Underclass: A Case Study of the National Welfare Rights Organization (NWRO)*. Chicago: University of Chicago.

Moynihan, Daniel P. 1965. *The Negro Family: The Case for National Action*. Washington, DC: Office of Policy Planning and Research, U.S. Department of Labor.

Nadasen, Premilla. 2002. "Expanding the Boundaries of the Women's Movement: Black Feminism and the Struggle for Welfare Rights." *Feminist Studies* 28, no. 2: 271–301.

———. 2005. *Welfare Warriors: The Welfare Rights Movement in the United States.* New York: Routledge.

Nadasen, Premilla, Jennifer Mittelstadt, and Marisa Chappell, eds. 2009. *Welfare in the United States: A History with Documents, 1935–1996.* New York: Routledge.

National Welfare Rights Organization (NWRO). Papers. Moorland-Spingarn Research Center, Howard University, Washington, DC.

Pope, Jacqueline. 1989. *Biting the Hand That Feeds Them: Organizing Women on Welfare at the Grass Roots Level.* New York: Praeger.

———. 1990. "Women in the Welfare Rights Struggle: The Brooklyn Welfare Action Council." In *Women and Social Protest*, edited by Guida West and Rhoda Lois Blumberg, 57–74. New York: Oxford University Press.

Reese, Ellen. 2005. *Backlash Against Welfare Mothers: Past and Present.* Berkeley: University of California Press.

Robeyns, Ingrid. 2008. "Introduction: Revisiting the Feminism and Basic Income Debate." *Basic Income Studies* 3, no. 3: 1–6.

Ross, Loretta J., Lynn Roberts, Erika Derkas, Whitney Peoples, and Pamela Bridgewater, eds. 2017. *Radical Reproductive Justice: Foundations, Theory, Practice, Critique.* New York: Feminist Press at CUNY.

Sanders, Beulah. 1969. "Statement to the Presidential Commission on Income Maintenance." June 5, 1969. Box 22, folder 4. Wiley Papers, State Historical Society of Wisconsin, Madison.

Sherwin, Wilson. 2019. "Rich in Needs: The Forgotten Radical Politics of the Welfare Rights Movement." PhD diss., CUNY Graduate Center.

Sreenivasan, Jyotsna. 2009. *Poverty and the Government in America: A Historical Encyclopedia.* Santa Barbara, CA: ABC-CLIO.

Stein, David P. 2016. "'This Nation Has Never Honestly Dealt with the Question of a Peacetime Economy': Coretta Scott King and the Struggle for a Nonviolent Economy in the 1970s." *Souls* 18, no. 1: 80–105.

U.S. Congress. 1968. *Income Maintenance Programs: Proceedings.* Joint Economic Committee, Subcommittee on Fiscal Policy. Income Maintenance Programs: Hearings, 90th Congress, second session. U.S. Government Printing Office.

West, Guida. Papers. Sophia Smith Collection, Smith College, Northampton, MA.

———. 1981. *The National Welfare Rights Movement: The Social Protest of Poor Women.* New York: Praeger.

———. 1998. "Women in the Welfare Rights Movement: Reform or
    Revolution?" In *Women and Revolution: Global Expressions*, edited by Marie
    Josephine Diamond, 91–108. Dordrecht: Springer.
Wiley, George Alvin. Papers. State Historical Society of Wisconsin, Madison.

Mildred Beltré. *Freedom Dreams*, 2014. Cotton, 5 x 5 in. Image courtesy of the artist.

Response to Sherwin and Piven's "The Radical Feminist Legacy of the National Welfare Rights Organization"

Premilla Nadasen

Abstract: This essay is a response to Wilson Sherwin and Frances Fox Piven's "The Radical Feminist Legacy of the National Welfare Rights Organization" in this volume of *WSQ: Together*. It argues for the importance of a politics of citation as part of feminist scholarly practice and discusses previous scholarship that has analyzed the radical, oppositional feminist activism of the welfare rights movement. **Keywords:** welfare rights, citation, feminism

Wilson Sherwin and Frances Fox Piven's essay in this volume of *WSQ: Together* purports to offer a new interpretation of the welfare rights movement. The authors claim to unearth a "unique style of feminism that departed from middle-class white feminists," a "subversive feminist politics," that "remains underappreciated" (Sherwin and Piven 2019, 144, 136). They propose to "reexamine some of the more distinctive features of the movement—their critique of waged work, their pro-sex attitudes, and their encompassing understanding of social reproduction" (136). The "avant-garde feminism" of the welfare rights movement, they argue, "has been either mischaracterized or completely ignored by scholars" (142).

The history of the welfare rights movement is relevant and timely in the current political climate. Sherwin and Piven are correct that in mainstream feminist discourse, there is little reference to the kind of radicalism articulated by the welfare rights movement. In an increasingly precarious labor market and at a moment when neoliberalism has whittled away any semblance of a welfare safety net, we can learn a great deal from recipients'

WSQ: Women's Studies Quarterly 47: 3 & 4 (Fall/Winter 2019) © 2019 by Premilla Nadasen.
All rights reserved.

critiques of wage work and their analysis of sexuality and social reproduction. As Sherwin and Piven assert, the welfare rights movement's "perspectives on everything from poverty, reproductive justice, work, and war provide illuminating alternatives for contemporary feminists" (148). Its version of feminism included economic security, bodily control, state support for care work, opportunities for community engagement, and a critique of foreign policy.

Despite the importance of the subject matter, I am troubled by the authors' lack of citation and misreading of earlier scholarship. The argument is presented as wholly original in response to a "silencing" by other scholars. However, many of the lines of inquiry that the authors claim are underappreciated have been discussed extensively by previous welfare rights scholars. Even as they seek to resurrect the voices of welfare rights activists, their failure to engage work by others contributes to another kind of invisibility—the invisibility of the labor of feminist academics, who have not been silent, but are being silenced in this essay. Just as we need to incorporate the radical views of welfare recipients in considering contemporary social policy, we also need to acknowledge the work of other feminist scholars as part of a feminist scholarly praxis.

Politics of Citation

The politics of citation are necessary for both good feminist praxis and rigorous feminist scholarship. The world of academia and academic publishing is competitive. Finding one's intellectual contribution has traditionally meant defining oneself against other scholars; identifying and debunking their ideas—a kind of search-and-destroy operation. The academy encourages people who most distinguish themselves as innovators and originators. In the process, it rewards individualism and undermines the collective project that ought to be central to feminism.

When I entered graduate school, the importance of citation was not evident to me. I learned, sometimes the hard way, through guidance (and criticism) from others. Citation is especially important when writing about subjects such as the welfare rights movement, which encounters its own marginalization within mainstream academia. I was dismissed by (some) more established professors who assumed that this movement's history was less significant than other kinds of political history. I came to learn that the larger body of feminist scholarship fortifies my work and helps create scholarly space for nontraditional subjects that have the potential to overturn the racialized and gendered hierarchies in academia. I was pushed by some advisers to think of myself as an individual, and I had to work to see myself in academia as part of a collective, as resting on the shoulders of previous feminist scholars.

Academic competitiveness manifested not only in my dealings with more senior people, but with students. Another graduate student urged me not to write about an underresearched topic because they believed they had ownership of it. My response was that so little had been written about the topic that we (and the discipline) would benefit from granting it more scholarly attention. My argument fell on deaf ears. I was dismayed. There was no discussion of ideas or how we might approach the topic differently. Rather, it was about territoriality—and reminded me of a settler colonial mentality.

Even as we should not claim ownership, we must recognize and engage the work that has come before us. Principled political and academic work means acknowledging how we are building upon the labor of others—even if we are taking it in a different direction and asking a different set of questions. Drawing on the work of Raymond Williams, Ruth Wilson Gilmore writes about the "selection and reselection of ancestors" as part of the radical process of finding . . . in "political practice and analytical habit, lived expressions of unbounded participatory openness" (2017, 236). How we understand our intellectual lineage and who we see as our "ancestors" is part of what Gilmore calls "a time-space freedom-making consciousness" that moves us "away from partition and exclusion" (2017, 237). The Cite Black Women initiative was established in 2017 in order to rectify the devaluation of Black women's scholarly contributions. It aims to "push people to engage in a radical praxis of citation that acknowledges and honors Black women's transnational intellectual production" (Cite Black Women 2018).

My aim in this essay is to not to silence or discredit new work, especially because I am fully aware of the power differential between one of the authors and myself. For that reason, I was hesitant to write this response. But I did so because the problem of academic citation extends far beyond Sherwin and Piven's essay and because of what I see as our shared investment in a radical feminist project. At the same time, I grappled with how to initiate a difficult dialogue with people whom I respect and want to support. I am indebted to Frances Fox Piven whose political labor and scholarly interventions have had an enormous influence on me since I was an undergraduate. Thus, my intention here is to raise questions about how power operates in the academy, consider the best way to make space for new and distinct voices, and contribute to a conversation about what a radical feminist praxis of citation might look like. I am grateful to the editors for inviting me to respond and creating space for such a dialogue. In that spirit, in the following section I will engage with some of the key themes raised in this important essay.

Rethinking the Welfare Rights Movement

In contrast to Sherwin and Piven's claim that welfare rights scholars have highlighted "aspects of the movement which are congruous with mainstream values" (2019, 150), the militancy and radical politics of the movement have been embraced by scholars. Mary E. Triece (2012; 2013), for example, writes about welfare recipients' confrontational style of speaking as a rhetorical intervention, which she argues was deeply influenced by race and class. Holloway Sparks, in her essay "When Dissident Citizens Are Militant Mamas: Intersectional Gender and Agonistic Struggle in Welfare Rights Activism," identifies the movement tactics and practice of dissident citizenship as "disruptive democratic activism" (2016, 624).

Previous scholarship has also analyzed the movement's claims for sexual freedom and reproductive justice, in particular women on welfare's assertion for a right to date, have intimate relationships with men, and access contraception. Deborah Gray White has written about how the movement's positions, particularly around sexuality, differed from the respectability politics advocated by middle-class African American women (White 1999). In my own work, I argue that they "vocally asserted their right to sexual freedom" and autonomy (Nadasen 2002, 284).

Sherwin and Piven suggest that scholars have interpreted the welfare rights movement as prioritizing motherhood and care labor with the objective of "staying home" and "lives centered on children." The discourse of motherhood was a central pillar of how welfare activists crafted their claims for assistance. Although welfare rights participants self-identified in multiple ways, voluminous evidence demonstrates that identifying as mothers and mother-recipients was perhaps most important (Boris 1998; Nadasen 2005; Triece 2012; Valk 2000; West 1981). The political claims to mothering made by the welfare rights movement cannot be equated to the maternalism of white middle-class women. Cynthia Edmonds-Cady (2009) argues that race and class shape how women understand maternalism. This was especially true for poor Black women whose mothering work had been denigrated and devalued. Black welfare recipients were cast as lazy, idle, and unfit mothers, and local, state, and federal officials were implementing policies to require them to take paid employment outside the home. The widespread public hostility directed at Black mothers in this period prompted them to embrace their status as mothers and insist on state support for this work, which brought recognition to this labor and shifted the focus "from work to income," as Eileen Boris has argued (1998, 29).

Although welfare rights activists demanded the right to mother their children, they never mandated or prescribed this role for anyone. Instead, they advocated that welfare recipients have a choice about entering the workforce or staying home with their children—the same choice available to women with economic means. As I argued: "Rather than prescribing that women either enter the workforce or stay home with children, choose to marry or reject marriage, welfare activists demanded that women have the power to define their own lives" (Nadasen 2002, 273). Their claim to maternalism was intended "to challenge social norms, not conform to dominant expectations" (Nadasen 2002, 280).

Although the claim to motherhood may be read as "legible to racist, capitalist, patriarchal society" (Sherwin and Piven 2019, 150), in fact, as Holloway Sparks argues, it "initiated political quarrels about the meanings of democratic citizenship, the American dream, the definition of work, and whose children and whose futures count" (2016, 633). Welfare recipients' embrace of motherhood as a political category subverted gendered norms about the proper role of poor Black women and contravened a labor market that relied on Black women's participation in the paid labor force. Black women's demand for economic support enabled them to withdraw from the labor market which fundamentally challenged core features of American racial capitalism. American capitalism is inextricably tied to a racial hierarchy, is dependent upon the labor of Black women (and men) and other people of color, and has historically denied Black women the right to be mothers. By demanding the right to choose to be mothers or not, welfare rights activists chipped away at the logic of racial capitalism.

This scholarship suggests that what on the surface looks like legibility, can be understood as radicalism because of who was making the demands for rights and inclusion. By turning to the politics of mothering and framing mothering as work, welfare recipients sought legibility in a country that made them illegible as mothers and citizens. Thus, their demands for inclusion were highly disruptive to the status quo.

Sherwin and Piven also urge us to step outside of a home/work dichotomy and acknowledge the community activism and political mobilization of welfare rights activists. They cite evidence of welfare recipients who insisted on state support for "childcare that will free them for community involvement." I appreciate the attention to the political roles of welfare rights organizers and their claims to utilize childcare for political engagement. In a moment when we are witnessing a crisis of American democracy, perhaps there are lessons here about how public support, not just for care work, but for participation in the political sphere, might be beneficial.

Although the reading of some of the evidence presented and the framing of the argument about childcare by Sherwin and Piven are new (to me at least), several scholars uplift welfare recipients' civic participation, their commitment to community improvement, and their roles in policy making (Williams 2005; Orleck 2006; Kornbluh 2007).

In her important book *The Politics of Public Housing*, Rhonda Williams (2005) recounts a struggle by public-housing residents—many of whom were on welfare—to develop leadership skills and influence housing policy. Williams discusses Baltimore's Resident Aide Program that put public-housing residents on payroll to maintain the buildings and serve as a liaison between staff and residents. Although initiated as a "self-help" program, Williams argued that the program "allowed black women to combine their motherly duties with community work, earn a salary, and hopefully shape while regulating residential behavior and attitudes" (2005, 115).

In *Storming Caesar's Palace*, Annelise Orleck (2006) traces the two-decade campaign by welfare recipients in Las Vegas to establish and run a social service agency designed to wage their own "war on poverty." It is a striking example of how with drive, determination, and government support, Black mothers on welfare became engaged civic participants. Welfare recipients can and did carve out avenues to get paid to engage in the community work that they saw as necessary.

For most welfare activists, civic participation was in tandem, not in tension, with mothering. Their involvement in the public sector was inextricable from their status as mothers, since they lobbied and engaged in policy making to push for adequate state assistance in order to expand their mothering capacities. But the significance of their claim to mothering extended far beyond that. For American society to fully acknowledge and support them in their work as mothers, it would be necessary to reallocate public funds—divert money from war-making to domestic spending—develop a new framework to determine who is entitled to public assistance, generate new ideas about what constitutes a proper family, and create new sensibilities about race and the social and economic role for Black women. Welfare rights activists' claims to motherhood were about much more than taking care of their children but served as a basis to critique foreign and domestic policy.

There is a great deal we can learn from the welfare rights movement. Perhaps most important is that class and economic inequality must take into account the politics of race and gender. This analytical perspective was expressed most clearly by the Combahee River Collective in 1977, which aimed to articulate the "real class situation of persons who are not merely raceless, sexless, workers, but for whom racial and sexual oppression are significant determinants in their working/economic lives." The Collective's analysis of a race/class/gender structural inequality—which scholars now refer to as *intersectionality*, a term coined by Kimberlé Crenshaw—illustrates how class is refracted through a lens of race, gender, and sexuality. The welfare rights movement similarly utilized an intersectional analysis, enabling it to develop a far-reaching and radical feminist agenda.

Conclusion

I look forward to reading more scholarship on the welfare rights movement at this critical moment in history. And there is much that can be written. As Wilson and Piven point out, transgender politics and climate change are underresearched lines of inquiry in this movement. A fuller account of the welfare rights movement could complicate how we understand working-class feminism and advance feminist discourse at this critical juncture.

The dominance of "lean-in" feminism can also be countered by uplifting multiple contemporary radical feminist activist voices. Home healthcare aides, domestic workers, nail salon workers, fast-food workers, the Movement for Black Lives, as well as countless grassroots community organizations, are crafting a robust feminism that integrates a reprioritization of government spending, economic justice, prison abolition, and bodily integrity. In the same way that the welfare rights movement was not always recognized for its feminist contributions in the 1960s and 1970s, these formations are complicating the landscape of feminism today, sometimes in unacknowledged ways. In the spirit of collective feminist struggle, in addition to resurrecting models from the past, we should direct our intellectual and material support to current manifestations of a radical feminist politics.

Premilla Nadasen is a professor of history at Barnard College, Columbia University, and the author of *Welfare Warriors: The Welfare Rights Movement in the United States*, *Welfare in the United States: A History with Documents* (with Marisa Chappell and Jennifer Mittelstadt), and *Household Workers Unite: The Untold Story of African American Women Who Built a Movement*. She is currently president of the National Women's Studies Association. She can be reached at pnadasen@barnard.edu.

Works Cited

Boris, Eileen. 1998. "When Work Is Slavery." *Social Justice* 25, no. 1: 28–46.

Cite Black Women. 2018. "Our Story." https://www.citeblackwomencollective.org/.

Crenshaw, Kimberlé. 1991. "Mapping the Margins: Intersectionality, Identity Politics, and Violence Against Women of Color." *Stanford Law Review* 43, no. 6: 1241–99.

Edmonds-Cady, Cynthia. 2009. "Mobilizing Motherhood: Race, Class, and the Uses of Maternalism in the Welfare Rights Movement." *WSQ* 37, nos. 3/4: 206–22.

Gilmore, Ruth Wilson. 2017. "Abolition Geography and the Problem of Innocence." In *Futures of Black Radicalism*, edited by Gaye Theresa Johnson and Alex Lubin, 225–40. London: Verso Press.

Kornbluh, Felicia. 2007. *The Battle for Welfare Rights: Politics and Poverty in Modern America*. Philadelphia: University of Pennsylvania Press.

Nadasen, Premilla. 2002. "Expanding the Boundaries of the Women's Movement: Black Feminism and the Struggle for Welfare Rights." *Feminist Studies* 28, no. 2: 270–301.

———. 2005. *Welfare Warriors: The Welfare Rights Movement in the United States*. New York: Routledge.

Orleck, Annelise. 2006. *Storming Caesar's Palace: How Black Mothers Fought Their Own War on Poverty*. Boston: Beacon Press.

Sparks, Holloway. 2016. "When Dissident Citizens Are Militant Mamas: Intersectional Gender and Agonistic Struggle in Welfare Rights Activism." *Politics and Gender* 12, no. 4: 623–47.

Triece, Mary E. 2012. "Credible Workers and Deserving Mothers: Crafting the 'Mother Tongue' in Welfare Rights Activism, 1967–1972." *Communication Studies* 63, no. 4: 1–17.

———. 2013. *Tell It Like It Is: Women in the National Welfare Rights Movement.* Columbia: University of South Carolina Press.

Valk, Anne M. 2000. "'Mother Power': The Movement for Welfare Rights in Washington, D.C., 1966–1972." *Journal of Women's History* 11, no. 4: 34–58.

Williams, Rhonda Y. 2005. *Politics of Public Housing: Black Women's Struggles Against Urban Inequality.* Oxford: Oxford University Press.

West, Guida. 1981. *The National Welfare Rights Movement: The Social Protest of Poor Women.* New York: Praeger.

White, Deborah Gray. 1999. *Too Heavy a Load: Black Women in Defense of Themselves, 1894–1994.* New York: W. W. Norton & Company.

Mildred Beltré. *Where my dream at?*, 2015. Linen and wool, 18 x 12 in. Image courtesy of the artist.

Response to Premilla Nadasen

Wilson Sherwin and Frances Fox Piven

The primary position we take in our article is that some scholars have overlooked a major insight of the welfare rights movement. As Nadasen notes, existing scholarship argues welfare recipients were militant in their pursuit of a right to the domesticity that they had long been denied (Denton 2012; Nadasen 2002; Reese and Newcomb 2003; Triece 2012; Sparks 2016). Departing somewhat from this analysis, we argue that the archival record suggests welfare activists wanted more than to just "stay home" (Nadasen 2002), and that they did not limit their demands and political vision to seeking recognition and income support (however radical those demands may have been). Rather, they asserted women "can be much more valuable doing something else . . . and that is out into the community, mixing with the people, finding out what their problems are, and trying to help solve those problems" (Sanders 1969). We believe the challenge these activists posed to the home/work binary as the only two options available to women is not only an important piece of the historical record of the movement but especially relevant to today's debates over safety net programs in the present, and the merits and potential pitfalls of Universal Basic Income (UBI) in the future. If a UBI is ever achieved, will it, as some critics fear, concretize a gendered division of labor relegating women to their homes, cloistered away from the real machinations of society? In reexamining the archival record, alongside Frances's recollections of the movement, we hope to have demonstrated that the prescient analyses of the welfare activists was a resounding no.

We, too, share an appreciation for the importance of citing Black women; it is one of many reasons why, rather than engaging exclusively with existing scholarship (of which there is a fortuitous abundance),

WSQ: Women's Studies Quarterly 47: 3 & 4 (Fall/Winter 2019) © 2019 by Wilson Sherwin and Frances Fox Piven. All rights reserved.

we have attempted to center the archival record and elevate some of the underappreciated insights they contain. If the citations were incomplete or inaccurate this is the purview of the peer review process.

It is heartening to see that we agree on numerous points, including the important political lessons to be learned from the welfare rights movement—lessons we should heed as we strive to build a political feminism that is broad and inclusive, and the essential backbone of the ongoing resistance movement in the United States.

Wilson Sherwin is an educator and activist. She recently received her PhD in sociology from the CUNY Graduate Center. Her dissertation, "Rich in Needs: The Forgotten Radical Politics of the Welfare Rights Movement," was supervised by Dr. Piven. She can be reached at wilsonsherwin@gmail.com.

Frances Fox Piven is distinguished professor of political science and sociology emerita at the CUNY Graduate Center. The books she has authored or coauthored include *Regulating the Poor*, *Poor People's Movements*, *Why Americans Don't Vote*, and *Challenging Authority*. She can be reached at fpiven@hotmail.com.

Works Cited

Denton, Georgina. 2012. "'Neither Guns nor Bombs – Neither the State nor God – Will Stop Us from Fighting for Our Children': Motherhood and Protest in 1960s and 1970s America." *The Sixties* 5, no. 2: 205–28.

Nadasen, Premilla. 2002. "Expanding the Boundaries of the Women's Movement: Black Feminism and the Struggle for Welfare Rights." *Feminist Studies* 28, no. 2: 270–301.

Reese, Ellen, and Garnett Newcombe. 2003. "Income Rights, Mothers' Rights, or Workers' Rights? Collective Action Frames, Organizational Ideologies, and the American Welfare Rights Movement." *Social Problems* 50, no. 2: 294–318.

Sanders, Beulah. 1969. "Statement to the Presidential Commission on Income Maintenance." June, 5 1969. Box 22, folder 4. Wiley Papers, State Historical Society of Wisconsin, Madison.

Sparks, Holloway. 2016. "When Dissident Citizens are Militant Mamas: Intersectional Gender and Agonistic Struggle in Welfare Rights Activism." *Politics and Gender* 12, no. 4: 623–47.

Triece, Mary E. 2012. "Credible Workers and Deserving Mothers: Crafting the 'Mother Tongue' in Welfare Rights Activism, 1967–1972," *Communication Studies* 63, no. 4: 1–17.

PART IV. **INSURGENT SOLIDARITIES**

"Sex Workers Unite!": U.S. Sex Worker Support Networks in an Era of Criminalization

Crystal A. Jackson

Abstract: This article analyzes how sex worker support networks exist at a nexus of support, friendship, and assistance for current and former sex workers, stemming from participation at the Desiree Alliance conference in 2010. During the conference, current and former sex workers engaged in peer-to-peer education on a range of issues and continued to support one another after the conference in ways that value both well-being and work. As social nodes of resilience and care in a neoliberal, carceral society, sex worker support networks embody broad meanings of harm reduction and resistance to traditional, institutionalized forms of protection and labor rights. **Keywords:** sex work, support networks, prostitution, activism

Sex workers supporting each other and organizing together is a relatively new topic of study, seldom situated as historically relevant or insightful, and only occasionally discussed in the histories of activisms in the United States (Chateauvert 2014; Ditmore 2010). This article builds on the feminist concept of "female support networks" (Cook 1977, 43) to explore sex workers' power as radical challenges to labor organizing and the carceral state. I propose that "sex worker support networks" are critical social nodes of resistance and resilience grounded in peer-to-peer skill sharing, valuing the individual and the work, and figuring out how to navigate an ontologically insecure world.

Feminist studies find that emotionality and community are not just important characteristics of activism, but important outcomes—outcomes not traditionally recognized as central to activism and organizing (see Fine

WSQ: Women's Studies Quarterly 47: 3 & 4 (Fall/Winter 2019) © 2019 by Crystal A. Jackson.

2006; Guenther 2009; or Hardy and Cruz 2019 for diverse examples of emotionality as an activist outcome). How do sex workers in the United States carve out strategies of support despite the lack of labor union support and in direct opposition to the criminalization of sexual labor (including current assumptions that legal sexual labors like erotic dance are suspect hubs of sex trafficking)? In an era of increasing criminalization of prostitution and sex trafficking in the United States (Bernstein 2018), sex worker support networks are a vibrant form of resistance and care.

Since 2006, the Desiree Alliance, a by-and-for-sex-workers organization, has hosted the only U.S. national rights conference for sex workers and their allies every few years. Stemming from participant observation at Desiree Alliance 2010 and postconference interviews, this article focuses on the sex worker support networks which were produced at and continued after the conference. The year 2010 represents a unique moment in time: after a decade of institutionalization of the federal Trafficking Victims Protection Act (TVPA) of 2000 but before the Act was used to target and shutter online sex worker screening tools and electronically mediated harm-reduction practices (for example, the government raids of sex work websites Rentboy.com and Backpage.com). The domestic uses and consequences of the TVPA on sex workers and sex workers' rights efforts were a hot topic at the 2010 conference.

The Whorephobia of Carceral Politics

In the United States, prostitution (the sale and purchase of sex) and prostitution-related activities (advertising, transporting, etc.) are wholly criminalized.[1] Criminalization is a traditional institutional response to protecting women and girls. But this approach has failed sex workers, not helped them. The physical, sexual, and emotional violence and stigma that people who engage in sexual labor (and people assumed to engage in sexual labor) experience at the hand of the state has been cataloged by scholars (e.g., Bass 2015) and activists alike (Alliance for a Safe & Diverse DC 2008; Ray and Caterine 2014; Torres and Paz 2012; see also Best Practices Policy Project, Desiree Alliance, and Sex Workers Outreach Project-NYC 2014). Individuals who sell sex/ual services are subject to punitive laws that situate them as criminals or victims, necessitating contact from law enforcement or entanglement in the "criminal justice–social service alliance" (Dewey and St. Germain 2016).

Additionally, legal businesses like strip clubs and massage parlors are raided regularly by law enforcement across the country as suspected sex trafficking hubs. Further, adult businesses in neighborhoods of color or businesses with majority Black, Latina, and Asian/Asian American work-ers are targeted with greater frequency (Ditmore and Thukral 2012). Yet there is little "accountability of governments, traffickers, or communities" when these raids are conducted (2012), and, according to sex workers, often result in arrest, violence, or death.[2]

Institutionalized support structures have not worked well for sex work-ers, unless grounded in harm-reduction ideology, which is the minority of social service provision in the United States today for sex workers and sex trafficking survivors (Dewey and St. Germain 2016; Musto 2016). Rely-ing partially or wholly on TVPA funding, U.S. anti-trafficking programs often refuse assistance unless the woman agrees to stop selling sex, and in some cases, to stop talking to people from "the life," the colloquial term that anti-prostitution and anti–sex trafficking activists use to refer to en-gaging regularly in sexual labor (Oselin 2014). Moreover, when Dewey and St. Germain studied what they term the "alliance" between the crim-inal justice system and social services that offer rehabilitation in lieu of imprisonment for prostitution charges, they found that "the criminal jus-tice system's financial and ideological dominance over the alliance and its ethos results in a punitive approach that fails to consider the gendered socioeconomic realities that make sex trading the best viable option" for some women, largely poor women and women of color (2016, 255). The criminal justice system, and the related alternatives to incarceration, have crystallized coalitions under the TVPA that are grounded in protectionist beliefs about what is "best" for women rather than realistic support for poor women.

The U.S.-based TVPA, first passed in 2000, has influenced prostitu-tion and sex trafficking policy and efforts domestically and internation-ally for almost two decades (Bernstein 2010, 2012, 2018; Chuang 2010; Ditmore 2005; Bromfield and Capous-Desyllas 2012; Limoncelli 2009; Weitzer 2007, 2011). The TVPA was written to "protect, prosecute, and prevent" trafficking, which is framed as synonymous with "modern slav-ery" (Office to Monitor and Combat Trafficking in Persons n.d.). But in-stead of helping survivors and victims of trafficking, scholars and activists alike have critiqued the TVPA for overly focusing on sex trafficking (the smallest group of trafficking victims), for criminalizing the choices of poor women of color, and for acting as an anti-immigrant regulation (Agustín 2007; Doezema 2010). To wit, trafficking raids are overwhelmingly sex trafficking raids, and tend to result in prostitution-related arrests and charges, rather than assisting trafficking victims, domestically and globally (Agustín 2007; Ditmore and Thukral 2012). In a sense, sexual labor and sex trafficking are conflated as a universal experience of violence.

The conflation of sexual labor and sex trafficking obscures the realities of sex trafficking victims/survivors and sexual laborers. Scholars have argued that this is not an accident. Rather, this is a continuation of the "feminist sex wars" that situates all sexualized commerce and sex work as a form of violence against women and girls. Beyond the local anti-porn and anti-prostitution politicking of the late twentieth century, today's carceral feminists situate the nation-state as the guarantor of gender equity and freedom from violence for women and girls, and enact a neoliberal reliance on the criminal justice system as arbiter of protection (Bernstein 2018). Subsequently, an extreme criminalization of prostitution and related activities has emerged in the United States (Bernstein 2018; Jackson, Reed, and Brents 2017). Relying on a carceral approach to sexual labor shifts the conversation about social problems away from poverty and economic inequalities, structural transphobia and homophobia, and the racist and classist U.S. criminal justice system (including alternatives to incarceration), thus manifesting an increasingly complex system of social control and punishment for poor women who sell sex or are suspected of selling sex (Dewey and St. Germain 2016; Oselin 2014).

Organizing

Sex workers' rights activists in the United States have made successful coalitions with numerous organizations on local levels, including local National Organization for Women chapters (Gilmore 2010). But large-scale inclusion in sizable unions or support from national, mainstream feminist organizations has not been achieved.[3] "Nontraditional workers" like sex workers or undocumented immigrants (and undocumented sex workers) are not traditional worker rights fodder (Gall 2006; Fine 2006). Yet issues with the occupation and industry, such as unsafe working conditions, violence, or arrest, are often primary mobilizing grievances for contingent and criminalized workers. Thus alternative forms of worker organizing are necessary for criminalized workers like undocumented immigrants because they "have always been underrepresented within the ranks of organized labor" (Fine 2006, 245).

Alternative nodes of worker organizing result in alternative types of support and alternative means of building membership. As social movement scholars point out, political consciousness and identity evolve over time (Barker and Lavalette 2002), and it is community that often keeps someone connected to an organization or effort. In her study of "emotional cultures of feminist organizations," Katja Guenther found that, different from "state-dependent organization[s]," an "autonomous organization encourages displays of feelings as part of consciousness raising, creating an emotion culture that reduces public appeal but produces especially loyal and active constituents" (2009, 337). Further, peer-to-peer support has been found to be uniquely suited to, and needed for, worker organizing within stigmatized and criminalized communities such as undocumented day laborers (Fine 2006). Peer-led workshops, know-your-rights trainings, and art as activism are some nontraditional types of worker organizing that lend well to identity building and emotive response.

Feminist historian Blanche Wiesen Cook first studied "female support networks" as a structural element of politically active women in the late 1800s and early 1900s, arguing that there is something viable and important beyond these women's "political contributions" (1977, 43). Cook argues that "networks of love and support are crucial to our ability as women to work in a hostile world where we are not in fact expected to survive" (44). There is a structural element here beyond pop-cultural ideals of sisterhood. Cook's theorizing of solidarity-driven connection helps us understand how and why activist success can be (and could be) measured in nontraditional ways—beyond, for example, changes to law.

A study of sex worker advocacy participation in the United States found that activist involvement produces identity building, which resists and challenges the master status of "victim-criminals" put upon sex workers (Majic 2014, 463). Indeed, Melissa Gira Grant (2014), journalist, author, and longtime sex workers' rights proponent, noted in her book *Play the Whore: The Work of Sex Work* that sex workers have a history of sharing skills and building connections with people new to sex work. Since the 1960s, U.S. sex workers' rights organizers have provided support for sex workers while also advocating for changes in society to destigmatize and decriminalize sexual labors (Chateauvert 2014; Gilmore 2010), and doing so as part of a global sex workers' rights movement (Mac and Smith

2018; Mgbako 2016). Globally and locally, the emotions of organizing are important (Hardy and Cruz 2018). Further, while the rise of affordable and accessible technology and internet at the time of the TVPA led to a flashpoint of sex worker organizing that is still in play today, scholars have noted that changes in technology are met with suspicion by anti–sex trafficking advocates who are concerned about new avenues of sex trafficking, vulnerability, and exploitation (Musto 2016).

Methods

Drawing on participant observation at the Desiree Alliance 2010 national sex workers' rights conference and seventeen semistructured interviews with attendees over the following eighteen months, this article explores how sex worker support networks exist at a nexus of support, friendship, and assistance for current and former sex workers. The Desiree Alliance is a sex workers' rights organization whose primary task is hosting a multiday national gathering of current and former sex workers, as well as sex workers' rights advocates and allies. The gatherings have taken place in 2006, 2007, 2008, 2010, 2012, and 2016. It is a coalition of other national and local sex workers' rights organizations, a place to bring everyone together. Organizational goals focus as much on worker development and support *within* the community, as they do on external or collective actions *for* the community. Per the Desiree Alliance website:

> The most important goal of the Desiree Alliance is to be part of efforts to reinvigorate the sex workers' rights movement in the U.S. Therefore, all of our actions in the last years focused on building leadership and constructive activism in the sex worker population. While the Desiree Alliance promotes rights and justice for people engaging in sexual commerce, we collaborate and stand with organizations working in overlapping struggles for the rights of sexual and gender minorities, sexual rights in general, reproductive rights and human rights. (n.d.)

The need to "reinvigorate" has been spurred by increasing online surveillance and subsequent raids or setups, as a result of the technological advances since the early 2000s and in response to the strength of carceral feminist efforts and the institutionalization of the TVPA. Indeed, as I have concluded elsewhere, "the U.S. anti–sex trafficking movement has galvanized and mobilized sex worker rights organizers as sex workers feel the impact of anti-prostitution policies enacted to end trafficking" (Jackson 2016, 40). Mainstream anti–sex trafficking efforts have forced sex workers' rights activists to frame their efforts in response to new contexts of criminalization and policing.

With hindsight, I can say I have been a sex workers' rights activist since around 2005. At the time, I was a graduate student; a white, cisgender, queer woman engaging in sex-positive sex activism. I was introduced to a local woman, Genesis, who, along with another organizer, wanted to create a national conference in the United States for sex workers and their allies to come together—what would become the Desiree Alliance. Genesis had approached my mentor, a professor at the University of Nevada, Las Vegas, to talk about allying over the conference. I interned with the Desiree Alliance and volunteered at the 2006 conference. I continued to be involved with local sex workers' rights efforts off and on over the next few years. Then, in 2010, I asked Genesis if I could attend the conference as a researcher to collect data, and she agreed. I was noted as a researcher on my badge; I left a flyer at the sign-in table letting folks know I was looking to do interviews with attendees. It soon became clear that there was no time to conduct interviews during the conference as people went from workshop to workshop, or grabbed coffee with a new or old friend. Some people agreed to be interviewed at a later date, most by phone, a couple in person. All the interviews were recorded with permission, and then transcribed; pseudonyms were used.

While the Desiree Alliance conference was quite diverse in terms of race and ethnicity, age, and sexual identity, the conference leaders were concerned that the most marginalized group of sex workers—street-based workers—were not well represented. It is important to note that street-based sex work is, likely, the smallest group of sexual laborers today—with the internet, there is less need to be street based (though this is changing, due to online policing and federal intervention) (Weitzer 2007, 2011). That, combined with racialization of class privilege (of having regular email access and a consistent phone number), and people's response to my own intersectional identities, skewed the interviewee data to majority white (fourteen of the seventeen participants). One identified as black, one as Latina, and one as multiracial Latina and white.

The majority of interviewees were cisgender (two cis men and thirteen cis women), with two identifying as trans women. The majority also identified as gay, queer, or bisexual, which makes sense given the historic intersections of sex workers' rights activism and LGBTQ+ activism (Chateauvert 2014), and given the impacts of homophobia and transphobia on a person's socioeconomic status. Indeed, many interviewees also had experience with organizing around LGBTQ+ rights, reproductive justice, and/or racial justice/antiracism activism. The age range was wide considering the stereotypes of sex workers as young: ages ranged from midtwenties to early fifties, with five participants in their thirties and eight participants in their forties. They lived across the United States and similar themes emerged across geography. Although the Desiree Alliance is national, interviewees spoke of local knowledge as useful and important to well-being.

While coding interview transcripts and field notes using grounded theory, I found that sex workers' narratives underscore the centrality of connection and coming together. Interviewees shared that participating in the conference impacted them long after the conference was over. Many reported friendship, business support, and opportunities for art and activism as continued experiences and connections postconference. What follows is analysis of how the conference itself and the attendees created sex worker support networks that valued labor, safety, and health through friendships, connections, and peer-to-peer trainings. Below, I show how peer socializing forms social nodes that a) fight stigma, b) set the framework for support network building, and c) affirm value in two categories: business and camaraderie intertwined, and emphasizing *value*, including the value of the person's safety and health, and the monetary value of the work itself.

Business and Camaraderie Intertwined: Fighting Stigma, Finding Friendship

The 2010 conference, themed Working Sex: Power, Practice, and Politics, consisted of ninety-nine panels, workshops, and talks over six days in July. The conference itself is a key component of community building centering peer-to-peer support. Workshops and panels addressed a range of issues that aim to increase sex workers' safety, enhance solidarity, reinforce safer-sex norms, encourage harm-reduction practices, and connect sex workers to (or teach sex workers how to find) less stigmatizing social services, legal aid, or a local sex workers' rights organization. Business development panels, which were led by and for sex workers (current or former), addressed a diverse range of business-related issues, with titles like, "A Taste of Leather: Incorporating Kink into Your Work," "Keeping Out of

Harm's Way: Sex Work and the Law," "Energetic Protection and Cleansing for Sex Workers," and "Developing a Screening Policy That Works for You, Keeping You Safe, and Ensuring Your Success!"

In interviewing conference attendees after the conference—some a month or two later, most about five to eight months after the fact—I was able to gain insights into the impacts of conference attendance. Astrid, a bisexual white cisgender woman in her early forties, shared that it was common for attendees, through bonding at the conference and afterward, to share contact information for local businesses that are sex worker friendly, which is important to her and her work as an escort. In our interview a few months after the conference, Astrid explained she was "more comfortable dealing with someone in their business if I know that they're sex worker friendly." Sex workers seek out nonjudgmental (or, less ideally, less judgmental) resources from an "accountant or chiropractor [to an] OB-GYN." Sex workers contend with fears of arrest or police harassment in both legal and criminalized labors, and fears of being outed as a sex worker against their wishes, even by a professional who is bound by certain ethics. Finding sex worker friendly resources and businesses is a relief, from a hairdresser one could chat with to a mental-health professional who does not obsess over sex work or push them to stop working. For Astrid and many others, sharing advice like this is not just about business, it is a form of activism that supports an individual holistically.

Catherine's interview took place almost a year after the conference. Catherine, a longtime sex workers' rights activist and a cisgender women in her forties who identified as half-white, half-Latina, surmised that "your activism might not even be traditional activism. It might be just giving someone a great idea online about how to screen somebody, or how to improve your website. That's activism too." In the "shadow economy" that is sexual labor, whether working as an independent contractor in a strip club, or advertising professional domination services online, or selling sex, networking and self-made business connections are necessary to replace the skill building, support, and general safety mechanisms that a company or manager would supply an employee.

Jana, a white cisgender woman in her twenties who worked both in strip clubs and as an escort, shared that she had gotten business support, client referrals, and learned new skills through her involvement with the Desiree Alliance and a local chapter of the Sex Workers Outreach Project (SWOP).[4] In an interview during the fall following the DA conference, she explained that "as a stripper, it's nice to have friends in that industry that I can hang out with. In terms of out-call or in-call, it's nice to have people know some of the customers and can attest to their personality or [tell] you about certain things." Whether it is about a client who takes "forever" to orgasm or advice on menstruating while sex working, sex worker support networks provide both practical advice and affirmation.

Making "lifelong friends," as one interviewee exclaimed, was what many current and former sex workers liked most about being an activist in the sex workers' rights movement. For example, while working at a West Coast sex workers' rights organization, Shawn started a support group for male sex workers that lasted from 1999 until he left the organization in the mid-2000s. Shawn noted gender differences in coming together, and acknowledged:

> I just felt like men were so, so far behind women in just basic organizing. I, to this day, if you went on a male sex worker website in a major city like New York or San Francisco, you could find men who don't know another sex worker, [men who] don't have friends who are sex workers. Like, the level of isolation is astounding. So we would have these very kind of sweet support group meetings.

Connection took on political meaning as (criminalized) sex workers came together. I often heard a sense of excited relief about finding similarly situated people. Jana, quoted earlier, remarked, "The people that I've met has been the most rewarding part of being an activist. It's really empowering to be around really passionate people, who want to reshape the world for the better." Catherine, who traveled the world as an erotic dancer, made some of her best friends through her involvement in sex workers' rights activism, said excitedly, "Some of my best friends! All of his aunties! [*motioning to her baby*] He's a product of the sex workers' movement! [*laughs*] Yeah, yeah . . . people I will always know and work with."

Friendships help ease the impact of stigma, in addition to providing practical business support and help. For example, Astrid lives in a midwestern state and often travels for work as an escort. In our interview several months after DA 2010 in July, she shared that she is happy to "have friends everywhere! Everywhere in the country, every state, I've got a friend now. . . . it doesn't matter if I stay in sex work or if I'm even an activist, I know I'm still going to have those friends forever." More than that, being able to offer a home to traveling sex workers, rather than a stay at hotel or motel, is another outcome of connecting sex workers together. Astrid went on: "It's just nice to be in a house. You can cook your own meals, it's comfortable, and you have, you know, that kind of bond." These bonds have formed over years. Astrid first attended the Desiree Alliance conference in 2006, but "didn't really meet a lot of people from the core organizational group at that time." She went on to say that she met DA organizers at other sex workers' rights events over the next couple of years, and was inspired to found a SWOP chapter in her home town, and eventually, attend DA again in 2010. This is evidence of how a sex worker support network builds via friendly connections.

In an interview in August, the month after the conference, Kennedy, a white, queer cisgender woman, former erotic dancer, and current artist in her midforties, also excitedly shared how she has found support, friendship, and caring in coming together as a community of sex workers and allies. As an artist, she felt that her work had benefited from her involvement with the Desiree Alliance, in addition to making new connections: "I have a whole bunch of new hooker friends!"

In this way, the sex workers' rights conference acts as a catalyst for different kinds of support around both business and friendship (or at least, friendliness). On one hand, for contingent, stigmatized workers, this is "workplace" organizing. This is also important for safety. Sex workers warn each other about problematic and violent clients, both informally through emails and texts to each other, and also formally through "bad client lists" published online by a local organization or an individual in a particular area. On the other hand, the Desiree Alliance does not have a formal membership process beyond the board and the director. Local chapters of SWOP or other local sex workers' rights organizations fill that role. Personal connections from the conference are what build much of the support networks, not formal committees or coordinated multistate political efforts. Interviewees were clear in labeling these microlevel forms of support as "activism."

Valuing the Individual: Their Health, Their Safety, and Their Moneymaking

Attending the Desiree Alliance conference becomes a signifier of safety and trust. Establishing connections and friendships, and exchanging advice and tips about work, in effect, values the work, health, and safety of each person. Peer-to-peer workshops and trainings at the conference ensure sex workers are comfortable with being there and trust the information being shared, as spaces for workers to address their needs on the job. Training each other and sharing information for safer, more lucrative work, holding know-your-rights trainings for police encounters, sharing ways to work with different clients (e.g., clients suffering from emotional or sexual trauma), and discussing experiences like coming out to family or balancing sex work and parenting were common throughout the six-day conference. These are classic characteristics of alternative modes of worker organizing: peer-to-peer education, broadening meanings of worker safety and support, discussing safety as avoiding the criminal justice system, and, frankly, ensuring they get paid. Further, coming together provides sex workers the space and time to value the individual not only as a person but also as a person who needs money to survive in a capitalist society.

For example, conference leaders conceptualized "harm reduction" in broad and holistic parameters. Harm-reduction approaches identify and work around barriers to safety, health, and well-being for marginalized communities like sex workers, drug users, or homeless youth by, for example, providing needle exchange or condoms to help people stay free of diseases or infections. This is in contrast to only offering services and support if the person stops working or stops using drugs. At the conference, there were traditional harm-reduction workshops that promoted sensible policies and realistic practices for sex workers, encouraged peer education, and offered venue-specific safety tips and advice on how to find and access nonjudgmental health care.

Yet, different from traditional worker rights conferences, attendees were provided information about local Alcoholics Anonymous and Narcotics Anonymous meetings, and directions to the closest methadone clinic. Further, many other activities and workshops were labeled as harm reduction, like spiritual development and parenting advice. Yoga was offered at the start and end of each conference day, led by and for sex workers, with no allies allowed. This broadening of what counts as harm reduction values the worker. Valuing the person's sense of self, wellness, and individual needs without demanding someone quit sex work if they want to be safe and happy is quite a juxtaposition from anti–sex trafficking programs that often refuse aid if someone continues with, or returns to, "the life" of sex work.

Given the criminal justice–social service alliance (Dewey and St. Germain 2016), harm reduction also means addressing the impact of criminalization on sex workers' lives. The Desiree Alliance conference had several know-your-rights trainings and best practices for interactions with law enforcement. (Local sex workers' rights organizations sometimes offer similar workshops.) Sex workers learned about how their labor is situated within the law, how to engage police, and, in a more holistic approach to valuing safety, how to articulate the impact of policing on their lives. Allies led some of the workshops, like a "Common Myths about Police Encounters" workshop led by someone from the ACLU of Southern Nevada. This latter workshop is a good example of strategically calling on allies for help; here, having the ACLU present correct and up-to-date information.

Most safety workshops were sex worker led. For example, Streetwise & Safe (SAS), an LGBTQ youth-of-color organization based in New York City, screened a short video made "by and for LGBTQ youth of color who have experienced quality of life policing and policing of sex work." Sex workers of color and queer sex workers are subject to heavier policing efforts, and often report police harassment, violence, and arrest as top issues of concern, along with more punitive outcomes in courtrooms.[5] Afterward, SAS representatives distributed specialized know-your-rights information to attendees, talked more about racism, homophobia, and violence in police interactions, and discussed, according to the conference program, "possibilities for nationally coordinated locally-based advocacy around policing policies and practices which adversely impact queer youth in the sex trades."

In addition to know-your-rights and safety workshops, there were also business-development workshops. Most, as with other workshops, were by and for sex workers. These workshops included "A Tax Workshop for the Cash-Based Professional," "How Much an Hour?," and "Clicking with Your Photographer: Journalizing Your Portfolio and Knowing Your Rights." Business-development workshops also addressed how to deal with burnout, how to advertise online, and how to maintain personal privacy and boundaries with clients. Another lawyer with the ACLU of Southern Nevada led a workshop on "contracts and what to look for," one of few business workshops that was not sex worker led.

Business advice at the gathering is somewhat outside the neoliberal model of profit increase, because increasing value and making more money is a social justice issue for sex workers. Workshops taught sex workers how to ask for payment, how to negotiate with a client, and how to build or strengthen screening efforts in person and/or online. In short, learning how to identify "the value of sex work"—another business-development workshop title—is key to worker empowerment. Valuing money is important. I asked Kennedy what the Desiree Alliance conference provides to attendees. In rapid-fire succession, she offered rhetorical questions that explain what she and ostensibly others at the conference think about:

> How am I going to be a better hooker? How am I gonna make money at this shit? And there's nothing wrong with a heavy dose of capitalism because money is power. . . . And, I think that networking for hookers—fuck yeah! And, "How I do my job?" That's awesome! And also, issues of safety. Also, issues of humanity. And how do we care for each other?

Here, money, support, and well-being intersect. Imbued with a sense of support and care, Kennedy underscored how "networking for hookers" can be empowering exactly because the conference provides a space to talk about work, self-care, relationships, and more. A large part of worker empowerment here comes in the form of peer-to-peer support and the outgrowth of sex worker support networks. Valuing labor and valuing the person as a smart, agentic, complicated individual destroys the criminal-victim master status (Majic 2014). This negates shame and the idea of "dirty work."

Value has multiple meanings here. The simple action of "I see you" validates a person's existence. Peer-to-peer support engenders a sense of togetherness and affinity. It affirms identity, fights isolation and alienation, names oppressive laws and policies, and proffers relief through sharing micro- and macroaggressions of everyday life with empathetic ears. Peer-to-peer support can be in the form of know-your-rights workshops, outlets for artistic expression, activist development, and workshops on autonomy, skills, and self-sufficiency. Valuing the person challenges the stigma and stereotypes that sex workers encounter. This is why social support nodes are central to alternative modes of worker organizing.

Further, explicitly valuing labor means exposing the intersection of gender, class, and sex itself in capitalist society—an action that makes many anti-prostitution advocates point to both sex workers' oppression and their false consciousness. But being able to see oneself as an actor and in control of one's life, and not as a passive victim, is a powerful out-come of sex worker support networks. Talking to each other about earning money to survive and live validates each other's decision-making abilities. Considering the social ostracization that people who engage in sex work experience, situating a sex worker as valuable, as important, as a decision maker, stands in stark contrast to the "prostitute" criminal/victim tropes recycled again and again in politics and media.

Going Forward Together?

"Sex Workers Unite!" is a popular sex workers' rights slogan at activist events. This is not to say all sex workers are friends or even friendly with each other; similarly, this article is not meant to portray a rosy picture of easy solidarity. Disagreements on big issues, like political strategies, were (and are) common, and who-dislikes-who rumors and realities abound at the conference. Demands to center sex workers of color pushed the De-siree Alliance to purposefully think through inclusion, reflective of pushes in many social justice circles over the last fifteen years. What that slogan is conveying, however, is that sex workers, current or former, can form fierce connections to survive the criminalization and stigmatization of a whore-phobic society.

Social support nodes are central to "nontraditional" workers' surviv-al and well-being, as scholars and activists for undocumented immigrant workers' rights have shown. This survival relies heavily on avoiding the criminal justice system. For sex workers, the criminal justice system is a potential source of violence, arrest, incarceration, and loss of family, not a source of protection. Sex worker support networks go beyond norma-tive ideals of harm reduction and idolization of state protection, and create practical, pragmatic, and personal forms of support for economic stability, physical health, mental health, and more. This is very different from the "3 Ps" of the TVPA: prosecution, protection, and prevention.

Mainstream efforts to discourage or forbid sex work actually devalue and chastise people's monetary and survival decisions. "Outlaw poverty, not prostitutes" is a sex workers' rights slogan that encapsulates the differ-ent ideological approaches to addressing the sale of sex as a social prob-lem. It is striking that the Desiree Alliance and other sex workers' rights organizations endure in the face of anti-prostitution public opinion, and in opposition to prostitution abolitionists who want to eradicate the sale of sex and sexualized services altogether, and who want to "save" or "rescue" people without listening to what it is they need.

The 2010 conference was a unique site where attendees connected to each other by valuing each other's safety and health, and individuals' decisions to work or not. By going beyond traditional organizational outreach efforts to get women "off the pole" or "off the streets" (stereotypical vernacular about strip clubs and street-based sex work), the conference strengthened sex worker support networks at local and national levels.

Almost ten years on from the 2010 conference, sex workers' online harm-reduction strategies and electronically mediated support networks have been chipped away at by anti–sex trafficking efforts encoded into law. Desiree Alliance's social media and website announced in summer 2018 that they were canceling the upcoming 2019 conference, themed Transcending Borders: Immigration, Migration, and Sex Work, out of concern that the federal Fight Online Sex Trafficking Act (FOSTA) may be applied to conference organizing efforts. The fear, partially, was that internet-mediated communication and messaging about the conference, such as conference travel and scholarships for sex workers, could be construed as trafficking and put the attendees and organizers at risk.

Their fears are not unfounded. The 2018 passing of FOSTA and the continued reauthorizations of the TVPA have laid the groundwork for federal raids on sex worker advertising websites Rentboy.com and Backpage.com (in 2015 and 2018 respectively), Craigslist's shuttering of adult ads in 2010, and, in response to FOSTA in 2018, their dating ads. Sex workers are losing critical arenas (some of which were free) to find and screen clients, and in some cases, to build community. External governmental and advocacy forces, shored up by carceral feminism, are impacting the longevity of, and ability to, come together.

Sex workers and sex workers' rights organizations continue to tell politicians, community leaders, academics, and activists that what they need is harm-reduction support, not rescue; that they need labor rights and decriminalization, not criminalization, harassment, and violence (Bass 2015). It is clear that sex worker support networks are vital social nodes of support that value sex workers' work, well-being, and sense of self. As social nodes of resilience and care in a neoliberal, carceral society, sex worker support networks embody resistance to traditional, institutionalized forms of protection and labor rights. This is what worker organizing looks like in the twenty-first century.

Acknowledgments

Many thanks to the Desiree Alliance and to my interviewees for their openness. Thank you to the CUNY Faculty Fellowship Publication Program reading group who read and reviewed earlier drafts of this manuscript. A special thanks to Debra Schultz for guiding me to Blanche Wiesen Cook's early work. Thank you to the reviewers and editors for their time and support of this manuscript.

Crystal A. Jackson is an assistant professor of sociology and affiliated Gender Studies Program faculty at John Jay College, CUNY. She is coauthor of *The State of Sex*, an ethnography of Nevada's legal brothels. She can be reached at crjackson@jjay.cuny.edu.

Notes

1. Nevada's legal brothels are allowed only in rural counties; this legalization model does not adhere to federal anti-prostitution legislation but is allowed within state and county regulations.
2. For example, in 2017, a woman immigrant from China jumped out of the fourth floor of a raided massage parlor in Queens, New York, to avoid arrest, and died; see Gira Grant and Whitford 2017.
3. However, sex workers in other countries have had more success with traditional union labor organizing (Gall 2006).
4. SWOP local chapters and SWOP national were partner members of the Desiree Alliance.
5. See sex worker community-based research projects cited earlier in this article for more information: Streetwise and Safe in NYC, Red Umbrella Project NYC, Sex Workers Outreach Project USA, along with others not named in reference with the interviewees to protect identities, organizations like local SWOP chapters and the St. James Infirmary in San Francisco.

Works Cited

Agustín, Laura. 2007. *Sex at the Margins: Migration, Labour Markets and the Rescue Industry*. London: Zed Books.

Alliance for a Safe & Diverse DC. 2008. *Move Along: Policing Sex Work in Washington, D.C.: A Report by the Alliance for a Safe & Diverse DC*. Washington, DC: Different Avenues. https://dctranscoalition.files. wordpress.com/2010/05/movealongreport.pdf.

Barker, Colin, and Michael Lavalette. 2002. "Strategizing and the Sense of Context: Reflections on the First Two Weeks of the Liverpool Docks

Lockout, September–October 1995." In *Social Movements: Identity, Culture, and the State*, edited by David S. Meyer, Nancy Whittier, and Belinda Robnett, 140–56. New York: Oxford University Press.

Bass, Alison. 2015. *Getting Screwed: Sex Workers and the Law*. Lebanon, NH: University Press of New England.

Bernstein, Elizabeth. 2010. "Militarized Humanitarianism Meets Carceral Feminism: The Politics of Sex, Rights, and Freedom in Contemporary Antitrafficking Campaigns." *Signs* 36, no. 1: 45–71.

———. 2012. "Carceral Politics as Gender Justice? The 'Traffic in Women' and Neoliberal Circuits of Crime, Sex, and Rights." *Theory and Society* 41, no. 3: 233–59.

———. 2018. *Brokered Subjects: Sex, Trafficking, and the Politics of Freedom*. Chicago: University of Chicago Press.

Best Practices Policy Project, Desiree Alliance, and Sex Workers Outreach Project-NYC. 2014. "Human Rights Violations of Sex Workers, People in the Sex Trades, and People Profiled as Such." Submission to the *United Nations Universal Periodic Review of the United States of America*. Submitted September 2014 for the Second Cycle of the 22nd Session of the Working Group on the Universal Periodic Review Human Rights Council (May 2015).

Bromfield, Nicole Footen, and Moshoula Capous-Desyllas. 2012. "Underlying Motives, Moral Agendas and Unlikely Partnerships: The Formulation of the U.S. Trafficking in Victims Protection Act through the Data and Voices of Key Policy Players." *Advances in Social Work* 13, no. 2: 243–61.

Chateauvert, Melinda. 2014. *Sex Workers Unite: A History of the Movement from Stonewall to SlutWalk*. Boston: Beacon Press.

Chuang, Janie. 2010. "Rescuing Trafficking from Ideological Capture: Prostitution Reform and Anti-Trafficking Law and Policy." *University of Pennsylvania Law Review* 158: 1655–728.

Cook, Blanche Wiesen. 1977. "Female Support Networks and Political Activism: Lillian Wald, Crystal Eastman, and Emma Goldman." *Chrysalis* 3: 43–61.

Desiree Alliance. n.d. "About Us." Desiree Alliance. Accessed May 30, 2019. http://desireealliance.org/about-us/.

Dewey, Susan, and Tonia St. Germain. 2016. *Women of the Street: How the Criminal Justice–Social Service Alliance Fails Women in Prostitution*. New York: NYU Press.

Ditmore, Melissa Hope. 2005. "Trafficking in Lives: How Ideology Shapes Policy." In *Trafficking and Prostitution Reconsidered: New Perspectives on Migration, Sex Work, and Human Rights*, edited by Kamala Kempadoo, Jyoti Sanghera, and Bandana Pattanaik, 107–26. Boulder, CO: Paradigm.

————. 2010. "Pushing Boundaries in Sex Work Activism and Research." In *Sex Work Matters*, edited by Melissa Hope Ditmore, Antonia Levy, and Alys Willman, 239–42. London: Zed Books.

Ditmore, Melissa, and Juhu Thukral. 2012. "Accountability and the Use of Raids to Fight Trafficking." *Anti-Trafficking Review*, no.1: 134–48.

Doezema, Jo. 2010. *Sex Slaves and Discourse Masters: The Construction of Trafficking*. London: Zed Books.

Fine, Janice. 2006. *Worker Centers: Organizing Communities at the Edge of the Dream*. Ithaca, NY: Cornell University Press.

Gall, Gregor. 2006. *Sex Worker Union Organizing: An International Study*. New York: Palgrave MacMillan.

Gilmore, Stephanie. 2010. "Strange Bedfellows: Building Feminist Coalitions around Sex Work in the 1970s." In *No Permanent Waves: Recasting Histories of U.S. Feminism*, edited by Nancy Hewitt, 246–72. Piscataway, NJ: Rutgers University Press.

Gira Grant, Melissa. 2014. *Play the Whore: The Work of Sex Work*. New York: Verso Books.

Gira Grant, Melissa, and Emma Whitford. 2017. "Family, Former Attorney of Queens Woman Who Fell to Her Death in Vice Sting Say She Was Sexually Assaulted, Pressured to Become an Informant." *The Appeal*, December 15, 2017. https://theappeal.org/family-former-attorney-of-queens-woman-who-fell-to-her-death-in-vice-sting-say-she-was-sexually-d67461a12f1/.

Guenther, Katja M. 2009. "The Impact of Emotional Opportunities on the Emotion Cultures of Feminist Organizations." *Gender & Society* 23, no. 3: 337–62.

Hardy, Kate, and Katie Cruz. 2019. "Affective Organizing: Collectivizing Informal Sex Workers in an Intimate Union." *American Behavioral Scientist* 63, no. 2: 244–61.

Jackson, Crystal A. 2016. "Framing Sex Worker Rights: How U.S. Sex Worker Rights Activists Perceive and Respond to Mainstream Anti-Sex Trafficking Advocacy." *Sociological Perspective* 59, no. 1: 27–45.

Jackson, Crystal A., Jennifer J. Reed, and Barbara G. Brents. 2017. "Strange Confluences: Radical Feminism and Evangelical Christianity as Drivers of US Neo-Abolitionism." In *Feminism, Prostitution and the State: The Politics of Neo-Abolitionism*, edited by Eilís Ward and Gillian Wylie, 66–85. New York: Routledge.

Limoncelli, Stephanie. 2009. "The Trouble with Trafficking: Conceptualizing Women's Sexual Labor and Economic Human Rights." *Women's Studies International Forum* 32, no. 4: 261–69.

Mac, Juno, and Molly Smith. 2018. *Revolting Prostitutes: The Fight for Sex Workers' Rights*. New York: Verso Books.

Majic, Samantha. 2014. "Beyond 'Victim-Criminals': Sex Workers, Nonprofit Organizations, and Gender Ideologies." *Gender & Society* 28, no. 3: 463–85.

Mgbako, Chi Adanna. 2016. *To Live Freely in This World: Sex Worker Activism in Africa.* New York: NYU Press.

Musto, Jennifer. 2016. *Control and Protect: Collaboration, Carceral Protection, and Domestic Sex Trafficking in the United States.* Oakland: University of California Press.

Office to Monitor and Combat Trafficking in Persons. n.d. "3Ps: Prosecution, Protection, and Prevention." U.S. Department of State. Accessed June 20, 2018. https://www.state.gov/j/tip/3p/.

Oselin, Sharon. 2014. *Leaving Prostitution: Getting Out and Staying Out of Sex Work.* New York: NYU Press.

Ray, Audacia, and Emma Caterine. 2014. *Criminal, Victim, or Worker?: NYC Human Trafficking Intervention Courts' Impact on People in the Sex Trade.* Red Umbrella Project. https://www.nswp.org/sites/nswp.org/files/RedUP-NYHTIC-FINALweb.pdf.

Torres, C. Angel, and Naima Paz. 2012. *Denied Help!: How Youth in the Sex Trade and Street Economy Are Turned Away from Systems Meant to Help Us & What We're Doing to Fight Back.* Young Women's Empowerment Project. https://ywepchicago.files.wordpress.com/2012/09/bad-encounter-line-report-2012.pdf.

Weitzer, Ron. 2007. "The Social Construction of Sex Trafficking: Ideology and Institutionalization of a Moral Crusade." *Politics & Society* 35: 447–75.

———. 2011. "Sex Trafficking and the Sex Industry: The Need for Evidence Based Theory and Legislation." *Journal of Criminal Law and Criminology* 101: 1337–70.

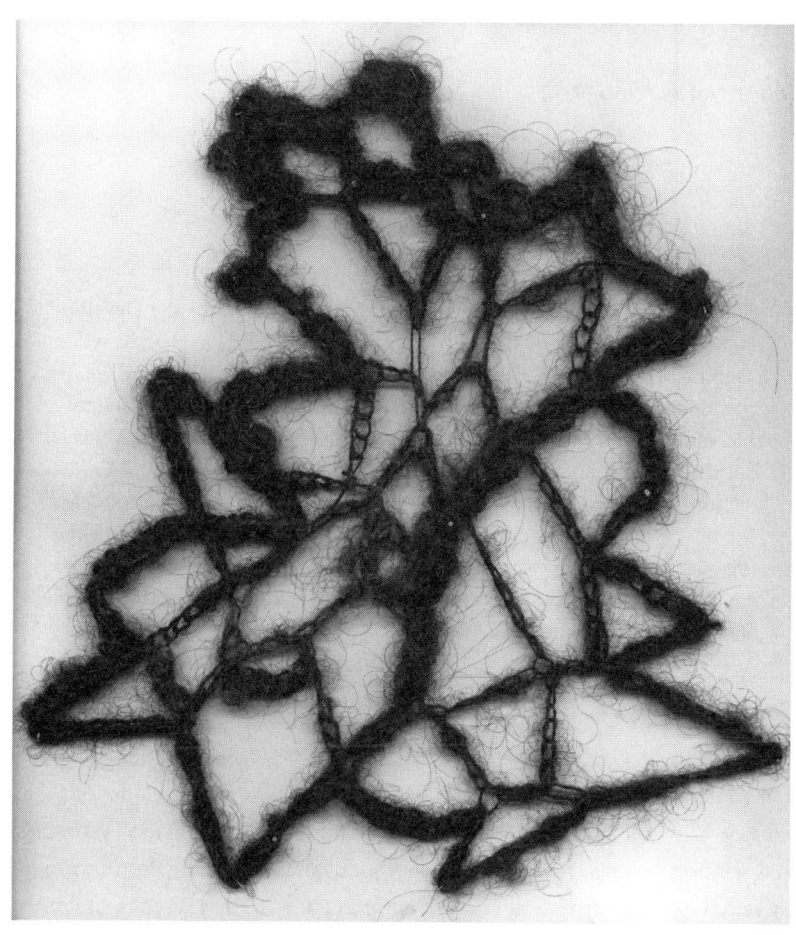

Mildred Beltré. *Constellation 2*, 2014. Human hair, approx. 3 x 6 in. Image courtesy of the artist.

Solidarity Economy Praxis in Limonade: Reintellecting Woman as Subject

Mamyrah A. Dougé-Prosper

Abstract: In 2013 the Limonade Women's Association for the Development of Agricultural and Craft Production (AFLIDEPA) in Haiti unveiled
its transformation center and seed bank. Invoking the Black radical *konbit*
tradition, the organization declared its commitment to food sovereignty
and called on its *fanm djanm* (valiant women) to contribute to the development of their home(land). In this article, I examine AFLIDEPA's formation and operations, and its relationship to the Haitian Platform for
Advocacy for an Alternative Development (PAPDA) to appreciate the
organization's pursuit to reconfigure woman, family, and nation in and beyond extractive zones. **Keywords:** solidarity economy, konbit, woman,
family, anti-capitalism

Introduction

On March 26, 2013, the *Asosyasyon Fanm Limonad pou Devlopman Pwo-
diksyon Agrikòl ak Atizana* (AFLIDEPA)—the Limonade Women's
Association for the Development of Agricultural and Craft Production—
unveiled its transformation center and seed bank in the presence of family
members, community residents, and government officials, and local, national, and international partners. Invoking the *konbit* tradition of work,
the federation declared its commitment to food sovereignty. AFLIDEPA
coordinator Olga Marcelin lauded members as *"fanm djanm*, as women
who have values, as women with principles" and called on them to serve
as models of "what is good, what is just, what is necessary for everyone
to be happy, for no one to regret being a woman, and instead to be proud

WSQ: Women's Studies Quarterly **47: 3 & 4 (Fall/Winter 2019)** © 2019 by Mamyrah A. Dougé-Prosper.

of being a woman, to be proud of being a person who contributes to her country's development and to the development of her home(land)."[1] Ricot Jean-Pierre from the *Platfòm Ayisyen Pledwaye pou yon Devlopman Altènatif* (PAPDA)—the Haitian Platform of Advocacy for an Alternative Development—recounted that PAPDA and AFLIDEPA are "in love . . . and remained faithful to one another" since the Association resisted becoming "a political tool for those seeking power . . . and money." Turning to the benches donated by his organization, *Collectif Citoyen pour le Développement et l'Intégration des Personnes Handicappées de Limonade* (CCDIPHL)—the Citizens' Collective for the Development and the Integration of Handicapped People of Limonade—coordinator and local doctor Romel Jean-Pierre asserted that "solidarity without profiteering" would lead to Limonade's development. The organizers then served *kasav ak manba* (cassava and peanut butter) sandwiches and *Lèt a Gogo*[2] yogurt, stressing the importance of consuming local products. This inaugural event signals AFLIDEPA's reintellection of sovereignty, democracy, and development, centered on the human (woman) and based on the values of solidarity and love.

In this article, I examine AFLIDEPA's solidarity economy praxis in Limonade through its structure and operations, and its relationship to PAPDA to appreciate its struggle to reorganize life in and beyond extractive zones. Though scholars of the solidarity economy point to its origins in the aftermath of neoliberal globalization, they also recognize that noncapitalist practices are not new. I contend that AFLIDEPA refashions century-old schemes of resistance to ongoing colonization and capitalism. Further, while critics of the solidarity economy underline its tendency to rely on women to fill in for an absent state, feminist economists nevertheless foresee women's liberation in cooperative economics. I invite readers to suspend purist critiques of AFLIDEPA's solidarity economy praxis and instead to visualize the horizon fanm djanm draw for us, that is the reformation of family and nation.

Solidarity Economy and the Black Radical Tradition

"Solidarity economy" is a concept that emerged in the 1990s out of Latin American social movements' experiences with not-for-profit arrangements of cooperative production, consumption, distribution, and land use, governed through collective decision-making processes and direct participation (Lechat 2013). Globally, the neoliberal turn engendered unemployment, deprivation, and resourcelessness (Wilkes 2004), and social movements the world over sought to generate a "humanist economy" (Dacheux and Goujon 2012) driven by community reciprocity rather than profit-based state redistribution (Nederveen Pieterse 1998). The structures and denominations these endeavors take vary according to the place's relationship to the market economy and the state, agricultural and climate issues, and its access to inter/national networks of people theorizing and experimenting with alternatives. Local conditions determine the varying scales at which they operate (Williams 2014). For example, the largest worker-cooperative in the world today, the Mondragon Cooperative Corporation, which regroups over thirty-five thousand worker-owners occupying one territory, was founded after World War II by isolated Basque people who leveraged Spanish state protectionism (Gibson-Graham 2006). In contrast, bankruptcy laws uphold Argentine worker-cooperatives resulting from worker takeovers of abandoned factories after the 2001 financial crisis (Ranis 2010). Even within one given nation-state, distinct configurations emerge (Lemaître and Helmsing 2012), as exemplified by Cooperation Jackson in the United States that strategizes to seize state power (Akuno and Nangwaya 2017) while Central Brooklyn Co-op operates as a civil society organization. Nevertheless, these grassroots formations with a profound critique of racial capitalism are a "series of experiments, becomings, emergent possibilities and prefigurative practices" (Williams 2014, 51). In this article, I bring to bear this tension between the possibilities that the solidarity economy promises and its limitations within the current configurations of state and power (Stahler-Sholk, Vanden, and Kuecker 2007).

The solidarity economy seeks to revalorize and formalize already existing non-market-based practices and to broaden the concept of economy beyond capitalist realism (Fisher 2009). It pluralizes the economy (Laville and Cattani 2005); other activities that do not take the form of wage labor, commodity production for a market, or capitalist enterprise are also economic. Most experimenters and observers identify its roots in century-old schemes organized by women, who still predominate in non-capitalist formations at the planetary level (Bell et al. 2018; Verschuur and Calvão 2018; Glave 2010; Escobar 1992). However, most studies of the solidarity economy remain "gender-blind" (Verschuur and Calvão 2018) and the few that take on a gendered perspective point to a lack of significant change in women's material conditions and decision-making power (Bauhardt 2014; Starr, Martínez-Torres, and Rosset 2011; Gibson-Graham 2006). Women's overwhelming participation in the care and subsistence economies ensures the social reproduction of the family and the community. Yet it does not always yield them autonomy over their own households and bodies (both in their productive and reproductive capacities). Formalizing women's othered economic practices into the solidarity economy further legitimizes the state's abandonment of surplus populations. Nevertheless, feminist economists anticipate the solidarity economy's capacity to liberate women (Federici 2012; Bennholdt-Thomsen and Mies 1999; Mies 1998). No economy can be solidary without being feminist (Matthaei 2009).

This article, and the larger project of which it is part, attempts to hold still an unfolding process. As such, I urge readers to exercise patience and restraint in their evaluation of AFLIDEPA women's innovative rebuttal to neoliberal predation and to see the alternative possibilities they present us. Following H. L. T. Quan (2005), who suggests we use Cedric J. Robinson's (1983) "vocabulary and grammar" of Black Marxism to reimagine a past and present marked by Black radical women, I situate AFLIDEPA women in the historical and present history of resistance to ongoing colonization and capitalism. To do so, I bring to light AFLIDEPA and PAPDA's coconstruction of solidarity economy praxis in Limonade as a refashioning of konbit in collaboration with their inter/nationalist comrades. Konbit is a mode of nonmonetized exchange of labor and resources between family members and neighbors occupying a given territory.[3] Though these labor and production arrangements varied in scale and took on different forms and appellations in different territories, they marked captive people's opposition to and transcendence of plantation politics, what Robinson calls the Black radical tradition. In these different places, African and African-descended people preserved and (re)constructed kinship relations based on solidarity and reciprocity. An African worldview that survived the transatlantic slave trade and chattel slavery animated resistance and rebellions in the Americas. In the "first Black republic," communalist practices not only endured the plantation system, they weathered the so-called postcolony, the longue durée of U.S. imperialism, dictatorship, and globalization. The solidarity economy in Haiti rests on these histories.

Constructing the "(Home)land" as the Field

I met Olga Marcelin (and other AFLIDEPA women) in May 2012 on my first trip to Limonade with PAPDA coordinator Ricot Jean-Pierre to study the praxis of solidarity economy. After the 2010 earthquake, in search of "new narratives about Haiti" beyond the tropes of poverty (Ulysse 2015), I turned to my network of Black Marxist militants in the United States to connect me to their homologues in the Caribbean country. At the time, PAPDA was already fifteen years into its struggle against neoliberalism, already experimenting with alternative-development models, and had renewed its campaign denouncing the United Nations military occupation. I sought to find out how cadres intellect sovereignty and citizenship, practice community-based autonomy, reconstitute gender regimes, form collective identities, and negotiate their uneven connections with other militants the world over. Heeding Dána-Ain Davis's (2013) reminder of our responsibility as feminist ethnographers to ensure that our research pursues social justice and the systemic transformation of our *subjects'* lives, I not only wanted to expose the workings of Empire in Haiti but also flaunt the places in which nonexploitative human relations are being forged.

Between April 2010 and August 2013, I conducted formal interviews with over forty leaders of PAPDA member and allied organizations at their offices, and I conversed with more than one hundred others at various gatherings mostly in the north of Haiti. All of my exchanges were carried out in Haitian Kreyòl. With PAPDA cadres, I traveled unpaved roads, scaled mountains, and traversed rivers to consort with a new generation of radicals. Out of the dozen solidarity economy practices with which PAPDA cogitates, AFLIDEPA, with a membership of almost one thousand women, most swayed me. I spent three months in Limonade, intermittently over a year, harvesting and grilling peanuts to transform into butter while telling stories and jokes, singing and debating over politics at organizational meetings and workshops, and drinking and eating at members' homes. I witnessed these militants in their roles as facilitators, moderators, orators, experts, expedition leaders, and caretakers. Overall, I reassembled an undertold thirty-year-old history of people rebutting against ongoing colonization. To un-"silence the past" (Trouillot 1995) and present that Haiti shapes as the first Black republic, I expressly name and situate the public actors who partook in my research.

Founding PAPDA: Toward a Feminist Tradition of Inter/nationalism

The Haitian Platform of Advocacy for an Alternative Development (PAPDA) was founded after the miscarriage of the *Revolisyon 1986*.[4] The transnational efforts that led to the removal of the twenty-nine-year dictatorship of the Duvalier family produced the necessary conditions for the rise of an anti-imperialist candidate, the (then) catholic priest Jean-Bertrand Aristide, who democratically secured the seat of the presidency in 1990 only to be deposed less than a year later by the U.S. Central Intelligence Agency (CIA)–trained Haitian Armed Forces and Police (Fatton Jr. 2014; Dupuy 2007). *Revolisyon 1986* radicals were further disillusioned with Aristide's restoration to power in 1994 by then U.S. president Bill Clinton and his United Nations multinational military entourage. Movement historian William Thélusmond from *Centre de Recherches Action et de Développement* (CRAD)—the Center for Action Research and Development (CRAD)—revealed to me that

> when Aristide came back, we experienced a strong neoliberal offensive, where nothing was clear and the whites [read: foreigners] had invaded the country, and then the neoliberal projects were launched. . . . There was a fragmentation on the Left . . . so we saw the necessity to at least have one discourse. That's where the alliance was born. All of us who were already strong . . . And we saw the need to get together so we can be stronger, so we can have a certain representation, so we can do certain things, so we could have an entity that was really doing things that would contribute to the construction of another type of economy in the country, another type of society using another framework, another perspective, you see. Anti-neoliberal. You see? (pers. comm., May 2013)

Aristide's homecoming indicated his commitment to implementing the Washington Consensus. *1986* revolutionaries reconsidered their participation in a proxied electoral process. In 1995, nine organizations retreated "to reinforce the capacities of our country's social movements especially in regard to their capacity to intervene on the political and social stage."[5] *Solidarite Fanm Ayisyèn* (SOFA)—Haitian Women in Solidarity—is among PAPDA's cofounders and serves on PAPDA's secretariat. Among the founders are lawyers, economists, sociologists, philosophers, and agronomists, "petit bourgeois" men and women, according to Chenet Jean-Baptiste from *Institut de Technologie et d'Animation* (ITECA)—the Institute of Technology and Animation—who, cognizant of their positionalities, instrumentalized their access to capital. They agreed that grassroots movements lacked coordination and that rural associations needed more training. They established PAPDA endeavoring to connect popular neighborhood (read: urban) associations and organizations of peasants, workers, and women across departmental lines and national borders in order to amplify resistance to the neoliberalization of the capitalist world order.

Many PAPDA founders studied abroad and developed networks with other militants, notably in France, Belgium, Venezuela, Brazil, Argentina, Mexico, Puerto Rico, Cuba, Guadeloupe, Saint Lucia, the United States, and Canada. PAPDA director Camille Chalmers cautioned me against antiquated concepts of nationalism. Chalmers explained,

> We noted that one of the obvious problems that we have is isolation. It is an isolation that functions in two ways. That means at the international level, no one knows about Haiti. So the quarantine that had been put in place by France and the other Western powers had worked well. It is total ignorance. Even among those who are professionals of history, even the folks who study slavery and revolutionary processes, they don't know the country's history. . . . Additionally, Haitians have in general a deformed vision of the world and of others. So it's a double difficulty that always plunges us into solitude. They don't understand us. But we, too, in defining our strategies, we are often clumsy on this issue of our relationship with the international, with the issue of international solidarity. So it's a double difficulty. . . . That's why within PAPDA, we decided that one work priority we had was to weave relations with movements, with international movements that share our vision, our analysis, that have almost the same critique of globalization, and that want to build alternatives. (pers. comm., November 2012)

Chalmers called for a "rupture with the colonial discourse" that convinces us to "think of ourselves as something separate, completely different than all the rest" (pers. comm., November 2012). Hence, liberation in Haiti is interlinked and contingent upon liberation everywhere else. In 1998, PAPDA solicited the collaboration of the Cuban *Asociacíon Nacional de Agricultores Pequeños* (ANAP)—the National Association of Small Farmers—to set up expert teams of Cuban and Haitian agronomists to cogitate on organic agriculture with a special focus on the rice-producing Department of Artibonite. In 2001, PAPDA participated in the "First Forum on Food Sovereignty" in Havana. That same year, the cadres presented themselves at the first World Social Forum in Brazil. Subsequently, the organizers hosted the Third Assembly in 2003 in Cap-Haïtien during which attendees visited the historical mythical site of *Bwa Kayiman*[6] and paid tribute to the transcendent figure of Boukman, who sparked the Revolution of 1804. PAPDA sat on the forum's international council for twelve years. Organizers also have ties with *Movimento dos Trabalhadores Sem Terra* (MST)—the Landless Workers' Movement. In 1999, PAPDA joined the transnational platform *Jubilée Sud* to denounce the practices of the International Monetary Fund (IMF) and the World Bank. It served on the coordinating committee of *Jubilée Sud-Amérique* for ten years. At every meeting of the Assembly of Caribbean People (ACP), leaders accompany a delegation of more than one hundred militants. PAPDA is also a member of the Committee for the Abolition of the Third World Debt (CADTM), as well as the World Forum for Alternatives (WFA). By engaging the international Left, PAPDA seeks to overcome the quarantine of the first Black republic. Cadres move across continents to exchange stories, experiences, and strategies, and act together with other militants. By doing so, they secure the necessary resources to support the development of solidarity economy in Haiti.

For over twenty years, PAPDA leaders journeyed throughout the country to identify potential allies and to abet peasant reimaginings of labor and land relations. Former PAPDA director of program Frank Saint-Jean insisted that

> when we select a pilot area, it involves a series of actions towards a type of experimentation . . . that serves us as an example to fuel our advocacy. The objective of the pilot for us, it's that there are actions being done, on the basis of alternative construction, you understand? And these alternatives are supposed to help us fuel our global advocacy work. This means that the advocacy work that we are doing at the global level is not that of an intellectual in an office. These are things firmly grounded in a reality. It is something fueled by local processes . . . A dialectic. (pers. comm., November 2012)

During the last four years, with the assistance of the *Groupe de Recherche et d'Appui en Milieu Rural* (GRAMIR)—the Research and Support Group in Rural Areas—PAPDA convened 153 peasant collectives at regional and national retreats to facilitate dialogues about their vision for an alternative Haiti and to formulate a *Kaye Nasyonal Revandikasyon Òga-nizasyon Peyizan ak Peyizàn Ayisyen yo* (National Notebook of Demands of Haitian Peasant Organizations). This dialectical consultation between local (peasant) and national (Western-educated) forms of knowing is what María Elena Martínez-Torres and Peter Rosset (2010) call a "dialogue of knowledges." Positing that food sovereignty is fundamental to self-determination,[7] the *Kaye* details a (popular) national proposal for an agroecological development centered around the (extended) family—the collective. Founding-member Allen Henry from *Association Nationale des Agro-professionnels Haitiens* (ANDAH)—the National Haitian Association of Agro-professionals—clarified in an earlier interview,

> We still encourage family-based agriculture. For a simple reason, because the social relations, the economic relations, they are very different than when you enter into massive production that are based on salary relations, which means classic relations of exploitation. We are not down with that. You see? Family-based agriculture is the best model for establishing healthy relations between people. (pers. comm., May 2013)

Family here is theorized as a "quality of relations, a principle of cooperation and responsibility" between human beings and not as exclusive biological relations (Federici 2012, 145). This reconceptualization of family reconjoins the processes of production, reproduction, and consumption that the social division of labor in capitalism divides and fetishizes (Federici 2012; Mies 1998). For PAPDA, family is a prefigurative formation that draws from preexisting ways of being and doing before and under capitalism. Former director of SOFA Carole Pierre-Paul Jacob specified in a separate exchange,

> Patriarchy is old but it is not tradition. Similarly, capitalism is old but it does not emanate, it is not an emanation of the people, meaning it is not the popular way of life, you see. So you have tradition that emanates, that is the emanation of the popular masses, meaning a reclamation of historical roots, historical things. (pers. comm., May 2013)

Tradition in Jacob's case stands outside of the "overrepresented Western bourgeois ethnoclass human figure," what Sylvia Wynter terms "Man" and his emanations of patriarchy and capitalism (2003, 260). SOFA feminists reclaim Man's centering of the human experience around himself.

Patriarchy and capitalism are not inevitable and timeless. Other subjectivities beyond Man are possible. It is this theory of a "popular" way of life as a "feminist" way of life that I try to ground below.

Locating and Uncovering AFLIDEPA

An hour drive southeast from Labadie, a private destination offered by the Miami-based Norwegian cruise line Royal Caribbean, the AFLIDEPA center is located in the commune of Limonade off the National Route No. 6, less than ten kilometers south of Haiti's second-largest city Cap-Haïtien, and up the road from the Dominican-funded State University King Henri Christophe Limonade Campus. Built in the early nineteenth century to defend independence from European reinvasion, the Citadel Laferrière rests 970 meters atop the Massif du Nord mountain chains, twenty-five kilometers south of Limonade, surveilling the Caracol Bay in which a free-trade industrial park financed by the United States Agency for International Development (USAID) disgorges chemical waste from the manufacture of Old Navy clothing. The fortress overlooks the Morne Bossa gold-mining project of U.S. company VCS Mining. Though Dubout is sited in the Department of Nord, it is only twenty kilometers from an old United Nations Stabilization Mission in Haiti (MINUSTAH) base in Terrier Rouge in the Department of Nord-Est, outside of the Blondin-Douvray copper mines of the Canadian company Majescor. Dubout is an hour drive away

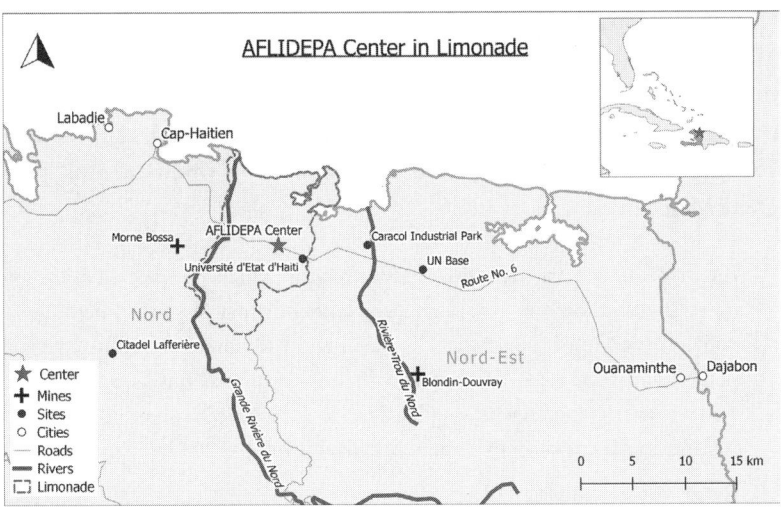

Fig. 1. Map of AFLIDEPA center in relation to extractive zones. Produced by author.

from the militarized border on the Massacre River where Haitians buy Dominican goods at the so-called binational market.

A few kilometers outside the Limonade city center stands a hand-painted sign with the organization's and supporting partners' logos. A narrow path large enough for the passage of one Nissan Patrol leads to the gate, above which hangs "*Byenvini nan Sant AFLIDEPA* (Welcome to the AFLIDEPA Center)." The seafoam green ranch-style edifice sits on six acres of land; it occupies less than one-fourth of the property. Its large porch serves as a stage during events and as a gathering space for assemblies and training workshops. A window on the left side of the center opens up to a shop. To its right sits a smaller building in which local seeds are stored. On the rest of the land, AFLIDEPA plans to erect another structure to house organizational activities and accommodate participants.

Founding AFLIDEPA: Woman as Subject

The center is a milestone in the vision of the six women who established AFLIDEPA in January 2004, the year marking the bicentennial of the Haitian Revolution. The founders are former members of the peasant collective *Asosyasyon Pwodiktè Lèt Limonad* (APWOLIM)—the Association of Milk Producers of Limonade. The separation was not the result of discord. They cite the most recent 2003 census to recognize that women comprise 52 percent of the population, and that 53 percent of all households are headed by women; 41.2 percent of households in the country include four to six people; and 31.2 percent of all women are unemployed (IHSI 2003). Marcelin explained, "When a woman has an economic activity, it is in fact the entire family [that benefits]" (pers. comm., November 2012). At the time of the inauguration, there were 224 cows in circulation, and fourteen young women had recently joined the "*manman bèf* (mother cow)" program. Marcelin elated:

> The manman bèf program, this is something in which we are greatly invested. Because before—I will give you a little history lesson . . . before, women didn't use to raise cows. It was men in Limonade. . . . But now women are integrated—as they should be—in animal husbandry, and there are many women who shepherd cows. . . . So this is something very exciting for the organization. (pers. comm., November 2012)

Cow husbandry (in Limonade) is traditionally the domain of men. AFLIDEPA challenges and seeks to dismantle this occupational segregation. Marcelin reminds us that women, too, labor—women, too, are peasants. Woman becomes subject; the world is imagined and ordered from her standpoint.

Volunteers coordinate the federation; Marcelin functions as its director. There are various committees that oversee the management of projects, popular education, and health, to name a few. AFLIDEPA holds monthly membership meetings. Every January, the Association organizes a General Assembly during which adherents reevaluate and recommit to its principles. In 2017, membership counted 520 adult women and 325 young women ages nine to twenty-five distributed over ten branches in varying communal sections of Limonade, or 3.11 percent of the female population. The organization integrates the disabled, the elderly, and children in all its activities, including laboring in the gardens. At the inauguration, a CCDIPHL spokesperson applauded the collective for believing "that all people are people." Every year, the federation honors a woman of Limonade who is almost one hundred years old. Life expectancy for women in Haiti is sixty-four years. The organization embraces single pregnant teens. Members also involve their children:

> We mentor them in all ways, in sports, in agriculture, animal husbandry, in all AFLIDEPA activities. These children are there to ensure continuity since we have noticed that times are modern, there are other things that are increasing and coming. So we are trying to orient them in it so that we may save them so that they may become a resource for the country—I won't only say Limonade—but for the country. (Marcelin, pers. comm., November 2012)

The organization subsidizes and monitors the schooling of members' children. Consider that 42.6 percent of children six years or older living in rural areas have never received formal schooling. AFLIDEPA started *Sous Espwa Limonad* (SEL)—Source of Limonade's Hope—for members' children five and over. The collective provides its youth with judo training though Romel Jean-Pierre's *Centre de Réflexion et d'Action sur les Problèmes Sociaux* (CRAPS)—the Center for Thinking and Acting on Social Problems. AFLIDEPA administers classes on cleanliness and behavior. With rivers compromised by chemical residues from mining expeditions and industrial projects like Caracol and by the MINUSTAH-derived cholera epidemic that killed ten thousand Haitians and sickened tens of thousands of others, organizers are vigilant. The collective also offers its younger members (so far up to eleven) "credit" to pursue higher education, especially in accounting, veterinary medicine, and agricultural technique. AFLIDEPA conducts workshops on women's reproductive health. Note that the maternal mortality rate in Haiti in 2017 is 529 deaths per one hundred thousand live births, and the infant mortality rate is fifty-nine deaths per one thousand live births (IHE 2017).

The organization owns four plots of land, controls previously unused governmental territory (through usufruct rights), and utilizes individual members' "private" property to cultivate mainly corn, beans, and peanuts using a tractor AFLIDEPA shares with APWOLIM. The federation buys crops from members' personal gardens and from other collective farms in Limonade. The women raise chickens, goats, and cows. Together, they also possess a bull with which they breed their cows. AFLIDEPA remains a partner in APWOLIM's *Lèt a Gogo Limonade*, which distributes milk to local schools. Their *chwal batay* (battle horse) is agriculture "to kick out foreign milk." AFLIDEPA also produces pastries and fruit preserves. It fabricates sandals, purses, belts, necklaces, and earrings with solid waste and string. The federation's national and international partners donated the stationary and the mobile equipment. Member contribution facilitated the purchase of organizational land. The peasant women sell their products at Limonade and surrounding marketplaces. AFLIDEPA relies on its members' social networks and its ties to other organizations for distribution.

The federation controls three mutuals, and plans to open another seven in the next ten years. Only members who regularly attend organizational meetings and volunteer on committees can partake. They convene once a month and contribute five gourdes (about seven U.S. cents) to an emergency fund that covers members' illnesses, deaths, and childbirths. AFLIDEPA also collects large sums from supporters to provide loans (for a period of time determined by the member herself) at a 2 percent interest fee (1 percent for AFLIDEPA proper and the other for the mutual). Marcelin testified that "the mutuals bring about solidarity because the women learn about one another's problems" (pers. comm., May 2013). Unlike in microcredit systems, money here is a commons; it is not simply accumulated for profit and consumption. The organization strategically appeals to individual women with opportunities for personal economic growth to inscribe them in a collective movement of creative work, wealth sharing, and self-determination through a ritualistic initiation it calls "*Pase Kado*," or passing on the gift.

> Pase Kado is: we give three goats and these three goats need to be returned. The person returns them once her original have had offspring by giving them to next member. This means that even if a partner ceases to be in the field, the activity will continue within the organization. We do this with everything . . . chickens. We do it with goats, we do it with cows, we do it with the gardens. So if you have a garden activity, you have beans, you give a woman four pots of beans to plant. After she plants, she harvests them and we do follow-ups. . . . So when the beans are harvested, not only does the person have beans to eat, she also has some to sell, as well as to return to the organization to benefit another. (Marcelin, pers. comm., November 2012)

AFLIDEPA's solidarity economy praxis resubjectivizes participants beyond the transactional and exploitative categories capital imposes on them. Cooperation and responsibility underpin "healthy relations."

Accordingly, the fanm djanm are careful and strategic about not getting swallowed in "projects that do not match who we are" (Marcelin, pers. comm., November 2012). Since 2006 AFLIDEPA and PAPDA have been friends. Marcelin affirmed at the inauguration of the mill that

> we don't need anyone dictating anything to us. Because this is ours. We have our own objectives, we know what we want. We don't want to mismatch what we believe, our acronym and all. We find that PAPDA has not come to dictate anything to us . . . We can say that PAPDA has always remained in the line of vision in which we believe. And we have stayed in the line in which PAPDA believes. This is why we are friends. (pers. comm., November 2012)

At every yearly assembly, AFLIDEPA invites PAPDA and CRAPS to muse together on ways to develop Limonade. AFLIDEPA coorganized the regional workshops for the Departments of Nord and Nord-Est, coordinated the follow-up meetings to ratify the regional Kaye Revandikasyon, and cofacilitated the national gatherings to approve the final text. Via PAPDA, AFLIDEPA is a member of the transnational peasant movement *La Via*

Campesina (The Peasant Way) and participates in inter/national conventions on the solidarity economy. Moreover, the federation's collective enterprise is made possible by funding from INGOs AgriSud, *Entraide & Fraternité* (Mutual Aid & Fraternity), and Grassroots International, to name a few allies. Grounded in Limonade, AFLIDEPA's solidarity economy operations involve a multifarious construction of the nation as unique but also tied to other nations in a larger project of human emancipation.

Woman as Subject: New Intellections of the Family

The 2013 opening of the complex (mill and bank) in the presence of government officials and community members firmly roots AFLIDEPA as a central actor in Limonade and in the Departments of Nord and Nord-Est, and indicates that the federation seeks to be influential, to serve as a model, to return to Marcelin's words, for "what is good, what is just." As such, AFLIDEPA counters the Rural Code[8] and free trade and mining laws that expulse peasants *andeyò* (outside) the national imaginary and dispossess them of ancestral lands. As in other Latin American countries (Petras and Veltmeyer 2007), the Haitian state's relationship with the peasantry has always been tumultuous (Casimir 2018; Dupuy 2007; Fick 1990). (Post)colonial elite men prove(d) they are "modern" by ignoring, underdeveloping, and abusing peasants, and by turning to development practices that promote industrialization. They construe(d) peasants as an inexhaustible unskilled labor pool of nonpersons deserving and capable only of menial and subservient work for capitalist accumulation (of transnational others). Conversely, peasant communities and movements resisted through marronage and armed rebellions (Hector 2000). Likewise, AFLIDEPA women refashion the Black radical tradition of konbit to scheme against the zones of extraction that envelop them.

In this imperfectly colonized space, abandoned people reintellect labor, land relations, and kinship. Land, labor use, and value are repurposed. The domestication of land is intentional and contingent upon ecologically sound, collectively driven projects. AFLIDEPA improves land according to its environmentalist commitment to resituating the human in nature. This revaluation of land engenders the reconceptualization of labor and the laboring body. In a solidarity economy, the worker and her labor are not commodities. Instead, labor is a distinctive commons, the application of "the human capacity to create" (Wainwright 2014, 74). AFLIDEPA rethinks people's capacity to labor and produce according to their creativity and for "everyone to be happy." Capacity is not reduced to the worker's corporeality as a factor in production. The worker directs her own actions. Work is thus not tedious and humiliating; the worker's body is not simply an "accumulation strategy" (Harvey 1998). The member's entire person (committed to a myriad of human relations) is engaged in the collective process.

For AFLIDEPA, kinship is based on reciprocity; people without biological attachments produce and distribute together in exchange for labor on personal gardens and the consumption of their harvest and products. As a refashioning of konbit, the solidarity economy advances a democratic mode of regulation that decommodifies human relations in order to transform households, lives, and livelihoods. Though AFLIDEPA's politics of the body seemingly point to the child as the horizon and beneficiary of political action, contrary to queer theorist Lee Edelman's (2004) claims, they are not inevitably heteronormative. The child here is not the product of compulsory marital relations. Biological reproduction is not to be bargained with husbands and national elites (whose interests align with those of Global North development agencies). AFLIDEPA affords women tools with which to design their own families. Accordingly, solidarity economy praxis in Limonade pushes against the bourgeois-liberal model of the nuclear family and the genre of human it constructs. These altered "bodily practices" (Harvey 1998, 99) dislocate "woman" from bourgeois conceptions that conjoin, oppose, and hierarchize men and women. Family here is a place where humans can reimagine and reorder their relationship to one another.[9]

AFLIDEPA offers us emanations of family and tradition that PAPDA lifts and amplifies nationally and inter/nationally as an alternative arrangement to patriarchal capitalism, and SOFA ensures that one hundred years of feminist struggles and intellections in Haiti ground this "dialogue of knowledges." Together, AFLIDEPA and PAPDA endeavor not only to create a robust civil society or a "third sector" (Laville 2010) but also to challenge the market economy and the underpinning ideology of growth in capitalism, a limitation of the solidarity economy critical scholars usually bemoan (Smith 2011; Coraggio 2011; Santos and Rodríguez-Garavito 2006). AFLIDEPA and PAPDA do not seek rapprochement to the colonial state but instead aim to expose the contradiction in the coupling of democracy and participation with capitalism. If we indeed interpret my findings in this article as an open-ended process, we inevitably see a movement in construction vying for control of state power rather than co-existence. We also recognize the revival of inter/nationalism at a time we desperately need it.

Conclusion

To remove Haiti from quarantine is to unsilence the past and present. It is to place Haiti at the center of modernity and its discontents—not in order to continue exceptionalizing the first Black republic, but rather to remind us that colonialism is alive and well, and that capitalism relies on the devaluation and exploitation of African people. Thinking through and with Haiti also offers an alternative to the capitalist system. For over five centuries, the people who have walked its land have intellected beyond Man. AFLIDEPA organizers pursue these revolutionary goals of relating to other human beings on a nontransactional basis. Fanm djanm invite women in extractive zones to experiment with a konbit economy. Living the "popular" way of life necessitates the reconstruction of family. AFLIDEPA recognizes the plurality of family composition; it extends its limits beyond (heterosexual) biological ties. Living the "popular" way of life involves the transformation of the body from a mere capitalist instrument for accumulation to a peasant subject who directs her productive and reproductive actions. The body's desired output is solidarity rather than productivity. Consequently, nonnormative bodies, too, can labor. AFLIDEPA counts among its members the disabled and the elderly, pregnant teens and children. Living the peasant way of life requires cogitations with national others. It also entails reimagining the nation beyond its territorial cage, as linked to other nations engaged in the struggle for human liberation.

Acknowledgments

I thank PAPDA and AFLIDEPA for their ongoing collaboration, and my colleagues at the Center for Place, Culture, and Politics at the CUNY Graduate Center for helpful comments. This research was supported by Florida International University.

Mamyrah A. Dougé-Prosper is a postdoctoral fellow with the Institute for Research on the

African Diaspora in the Americas and the Caribbean at the CUNY Graduate Center. Her research program focuses on the construction of neocolonial nationalist ideologies and collective identities in relation to race and class, gender and sexuality, education and language, and religion. She can be reached at mprosper@gc.cuny.edu.

Notes

1. *Lakay* in Haitian Kreyòl stands for one of two words: "home" and "homeland."
2. *Lèt a Gogo* (Haitian for "milk in abundance") transformation centers produce dairy products.
3. Though Haitian anthropologists Rachel Beauvoir and Didier Dominique ([1989] 2003) clarified in their Haitian Kreyòl–language book *Savalou E* that democratic modes of organizing life varied and took on different appellations—*eskwad, asosye, sosyete travay, kòve, gwoupman peyizan*—it is precisely because konbit enjoys colloquial use across Haiti that I retain it here. U.S. anthropologist Jennie Smith's (2001) most recent English-language text *When the Hands Are Many: Community Organization and Social Change in Haiti* reconfirms this diversity.
4. Radical social movement thinkers refer to the three-decade-long struggles against and subsequent removal of the Duvalierist dictatorship in 1986 as *Revolisyon 1986*.
5. See www.papda.org for PAPDA's mission statement.
6. *Bwa Kayiman* in the Department of Nord, a few miles from Cap-Haïtien, is the site where a Vodou ceremony took place in 1791 and ignited the Revolution of 1804. See James 1989.
7. According to the World Bank, in 2016, 51.2 percent of Haiti's GDP was comprised of imports of goods and services.
8. The current Rural Code of 1962 is president François Duvalier's version, which arranges and governs peasant life in contradistinction to urban life administered by the Civil, Penal, Commercial, and Criminal codes.
9. Research on the Cuban peasant movement after the Special Period reveals that over time family-based cooperative practices make women's emancipation possible (Rosset et al. 2011). Family then promises to be an emancipatory space for peasant women.

Works Cited

Akuno, Kali, and Ajamu Nangwaya. 2017. *Jackson Rising: The Struggle for Economic Democracy and Black Self-Determination in Jackson, Mississippi.* Jackson, MS: Daraja Press.

Bauhardt, Christine. 2014. "Solutions to the Crisis? The Green New Deal, Degrowth, and the Solidarity Economy: Alternatives to the Capitalist Growth Economy from an Ecofeminist Economics Perspective." *Ecological Economics* 102: 60–68.

Beauvoir, Rachel, and Didier Dominique. (1989) 2003. *Savalou E.* Montréal, QC: Editions du CIDIHCA.

Bell, Myrtle P., Joy Leopold, Daphne Berry, and Alison V. Hall. 2018. "Diversity, Discrimination, and Persistent Inequality: Hope for the Future through the Solidarity Economy Movement." *Journal of Social Issues* 74, no. 2: 224–43.

Bennholdt-Thomsen, Veronica, and Maria Mies. 1999. *The Subsistence Perspective: Beyond the Globalised Economy.* London: Zed Books.

Casimir, Jean. 2018. *Une Lecture Décoloniale de l'Histoire des Haïtiennes. Du Traité de Ryswick à l'Occupation Américaine (1697–1915).* Port-au-Prince: Bibliothèque Nationale d'Haïti.

Coraggio, José Luis. 2011. *Economía Social y Solidaria: El Trabajo Antes que el Capital.* Quito: Fundación Rosa Luxemburg.

Dacheux, Eric, and Daniel Goujon. 2012. "The Solidarity Economy: An Alternative Development Strategy?" *International Social Science Journal* 62, nos. 203/204: 205–15.

Davis, Dána-Ain. 2013. "Border Crossings: Intimacy and Feminist Activist Ethnography in the Age of Neoliberalism." In *Feminist Activist Ethnography: Counterpoints to Neoliberalism in North America,* edited by Christa Craven and Dána-Ain Davis, 23–38. Lanham, MD: Lexington Books.

Dupuy, Alex. 2007. *The Prophet and Power: Jean-Bertrand Aristide, the International Community, and Haiti.* New York: Rowman & Littlefield Publishers.

Edelman, Lee. 2004. *No Future: Queer Theory and the Death Drive.* Durham, NC: Duke University Press.

Escobar, Arturo. 1992. "Imagining a Post-Development Era? Critical Thought, Development and Social Movements." *Social Text,* nos. 31/32: 20–56.

Fatton Jr., Robert. 2014. *Haiti: Trapped in the Outer Periphery.* London: Lynne Rienner Publishers, Inc.

Federici, Silvia. 2012. *Revolution at Point Zero: Housework, Reproduction, and Feminist Struggle.* Brooklyn, NY: Common Notions.

Fick, Carolyn. 1990. *The Making of Haiti: Saint Domingue Revolution from Below.* Memphis: University of Tennessee Press.

Fisher, Mark. 2009. *Capitalist Realism: Is There No Alternative?* Winchester: Zero Books.

Gibson-Graham, J. K. 2006. *A Postcapitalist Politics.* Minneapolis: University of Minnesota Press.

Glave, Diane. 2010. *Rooted in the Earth: Reclaiming the African American Environmental Heritage.* Chicago: Chicago Review Press.

Harvey, David. 1998. "The Body as Accumulation Strategy." *Environment and Planning D: Society and Space* 16, no. 4: 401–21.

Hector, Michel. 2000. *Crises et Mouvements Populaires en Haïti.* Montreal, QC: Editions CIDIHCA.

Institut Haitien de l'Enfance (IHE). 2017. "Enquête Mortalité, Morbidité et Utilisation des Services (EMMUS-VI 2016–2017)."

Institut Haitien de Statistique et d'Informatique (IHSI). 2003. "La Population." *Ministère de l'Economie et des Finances, Haiti.* http://www.ihsi.ht.

James, C. L. R. 1989. *The Black Jacobins: Toussaint L'Ouverture and the San Domingo Revolution.* 2nd ed. New York: Vintage Books.

Laville, Jean-Louis. 2010. "Solidarity Economy." In *The Human Economy,* edited by Jean-Louis Laville and Antonio David Cattani, 225-235. Cambridge, UK: Polity Press.

Laville, Jean-Louis, and Antonio David Cattani. 2005. *Dictionnaire de l'Autre Economie.* Paris: Desclée de Brouwer.

Lechat, Nöelle. 2013. "Organizing for the Solidarity Economy in South Brazil." In *The Social Economy: International Perspectives on Solidarity Economy,* edited by Ash Amin, 159-175. London: Zed Books.

Lemaître, Andreia, and A. H. J. (Bert) Helmsing. 2012. "Solidarity Economy in Brazil: Movement, Discourse and Practice Analysis Through a Polanyian Understanding of the Economy." *Journal of International Development* 24: 745–62.

Martínez-Torres, María Elena, and Peter Rosset. 2010. "La Via Campesina: The Birth and Evolution of a Transnational Social Movement." *Journal of Peasant Studies* 37, no. 1: 149–75.

Matthaei, Julie. 2009. "Beyond Economic Man: Economic Crisis, Feminist Economics, and the Solidarity Economy." Paper presented at the *International Association for Feminist Economics Conference,* Boston, June 2009.

Mies, Maria. 1998. *Patriarchy and Accumulation on a World Scale: Women in the International Division of Labour.* London: Zed Books.

Nederveen Pieterse, Jan. 1998. "My Paradigm or Yours? Alternative Development, Post-Development, Reflexive Development." *Development and Change* 29: 343–73.

Petras, James, and Henry Veltmeyer. 2007. "The 'Development State' in Latin America: Whose Development, Whose State? *Journal of Peasant Studies* 34, nos. 3/4: 371–407.

Quan, H. L. T. 2005. "Geniuses of Resistance: Feminist Consciousness and the Black Radical Tradition." *Race & Class* 47, no. 2: 39–53.

Ranis, Peter. 2010. "Argentine Worker Cooperatives in Civil Society: A Challenge to Capital-Labor Relations." *Journal of Labor and Society* 13, no. 1: 77–105.

Robinson, Cedric J. 1983. *Black Marxism: The Making of a Black Radical Tradition.* Chapel Hill: University of North Carolina Press.

Rosset, Peter Michael, Braulio Machin Sosa, Adilén Maria Roque Jaime, and Dana Rocio Avila Lozano. 2011. "The *Campesino*-to-*Campesino* Agroecology Movement of ANAP in Cuba: Social Process Methodology in the Construction of Sustainable Peasant Agriculture and Food Sovereignty." *Journal of Peasant Studies* 38, no. 1: 161–91.

Santos, Boaventura de Sousa, and César Rodríguez-Garavito. 2006. "Introduction: Expanding the Economic Canon and Searching for Alternatives to Neoliberal Globalisation." In *Another Production Is Possible: Beyond the Capitalist Canon,* edited by Boaventura de Sousa Santos. London: Verso Books.

Smith, Jennie M. 2001. *When the Hands Are Many: Community Organization and Social Change in Rural Haiti.* Ithaca, NY: Cornell University Press.

Smith, Richard. 2011. "Beyond Growth or Beyond Capitalism?" London: Institute for Policy Research and Development. http://iprd.org. uk/?p=6859.

Stahler-Sholk, Richard, Harry E. Vanden, and Glen David Kuecker. 2007. "Globalization Resistance: The New Politics of Social Movements in Latin America." *Latin American Perspectives* 34, no. 2: 5–16.

Starr, Amory, María Elena Martínez-Torres, and Peter Rosset. 2011. "Participatory Democracy in Action: Practices of the Zapatistas and the Movimento Sem Terra." *Latin American Perspectives* 38, no. 1: 102–19.

Trouillot, Michel-Rolph. 1995. *Silencing the Past: Power and the Production of History.* Boston: Beacon Press.

Ulysse, Gina Athena. 2015. *Why Haiti Needs New Narratives: A Post-Quake Chronicle.* Middletown, CT: Wesleyan University Press.

Verschuur, Christine, and Filipe Calvão. 2018. "Feminist Analysis of Social and Solidarity Economy Practices: Views from Latin American and India." United Nations Research Institute for Social Development. http://www. unrisd.org/80256B3C005BB128/(httpProjects)/25E19977A47FFC96 C1257F110054BCB5?OpenDocument.

Wainwright, Hilary. 2014. "Notes for a Political Economy of Creativity and Solidarity." In *The Solidarity Economy Alternative: Emerging Theory and Practice,* edited by Vishwas Satgar, 64–100. Durban: University of KwaZulu-Natal Press.

Wilkes, Rima. 2004. "First Nation Politics: Deprivation, Resources and
    Participation in Collective Action." *Sociological Enquiry* 74, no. 4: 570–89.
Williams, Michelle. 2014. "The Solidarity Economy and Social Transformation."
    In *The Solidarity Economy Alternative: Emerging Theory and Practice*, edited
    by Vishwas Satgar, 37-63. Durban: University of KwaZulu-Natal Press.
Wynter, Sylvia. 2003. "Unsettling the Coloniality of Being/Power/Truth/
    Freedom: Towards the Human, After Man, Its Overrepresentation—An
    Argument." *New Centennial Review* 3, no. 3: 257–337.

PART V. **POETICS OF EMBODIED POLITICS**

Tillsammans Means Overlapping Edges, as in Tiles or Scales: *Feeling Translation*

Jennifer Hayashida

But there's a way in which, trying to translate from your experience to mine, I do need to hear chapter and verse from time to time. I'm afraid of it all slipping away into: "Ah, yes, I understand you."
—Audre Lorde, "Audre Lorde and Adrienne Rich:
An Interview with Audre Lorde"[1]

I started writing in my sophomore year after reading the poet Adrienne Rich and thinking: this is almost right but does not quite say what I want to say . . .
—Claudia Rankine[2]

1.

"We were hoping for an essay about Claudia Rankine's work and tentatively about *Citizen*.
We would love if you would write for _____ regarding this."

For, or together with, a selection from the Swedish edition of Claudia Rankine's *Citizen*.

1. Audre Lorde and Adrienne Rich, "An Interview with Audre Lorde," *Signs* 6, no. 4 (1981): 713–36.
2. Kate Kellaway, "The New Review Q&A: Claudia Rankine: 'Blackness in the White Imagination Has Nothing to Do with Black People,'" *The Guardian* (International edition), December 27, 2015.

WSQ: Women's Studies Quarterly 47: 3 & 4 (Fall/Winter 2019) © 2019 by Jennifer Hayashida.
All rights reserved.

A kind of transnational solidarity work, repeated attempts by the editors and I to compare our analyses regarding language, race, and migration, a joint poetics of *here* and *there*.

It is always a different thing to consider the afterlife of the translated text, how it is read—by *whose* bodies and *for whom*?

I consider the racialized body an instrument in the work of translation, a potential decolonial saboteur.

The translator can be an (un)settler. The translator can be a settler.

This is a translation from the Swedish, my translation of a failure, a recycling of the disaster.[3]

---

3. Ann Lauterbach, "Use This Word in a Sentence: 'Experimental,'" in *The Night Sky: Writings on the Poetics of Experience* (New York: Viking, 2005), 8–11.

2.

Racism and xenophobia. Apart and Together. In Sweden—*here*—the latter is seen as part and parcel of the former. Any distinctions made between the two may be perceived as undermining the political claims of both.

Acknowledge the situational *imbrication* of the two terms. Try to explain how they are weaponized as both together and apart in U.S. antiblack and yellow peril discourse.

Use 1996, Bill Clinton's second term, to illustrate *overlapping edges, as in tiles or scales*:
~~The Personal Responsibility and Work Opportunity Act~~
~~The Anti-Terrorism and Effective Death Penalty Act~~
~~The 1996 Illegal Immigration Reform and Immigrant Responsibility Act~~

The strategic deployment of overlapping edges against nonwhite bodies within U.S. logics of empire and racial capitalism.

"*An   Dilemma: The   Problem and   Democracy* was, Mr. Myrdal once said, 'not a study of the but of the American from the viewpoint of the most disadvantaged group.'"[4]

Swedish concern about the "American dilemma" while Sweden still operated the State Institute for Racial Biology (1922–1958), brainchild of the Swedish Society for Eugenics.

4. "Gunnar Myrdal, Analyst of Race Crisis, Dies," *New York Times* (National edition), May 18, 1987: A1.

3.

Fig. 1. Nina Mangalanayagam, "Balancing Act," 2012. Black-and-white still image taken from ten-minute split-screen HD video installation.

Translation is the method by which I gather the data of my embodiment.[5]

Attempt to translate *Black Lives Matter* into Swedish:
a) *It's about Black Lives*
b) *Black Lives Are Important*
c) *Black Lives Affect*

A BLM solidarity video produced by the political party *Feministiskt Initiativ* (FI!) transforms the rallying cry into a solemn *Black ... Lives ... Matter*, the protracted enunciation a method of translation.[6]

---

5. "I'm saying physical perception is the data of my embodiment." Mei-Mei Berssenbrugge, *Hello the Roses* (New York: New Directions, 2013).

6. *Death Row* is sometimes, but not always, an actual row. Translation as analytical method can here clarify both the metaphorical and the literal embedded in an institutional reality, the conditions people live under as they await a state-sanctioned death, timed by a bureaucratic and legal clock. *Deathlength. Deathstretch. Deathpace.*

English should not be the language of solidarity.

I am twenty-two years old, watching the OJ Simpson trial on Swedish television. One of the LAPD detectives is on the stand.
—*Did you collect swatches on the crime scene?*
—*Yes, we took Swatch watches,* the on-screen captioning (un)translates.

The racialized spectacle of the trial reminded me of where and what I came from, my cultural and political heritage, my racist homeland. Swedish liberal claims of *tillsammans* suddenly more sinister than that LA courtroom.

Perhaps what is true for the untranslatability of *fuck you* is also true for BLM: it's English-only, even in translation.

A language where *afrofobi* can contain a chasm of antiblack feelings in atonal harmony with *afrofili*, white Swedes' delight when they shop at AfroArt.

Zora Neale Hurston translated by Glenn Ligon: (*I Feel Most Colored When I Am Thrown Against a Sharp White Background*), a piece from *Untitled Four Etchings* (1992), included in the first section of *Citizen*.

After FI!'s BLM solidarity video, YouTube's algorithm recommends something else: two hunched-over white men in baseball caps. Racist commentary on the FI! video (un)translates as if referring to Ligon's *Untitled Four Etchings* (1992): "We have a monochrome film . . . it is black."

4.

Fig. 2. Still image taken from "Black Lives Matter: Sweden," a video produced by the Swedish feminist party FI! Feministiskt Initiativ (2016).

Rankine translates the racist tennis world surrounding Serena Williams, a black body which lends form, power, value to whiteness, *tennis whites* denoting the white regulation clothing along with the players, viewers, and judges who define this elite sport.[7]

In translation, the Swedish language and welfare state outline Rankine's project: How is the book's black-and-white terrain read against the often blindingly white backdrop of the literary landscape *here*?

Rankine states that the title is a question concerning how citizenship is "embodied and honoured."[8]

7. Toni Morrison, *Playing in the Dark: Whiteness and the Literary Imagination* (Cambridge, MA: Harvard University Press, 1992).
8. Kate Kellaway, "The New Review Q&A: Claudia Rankine: 'Blackness in the White Imagination Has Nothing to Do with Black People,'" *The Guardian* (International edition), December 27, 2015.

Can *Medborgare* be read as a study of the Swedish society from the viewpoint of the most disadvantaged group?

As a process of *reconsidering Citizen*, literary scholar Maria A. Windell wonders if the book's analytical reach reproduces a hegemonic focus on binary black-white race relations, especially since citizenship inevitably stands at its center.[9]

How would my reading of *Citizen* shift if *you* were also someone who had crossed the border between Ciudad Juárez and El Paso, if *you* were a Cambodian refugee facing deportation?

Citizen and the foreigner, "like a foreigner with a newly minted 'fuck you.'"[10]

Who are the poetic foreigners to emerge from a book like *Citizen*, not as the economic and political opposites of black lives, but as their twins in migratory translation?[11]

9. Roderick A. Ferguson, Evie Shockley, Maria A. Windell, and Daniel Worden, "Reconsidering Claudia Rankine's *Citizen: An American Lyric*. A Symposium, Part I," *Los Angeles Review of Books*, January 6, 2016.

10. Claudia Rankine, *Citizen: An American Lyric* (Minneapolis, MN: Graywolf Press, 2014), 72.

11. Don Mee Choi, "Translation Is a Mode=Translation Is an Anti-Neocolonial Mode" (keynote address, American Literary Translators Association, Oakland, CA, October 8, 2016).

5.

"Each moment is like this—before it can be known,
categorized as similar to another thing and dismissed, it has to be
experienced, it has to be seen."[12]

~~(Rankine on translation and the data of embodiment)~~

I want to know what happens to Rankine's use of *n-ordet* in translation:
What does it mean for another body to translate the historical violence of
that word—but also its potential expressions of "contingency, irony, and
solidarity"?[13]

What does it mean if the translator resists that work?

Which bodies are redacted in translation? Which bodies redact?

What happens if *you* (un)translate the historical heart of a beating inquiry?

When things don't go the way I want them to, that just makes me work even
harder.[14]

12. Claudia Rankine, *Citizen: An American Lyric*, 9.
13. Jody Armour, "Nigga Theory: Contingency, Irony, and Solidarity in the Substantive Criminal Law," *Ohio State Journal of Criminal Law* 12, no. 1 (2014): 9–56.
14. Darnell L. Hudson, Harold W. Neighbors, Arline T. Geronimus, and James S. Jackson, "Racial Discrimination, John Henryism, and Depression Among African Americans," *Journal of Black Psychology* 42, no. 3 (2016): 221–43.

No, translation does not allow *us* to imagine a world without borders. Translation cannot rehumanize the body, the border, the cage.

"Though the white liberal imagination likes to feel temporarily bad about black suffering, there really is no mode of empathy that can replicate the daily strain of knowing that as a black person you can be killed for simply being black . . ."[15]
(Rankine, again)

Is that daily strain—the embodied method of gathering racial data—a vital qualification for the contemporary translator?

How is Rankine's "panorama of micro-aggression" read in Swedish when, *here*, xenophobia and antiblack racism are not instrumentalized in strategic antagonism, but together?[16]

John Henry was a legendary folk hero who worked tirelessly and, in an extraordinary and embodied critique of industrialization, decided to compete against a steam engine. John Henry died of exhaustion.

15. Claudia Rankine, "The Condition of Black Life Is One of Mourning," *New York Times Magazine*, June 22, 2015.
16. Lisa Uddin, Catherine Zuromskis, Daniel Worden, and Kenneth W. Warren, "Reconsidering Claudia Rankine's *Citizen: An American Lyric.* A Symposium, Part II," *Los Angeles Review of Books*, January 6, 2016.

Rankine's unrelentingly dialectical reasoning. *You* are always watching and watched, actor and acted upon.

In *Against World Literature*, literary theorist Emily Apter considers how translation can provide an opportunity whereby the text can resist a reader's racialized and colonial expectations, often marked by an anthropological desire to experience the exotic.[17]

I experience nonwhite Swedes who speak regional dialects as *exotic*, as a decolonial intervention, a refusal to participate in the neocolonial project of uniform languaging that is *Rikssvenska*, "National Swedish."

This dialectical variation appears to me in the FI! solidarity video, in its appeal for me to understand the meaning of *together*: seven hundred Africans dead in the Mediterranean and black Americans executed on the streets of U.S. cities, large and small.

As in, overlapping tiles or scales.

17. Emily Apter, *Against World Literature: On the Politics of Untranslatability* (New York: Verso Books, 2013).

6.

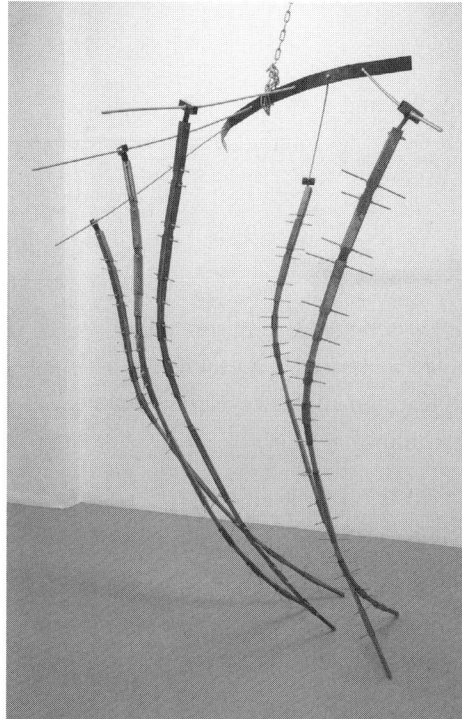

Fig. 3. Hanni Kamaly, *Freddie Gray*, 2016. Photograph by Jenny Ekholm. Originally shown as part of the exhibition *EVERY NAME IN HISTORY IS I* at KHM Gallery (Malmö, Sweden) in 2016.

What kind of worlding do we engage in if *you* translate without access to the embodied data of racism?

Can translation expand *Citizen*'s analytical reach so it is possible to see in it both Dylann Roof and John Ausonius, *Lasermannen*, "The Laser Man," who in the early 1990s terrorized Swedish POC communities armed with a laser-sighted rifle?

At the same time, brown, yellow, and black lives in Sweden do not necessarily require U.S. blackness as an analytical link, so can a Swedish translation challenge *Citizen* to be more than Ferguson as world literature? Can it redirect our gaze?

"We do not get to become human by reading this book."[18]
(Lisa Uddin)

Repeated attempts to burn Swedish refugee housing to the ground, barracks built by private contractors engaged in the neoliberal task of housing unaccompanied Syrian minors.

Decades earlier, the backdrop as I watch the OJ Simpson trial: BSS[19] on the elskåp, on the pebbled walls of the gångtunnel, outside the syo-konsulent, on the subway to Ropsten, three neo-Nazi fists pump toward me through a half-open window.

A white self gives a gift to a black self—using Rankine's logic, the other is by necessity also a self—but in turn expects a kind of gratitude where racialized power becomes (un)translated as a political gift.[20]

18. Lisa Uddin, Catherine Zuromskis, Daniel Worden, and Kenneth W. Warren, "Reconsidering Claudia Rankine's *Citizen: An American Lyric*. A Symposium, Part II," *Los Angeles Review of Books*, January 6, 2016.
19. "BSS" stands for "Bevara Sverige Svenskt" ("Keep Sweden Swedish"), the name of a Swedish Nazi organization founded in the late 1970s with the fascist British National Front as its model. The group promoted a deeply racist and xenophobic agenda, eventually reconstituting itself into what is the contemporary mainstream party Sverigedemokraterna, the Sweden Democrats, who today occupy nearly 20 percent of seats in Swedish parliament.
20. In her book *The Erotic Life of Racism*, Sharon Patricia Holland describes how she and a good friend's fifteen-year-old daughter sit in the car in the parking lot outside the grocery store Safeway. Holland is in Northern California, in the affluent Palo Alto, and it is just a few days after Tupac Shakur has been shot to death. The radio plays Shakur's music, and Holland and the younger woman discuss what has happened. A white woman approaches Holland and asks that Holland move her car so that the woman can more easily move her grocery bags into her car. Holland responds that she will happily wait to get out of her car until the woman is done unloading her cart. The woman appears surprised by Holland's response but says nothing. Holland and her young friend continue discussing Shakur, and when they soon thereafter leave the car in order to enter the store, the woman exclaims, "And to think that I marched for you!" Holland's response, "You didn't march for me, you marched for yourself—and if you don't understand that, I can't help you." (Thank you to Melissa Phruksachart for suggesting this reading to me during one of our many AASP office conversations at Hunter College.)

Grateful Southeast Asians who fled the American wars in Viet Nam, Cambodia, and Laos—today wars in Afghanistan, Iraq, and Syria—transformed into the "vulnerable" subjects necessary in order for U.S. military force and imperial benevolence to remain visible, domestically as well as internationally.

Mimi Thi Nguyen terms this *the gift of freedom*, enacted via an unrelenting cycle of U.S. warfare and asylum which continuously produces new refugees and new gifts to be granted and regulated, through, for example, welfare reform.[21]

What is the gift—the political and the lyric—offered Swedish readers of *Citizen*? Who is expected to say *thank you*, and in what language?

Brown Romanian bodies begging outside the sliding glass doors of each and every grocery store in Swedish cities, large and small.

I am instructed to not call them "beggars": they are "utsatta EU medborgare," that is, "vulnerable EU citizens" whose European right to free movement has brought them to this sidewalk.

My translation of the Swedish "utsatta" does not fully take into account many Swedes' feeling that the gift of free movement is being abused.

---

21. Mimi Thi Nguyen, *The Gift of Freedom: War, Debt, and Other Refugee Passages* (Durham, NC: Duke University Press, 2012).

Swedish municipal governments begin to institute prohibitions on begging, since it is "unpleasant" to shop in stores where vulnerable EU citizens sit on the ground outside.

What does it mean for a nation-state to *need* a book? How might translation reproduce or problematize that need?

Can Rankine's shifting *you* live in "particularly vulnerable areas" such as Biskopsgården, Rinkeby, Rosengård? Does *you* teach in Stockholm or Gothenburg, two of Europe's most segregated cities?

"Vulnerable," here, means subject to military-style policing or, alternately, that the police refuse to respond to calls at all.

7.

U.S. reviews of *Citizen* are primarily authored by white male critics. In 2015, the *New York Review of Books* had nearly three times as many male critics as it did female.[22]

Nick Laird in the *NYRB*: "One problem with writing poetry about political or historical issues is that poetry proves a terrible method for transmitting real information."[23]

What constitutes *real* information is not a neutral question: Who determines what information is real? *You* or *you*? For whom is Rankine's translation of the real too conceptual or not conceptual enough?[24]

Perhaps a translation of *Citizen* is already a translation twice removed.

Laird intimates that abstraction functions only when the reader has some knowledge of what is abstracted, and I am reminded of the uneven distribution of certain epistemological data.[25]

22. 2015 VIDA Count (Women in Literary Arts): https://www.vidaweb.org/the-2015-vida-count/.

23. Nick Laird, "A New Way of Writing About Race." *New York Review of Books*, April 23, 2015.

24. Michael Leong, "Conceptualisms in Crisis: The Fate of Late Conceptual Poetry," *Journal of Modern Literature* 41, no. 3 (2018): 109–31.

25. Laird, "A New Way of Writing About Race," 2015.

~~Experiences outside~~ the white male body are often characterized as abstract, as feelings and not facts, whereas, as Yvonne Rainer has observed, feelings of course are facts.[26]

What does it say about abstract art if it is *real* only to some bodies and not others?
Or, what does it say about reality that its abstraction is only *real* to some bodies and not others?

"What do we do with the fact that the qualities that mark *Citizen* as 'experimental' poetry are precisely the qualities that make it inviting, despite its disturbing subject matter, to a generally poetry-phobic public?"[27] (Evie Shockley)

Abstract or concrete: A Swedish taxi driver imprisoned for human trafficking after driving refugees across the Öresund bridge from Denmark to Sweden.[28]

26. Yvonne Rainer, *Feelings Are Facts: A Life* (Cambridge, MA: MIT Press, 2006).

27. Roderick A. Ferguson, Evie Shockley, Maria A. Windell, and Daniel Worden, "Reconsidering Claudia Rankine's *Citizen: An American Lyric*. A Symposium, Part I," *Los Angeles Review of Books*, January 6, 2016.

28. If you are a taxi driver and need to understand if you should request ID in the event that you suspect someone is a refugee: "It depends on the circumstances. If you arrive with suitcases straight from the airport, the imperative is not as great as if you arrive in slippers and aren't dressed for the winter" (Jimmy Serrano, district prosecutor in Malmö). Hannes Delling, "Åklagare: Taxiförare bör kolla id-handlingar," *Svenska Dagbladet*, January 4, 2016.

Abstract or concrete: Acquitted neo-Nazis assembled outside a courthouse in the rain, their newspaper faces obscured by black rectangles.

Abstract or concrete: "When the municipality needed private contractors to house unaccompanied minors, minimal risk was involved. That market is very competitive."[29]

Who translates the overlapping and ongoing afterlives of bodies, language, and borders. This is not a question.

Jennifer Hayashida is a poet, translator, and visual artist. She is currently a PhD candidate in artistic research at Valand Academy, the University of Gothenburg, Sweden. Her research focuses on translation, dislocation, race, and affect. From 2010 to 2017, she served as director of the Asian American Studies Program at Hunter College, CUNY. She can be reached at jennifer.hayashida@gu.se.

29. Jan Johansson, "Flyktingboende på entreprenad," *Västerbottens-kuriren*, September 3, 2012.

Public Sexuality and the Feminist Poetics of Redevelopment in Leslie Scalapino and Adrienne Rich

Davy Knittle

Abstract: This article works toward a reading theory of public sexuality, feminist activism, and urban redevelopment through an analysis of the poetry of Leslie Scalapino and Adrienne Rich. Scalapino's and Rich's poems each describe sexualized experiences of public space in dialogue with the physical transformation of their cities. I use their embodied accounts of sexual responses to urban space to situate a reading of feminist anti-pornography activism within a material attention to cities and their redevelopment. In short, I use the poems' focus on the city and its sexualized and rapidly transforming set of spaces to argue that urban sexual history is planning history, and that a reading of either one requires a reading of the two together. **Keywords:** anti-pornography feminism, urban space, gentrification, public sexuality, Leslie Scalapino, Adrienne Rich

"coming sequence," the final long poem in Leslie Scalapino's 1982 poetry collection, *Considering How Exaggerated Music Is*, documents people moving around an urban public space. As they move, the speaker speculates about their past and future sexual experiences and desires. The "coming" of the poem's title references both the expected sequence of people and buildings, and the poem's sequence of sexual activity and orgasms. Scalapino presents sexual responses to public space as both a necessary aspect of urban life and as inherently oppositional to the equitable use of the city. Her speaker notes, "People sat waiting at the bus stop in the sun and there was no traffic going by at the time so that I had the sense that they should be satisfied sexually by others and not by me or the others there." And later, "They shouldn't move or should walk around some though their sexual life should occur with someone from outside" (Scalapino 1982, 135). The poem raises the problem that urban space is populated by people who

WSQ: Women's Studies Quarterly 47: 3 & 4 (Fall/Winter 2019) © 2019 by Davy Knittle. All rights reserved.

could be sexual partners, and so the movement of bodies through urban space is or can be sexualized. Scalapino references sexual practices broadly and describes in detail neither those practices nor the gender, sexual preferences, or bodies of the people engaged in them. Rather, central to the poem are private, often speculative, and often problematic sexualized experiences of public space. "coming sequence" asks how sexual responses to cities affect the way people come together, in dialogue with how the built environment alternately coheres and comes apart.

Considering How Exaggerated Music Is was published as early redevelopment efforts began to selectively gentrify large American cities, and in the midst of debates around pornography that severed urban feminist communities including those in Scalapino's Bay Area and in New York, as recorded in the poetry of activist Adrienne Rich. In the late 1970s and early 1980s, New York and San Francisco, along with other major U.S. cities, had begun a selective financial recovery from the deindustrialization and disinvestment produced by the clearance logics of urban renewal and the mass suburbanization and highway development of the 1950s and 1960s. Even so, many cities and many neighborhoods remained largely in decline.[1] Furthermore, the selective recovery of the 1970s and 1980s presaged what geographer Neil Smith describes as the "class conquest of the city" (1996, 27). At stake in urban economic recovery was the valuation of the prospective capital accumulation of developers and the potential for cities' own uneven economic gain at the expense of the needs and rights of intersecting and overlapping groups including residents of color, queer residents, low-income residents, and others variously forced from and refused access to redeveloped urban areas.

Debates about pornography in these early moments of redevelopment often framed it as an urban problem, symptomatic of the widespread poverty and infrastructural decline of urban disinvestment. Anti-pornography activists' efforts to eradicate pornography from cities often rhymed or explicitly collaborated with governmental and private efforts to displace evidence of poverty, homelessness, sex work, and other contexts and practices positioned as damaging to the financial viability of redevelopment from the highly visible commercial districts where pornography was concentrated, including Times Square in New York and the North Beach neighborhood of San Francisco. Where anti-pornography activists and urbanists differed was in their relationship to sex and sexuality and its role in public life. Real-estate developers, urban planners, and advocates for the cultivation of tourism appealing to white, heteronormative families often argued for the eradication of public sexuality altogether. Commenting on the policing of public sexuality and its fracture of the gay male community who used pornographic theaters for casual sex, Samuel R. Delany argues of Times Square, "The Forty-second Street Development Project wants families to spend their money here. So the visible signs of sex have got to go" (1999, 95). The displacement and transformation that anti-pornography feminist activism helped facilitate contributed to the concentration of poverty in other areas of the city. By the late 1990s, while pornographic theaters had been closed in Times Square and the poverty level in the area had decreased from its 1980 levels—in some census tracts by more than 50 percent—the percentage of people living in poverty across Manhattan had improved by just 2 percent since 1980, and poverty levels in the Bronx and Brooklyn had both increased.[2]

While urban developers and city officials sought to displace public sexuality, debates over the representation of sexuality also severed ties within feminist organizing communities. Some anti-pornography feminists argued that all sexual desire and its expression were marked by the internalization of a sexual culture that equated heterosexual contact with violence against women. Others stressed the importance of feminist engagements with public sexuality and the separation of sex and violence.[3] In accordance with this latter view, Scalapino emphasizes the inherent entanglement of sexuality and urban space. In the presence of advocacy that equates public sexuality with violence and decline, her poems argue that sexuality is impossible to cleave from the city, and must therefore be a part of a feminist urban intervention.

Sexual responses to urban space are also central to Adrienne Rich's sequence "21 Love Poems," in her 1978 collection *The Dream of a Common Language*. "21 Love Poems" addresses alternately a lesbian couple and a single speaker moving through and against the backdrop of disinvested 1970s Manhattan. While Scalapino portrays sexuality as complexly and often undesirably inherent in urban spaces, Rich describes the streets of Manhattan as a site for the productive performance of a lesbian feminist public sexuality. When *The Dream of a Common Language* was published, Rich was involved as an early supporter of the organization Women Against Pornography (WAP), which staged a landmark protest in Times Square on October 20, 1979, that gathered five thousand protesters to advocate for the eradication of pornography from the area (Potter 2010, 67).[4] Where others have focused on WAP's effect on Times Square, or on its appeal to the city's civic life, I instead read anti-pornography organizing in New York and San Francisco together with the history of the social, political, and built environmental transformation of both cities, and with Rich's and Scalapino's descriptions of their gendered and sexualized experience of their cities as they changed. In so doing, I seek to further a conversation about the embeddedness of public sexuality and urban transformation.

A feminist reading of urban change needs to engage accounts of spatial and social marginalization that reflect how the presence and degree of the negative effects of redevelopment are racialized and classed. To do so, it must engage with material experiences of the city and with its history as a social and physical environment built and rebuilt in accordance with a changing set of expectations about the economic and relational models that constitute the normate urban resident and kinship networks. Understanding how public narratives of normative relational and kinship models change—how we make friends, build and describe our families, interact with our neighbors, use public space, and have sex—is necessary to understanding the kinds of spaces and policies those normative models might create to accommodate some kinship relations, or to protect them from other relations socially identified as deviant. It is necessary, too, to understand how the physical spaces available to us in cities and in suburbs themselves help constitute what is made to be socially normative and what is made to be deviant.

I argue that Scalapino's and Rich's poems concretize the presence of sexuality in all interactions between people in urban space and between individuals and the city itself. I locate sexuality as a key subject of analysis for studies of urban change across disciplines and methods by illustrating that sexual experiences of space are constitutive of cities and are the subject of control or policing during redevelopment. I read the poems as examples of feminist approaches to public sexuality in a moment where debates about pornography by both feminist activists and urban developers and city officials threatened to sideline accounts of feminist sexual perception and experience, or to note them as synonymous with urban decay. Additionally, these literary accounts of public sexuality provide a record of feminist relationships to redevelopment. Where anti-pornography feminists tend to frame the built environment as symbolic and static, Scalapino's and Rich's accounts of the city view it as material and dynamic. Scalapino and Rich each use a sexual materialist reading practice to document the physical and emotional experiences of women in these dynamic urban spaces. I argue that their accounts of their cities foreground the intimate relationship between public sexuality, feminist activism, and redevelopment, and demonstrate how feminist relationships to urban change are most visible when their embodied, material, social, and cultural histories are read together.

Both Scalapino and Rich were involved in feminist aesthetic and political communities split between the Bay Area and New York. And both poets identified their poetic work as the origin of their political commitments. Scalapino, whose poetry and essays included work in what she referred to as the "erotica genre," was active in the Bay Area experimental poetry community, and affiliated with the L=A=N=G=U=A=G=E poetry movement, many of whose members were based in New York. Scalapino's poetics aligned with the movement's wager that refusing normative syntax allowed for refusals of power communicated through received structures of meaning. However, Scalapino resisted being labeled a L=A=N=G=U=A=G=E poet. She argued that the term implied an experience of male homosociality and power unavailable to her. In a 1979 letter to Charles Bernstein and Bruce Andrews, the editors of *L=A=N=G=U=A=G=E* magazine, she wrote, "Women who vary or 'do their own work'—given some difference between the social milieu of men and women—will automatically be outside the category of language poetry as defined by the standards of those men" (Scalapino 1979). Writing in the "erotica genre" supported a feminist experimental practice focused on accurate descriptions of the simultaneity of external events and private human thought, a preoccupation she maintained throughout her career. Although she considered herself an erotic writer, the language Scalapino uses to describe sexual thoughts and experiences is often anti-erotic. In a 1996 interview with Elisabeth A. Frost, Scalapino said of writing erotic literature, "I wanted to take erotica as the thing that it is—a form or genre that consists of particular actions—because it can't be anything else and isn't a symbol of anything" (5). As I explore Scalapino's clinical descriptions of embodied experiences of sexuality, I use the term "sexual" rather than "erotic." Scalapino describes sexual attention and activity to articulate the role of private thought in her ethnographic cataloging of events in space and between bodies. Her clinical language also allows her to describe her speaker's frequent disidentification with experiences of public sexuality.

While her activist practice focused on debates within communities organized around feminist activism more than poetic production, Rich's feminist consciousness also developed in dialogue with her poetry. In the essay "Blood, Bread, and Poetry: The Location of the Poet," Rich reflects:

> Even before I called myself a feminist or a lesbian, I felt driven—for my own sanity—to bring together in my poems the political world "out there"—the world of children dynamited or napalmed, of the urban ghetto and militarist violence, and the supposedly private, lyrical world of sex and of male/female relationships. (1986, 181)

Rich, like Scalapino, sees the poem as the genesis of her feminist orientation. And she argues that staging the meeting in her poems of "the urban ghetto" and "the supposedly private, lyrical world of sex" was integral to her feminist poetics, and to her political development.

The question of how to represent feminist accounts of sexuality was the hinge point in debates about pornography in the late 1970s and early 1980s in which Rich participated. While WAP argued in the late 1970s that consensual sex and sexual violence should be clearly differentiated, their subsequent advocacy was unclear on this distinction, such that in the mid-1980s the Feminist Anti-Censorship Taskforce (FACT) differentiated itself from WAP by advocating for consensual sex and sexual expression as integral to feminist advocacy. Rich followed the support for sexual expression, shifting her allegiance from WAP to FACT. She signed a 1985 amicus curiae brief authored by FACT, which supported the decision of an Indianapolis judge to overturn a proposed piece of anti-pornography legislation. The brief expressed that what legal scholars Paul Brest and Ann Vandenberg term "sexual speech" was important to advocacy for women's rights. The brief argues: "Even pornography which is problematic for women can be experienced as affirming of women's desires and of women's equality.... The range of feminist imagination and expression in the realm of sexuality has barely begun to find voice" (quoted in Brest and Vandenberg 1987, 655). In a 1985 statement in the feminist journal *off our backs* entitled "We Don't Have to Come Apart Over Pornography," in which she explained her decision to sign the brief, Rich's objections to the legislation were grounded in concerns about sexual speech and particularly lesbian sexual speech, and in a consideration of whether pornography was at the root of urban problems that shaped women's lives. Rich wrote, "I have little reason to believe that legislation banning pornography from our cities ... would have the effect its proponents wish for: to give women recourse against suffering, to abolish the presumed central cause of that suffering"

(1985, 32). This "presumed central cause" is, of course, pornography, but also the disinvestment of which pornography was emblematic to anti-pornography protesters.

Rich's separation from WAP was reflective of her conviction that banning pornography would not address the range of urban problems that caused women to suffer. Her split from WAP also reflected her commitment to lesbian feminist politics and to racially inclusive organizing. She left WAP in September 1979, citing organizer Susan Brownmiller's homophobia (Bronstein 2011, 233). Her subsequent work stressed her interest in coalitional feminist politics. In her 1981 keynote address with Audre Lorde at the annual conference of the National Women's Studies Association (NWSA), Rich argued, "So long as we can identify only with white women, we are still connected to that system of objectification and callousness and cruelty called racism" (5). Her support of FACT in 1985 was fueled by a belief that feminist organizing championing the rights of white, heterosexual women did so at the expense of the rights of all other women.

Feminist anti-pornography organizing in the late 1970s and early 1980s read pornography as a synecdoche for urban decay, although WAP's primary intervention was focused not on urban improvement but on cycles of violence that they believed tethered the disinvestment of public space to women's domestic endangerment. As organizer Dolores Alexander explained in July 1979, "One thing we're trying to do is to make the public aware that violence in pornography leads to violence in the street, in the bedroom, and in the office" (Dullea 1979). The group began their formal work in Times Square, which they dubbed the "pornography capital of America" focused on violence against women, but what made their work possible was their relevance to a campaign for Times Square's economic development (Potter 2010, 67). The mayor's Midtown Enforcement Project, which deployed an inspection team consisting of a health inspector, a police officer, a fire lieutenant, and a building inspector to many businesses in the Times Square Area, donated WAP's New York office, and financial contributors included the League of Theater Owners and the Forty-Second Street Development Project, who believed that WAP's efforts could improve tourism, and also "associated the sex trades with urban decline" (Potter 2010, 71, 72; Kaiser 1979).

On October 14, six days before WAP's October 20 anti-pornography march, WAP organized a Broadway benefit performance in partnership with actress Jessica James. In a fundraising announcement signed by James, Brownmiller, Alexander, and fellow WAP organizer Barbara Mehrhoff, James explained in fiscal terms the need to "get rid of the pornography blight in the Times Square area." She wrote, "As a theatre person, you understand better than most that . . . a cleaned-up Times Square would be a big inducement to theatre-goers who in recent years have been reluctant to set foot in the Broadway area" (Records of Women Against Pornography 1979a). While WAP advocated for equality for women, they were supported by and contributed to revitalization efforts that exacerbated unequal development in Times Square, which by 1999 was as symbolic of gentrification in the interest of "family-friendly" tourism as it was of pornography in the late 1970s.

Beyond Times Square, in the years before the WAP protests, New York was faced with widespread economic and social crisis. In December 1975, President Gerald Ford signed a $2.3 billion loan-authorization bill to the city in order to prevent its filing for bankruptcy (Tolchin 1975). In 1977 the burning or abandonment of nearly two in five houses in the South Bronx prompted the unannounced visit of President Jimmy Carter (Dembart 1977). As has been well-documented, landlords across the city abandoned or burned for insurance money properties that were no longer profitable to rent (Starecheski 2016, 16). In the wake of the fires, Carter and his administration stressed the imperative to revitalize the area (Dembart 1977).[5] One of the Carter administration's strategies for revitalization was the federal program of "planned shrinkage," which under Director of the Department of Housing and Urban Development Roger Starr diminished city services in low-income neighborhoods. The program justified the uneven distribution of public resources by arguing that the concentration of resources in affluent neighborhoods with strong tax bases would best support the viability of redevelopment (Gotham and Greenberg 2014, 47). In tandem with "planned shrinkage," city, state, and federal governments offered a brief window of support for community-control efforts in the late 1970s in a desperate attempt at revitalizing neighborhoods even as those same government entities facilitated the removal of their public resources.[6]

Anti-pornography feminists' portrayals of disinvestment tended toward symbolic readings of the city most available to white women that brushed past issues that disproportionately disadvantaged urban residents of color, including housing, transportation access, and access to jobs.

The stigmatization of public sexuality in Times Square also problemati-cally overlooked the importance of sex work as a mode of employment whose criminalization unevenly affected cisgender and trans women of color, whose rights and needs WAP largely ignored (Bronstein 2011, 213). Additionally, when anti-pornography activists' desires to eradicate pornography from urban centers like Times Square were adopted by rede-velopment efforts, the activists' support of nonviolent sexuality was often lost. Scalapino's and Rich's poems describe sexual experiences of the city, positive and negative, and provide a context in which to read sexuality as constitutive of urban placemaking beyond anti-pornography organizing.

In Rich's sequence "21 Love Poems," the first sentence of the first poem, split over its opening six lines, establishes the action of the poem in an urban environment in which pornography suggests the presence of urban decline. The poem opens:

> Whenever in this city, screens flicker
> with pornographers, with science-fiction vampires,
> victimized hirelings bending to the lash,
> we also have to walk . . . if simply as we walk
> through the rainsoaked garbage, the tabloid cruelties
> of our own neighborhoods.
> (1978, 25)

The poem's first sentence draws a comparison between pornography and disinvestment as impediments the speakers must walk through. And yet the screens show "pornographers," not pornography. Available on the screens is a power relationship between vampirism, or violent consump-tion, and victimization. The speakers' walking is in dialogue with the pornography and also with its setting, "the tabloid cruelties / of our own neighborhoods." "Tabloid cruelties" suggests that the degree of disinvest-ment visible on the streets mirrors the sensationalized account of urban decay that a tabloid newspaper might present. Through a comparison of the "tabloid cruelties" of the streets and the "victimized hirelings" who are the subjects of pornographers, Rich establishes a relationship between the cruelty to urban residents caused by disinvestment and the cruelty to women leveraged by pornography. In the first sentence's final phrase, the speakers take ownership of this disinvested landscape. The "rainsoaked garbage" describes "our own neighborhoods." As the speaker argues, decline and pornography occur not at a distance from women, but where they live, and shape their public and intimate lives.

The final four lines of the poem conversely sexualize the speakers' experience of the city. They read:

> No one has imagined us. We want to live like trees,
> sycamores blazing through the sulfuric air,
> dappled with scars, still exuberantly budding,
> our animal passion rooted in the city.
> (1978, 25)

To live "like trees . . . blazing through the sulfuric air" is to live at odds with the city. The sexualized "exuberant budding" of the speakers is in contrast to the "victimized hirelings" who open the poem. A register of sexuality never appears in relation to pornography in the poem, but rather in these final lines, as Rich describes "our animal passion" as "rooted in the city." The rootedness of the passion establishes the entanglement of the lesbian sexual life of the speakers and the urban systems in which they take part. As the "animal passion" of the speakers is shared, the contrast it draws to the "victimized hirelings" is not on the grounds of physicality, but of power and consent. In the poem, pornographic violence and sexual perception are at odds. The former flickers on the surface of the city, while the latter is deeply set in the built environment. Rich establishes urban life as a relationship between the endurance of violent images and cathexis to hopeful ones, and between the systems shaping and blurring the domestic and public spheres. Rich centers her own lesbian relationship in order to explore the public life of pornography as opposed to the sustaining and generative forms of sexuality in her partnership. This lesbian feminist reading of public sexuality illustrates her pro-sex and queer-inclusive position that lead to her split with WAP in 1979. Rich argues in the poem that both violent and nonviolent sexuality are complexly embedded in urban spaces and in how urban residents constitute and are constituted by them.

While Rich focused on the disinvested urban landscapes of New York, Scalapino wrote in and about changes to the Bay Area. In the late 1970s, Scalapino was composing the sexually descriptive poems in *Considering How Exaggerated Music Is* and living in Berkeley. Elsewhere in the Bay Area, the first feminist American anti-pornography organizing was cohering around the group Women Against Violence in Pornography and Media

(WAVPM) (Bronstein 2011, 129). The anti-pornography movement gathered steam in San Francisco, and fueled the New York–based movement several years later.[7] WAVPM's first protest in 1976 targeted the North Beach neighborhood of San Francisco. WAVPM protested what urban historian Alison Isenberg refers to as "nudie theaters" and "pornographic magazines" as symbols of "supposed urban-rooted moral decay" (2017, 106). The anti-pornography movement was one of a number of activist projects vying to influence the city's redevelopment. It was also one of several projects linking San Francisco to New York. While anti-pornography activists marched through North Beach, Isenberg notes that anti-high-rise activists continued a decades-long protest against what they termed the "Manhattanization" of San Francisco (2017, 346). These two projects presented opposing visions of the city's future. Where anti-pornography activists focused on the city's social future, the anti-high-rise activists aimed at the city's infrastructure, and protested the sale of public land for private development, as well as the construction of skyscrapers. The anti-pornography activists aimed their critiques at urban blight, while the anti-high-rise activists aimed theirs at stratifying forms of redevelopment, including urban renewal and the community-focused redevelopment efforts that followed.

WAVPM's focus on North Beach also cast public articulations of sexuality—violent and nonviolent—as synonymous with urban decline. In contrast, Scalapino's poems in "coming sequence" depict sexual information as part of all urban spaces, rather than indicative of blighted or decayed ones. For instance, later in "coming sequence," Scalapino describes affluent neighborhoods in which construction is taking place. In her descriptions, redevelopment evidences often incongruous or problematic sexual relationships to urban space, rather than eliminating them:

> I saw some men doing construction work in the street and the feeling I had was that they shouldn't do the work then or walk around. There should be a lack of skill or at any rate no movement occurring so that the surroundings were not pleasant and the area they were in then was affluent, was well-off. Someone who ordinarily was skilled at the time has a lessening or crippling of his ability so that he comes sexually, and people just walking around have this sensation only not strong. (1982, 136)

As in the earlier section, the speaker feels that an action occurring within urban space should not be happening. Scalapino narrates an experience of public sexuality and a received expectation of redevelopment. Areas that "were not pleasant" cohere into an area that "then was affluent" through the presence of construction workers and the creation of new buildings. Does the speaker feel that the men doing construction should not be there because she is wary of redevelopment, or because their movement is sexual? Or both? Should they not move because their movement facilitates redevelopment? Or because it risks orgasm? Construction and sexuality are impossible to disentangle. Scalapino establishes a binary between "skill" and its diminishment or disabling by orgasm. She problematically uses the language of disability as a metaphor for the effects of orgasm, which produces "a lessening or crippling" of ability. Scalapino is suspicious of the men's public sexuality because it is bound up in the production of redevelopment for which as construction workers they are the metonym, rather than the audience. In the lines "[t]here should be a lack of skill so that . . . the surroundings were not pleasant," the "pleasure" of orgasm is synonymous with the pleasantness produced as the neighborhood becomes affluent. Both the construction and the workers' performed sexuality are the catalysts for these changes. Both are unwanted. In "coming sequence," public experiences of sexuality are often undesirable or threatening to the poem's speaker, and are yet constitutive of urban space.

Scalapino's interest in describing sexual responses to urban space is part of her larger project of representing the embodied experience of woman-identified speakers. For Scalapino, writing crystallizes the social and political life of language by detailing embodied experiences. Feminist experimental writing must resist not only received ideas of perception but also received ideas about feminism. Scalapino argues of the politics of feminist experimental poetry:

> Some complexity got into this also stemming from the sixties and from the women's movement arising from the earlier radical movement, that is that many of the men claimed to be champions of feminism, so . . . they begin telling you what feminism should be. (1998, n.p.)

Scalapino sets changes in the American experimental poetry community directly in dialogue with the results of the women's movement. The connective thread for Scalapino is a gender politics of perception. She argues that the political ideas that man-identified poets made room for women to express were bound up in the aesthetic and perceptual experiences that those man-identified poets supported. Consequently, a feminist experimental poetics requires an articulation of sexual perception as part of embodied experience.

Rich's poetics also strive for a feminist politics of perception, even as they hew toward lyric convention where Scalapino's employ experimental fracture. For Rich, as for Scalapino, troubling the line between public and private is a process of refuting divisions she views as anti-feminist, and is a common project of feminist poetry and women's liberation. The promise of the women's movement for Rich was one of synthesizing the public and the private by identifying the entanglements of the sexual and the political. As Rich writes in 1984, "By the end of the 1960s. . . . Breaking the mental barrier that separated private from public life felt in itself like an enormous surge toward liberation" (1986, 182). Sexuality, for both Rich and Scalapino, offers a means of productively blurring received separations of public and private language and life. These separations were enforced both by urban redevelopment efforts that advocated for the eradication of public sexuality, and by academic receptions of poetry, and particularly poetry by women, that consigned it to a focus on subjectivity and interiority. The representation of sexuality in their poetry is therefore crucial to a feminist depiction of urban space and how it changes.

My argument that Scalapino's and Rich's poetry offers accounts of sexualized, feminist responses to the changing urban environments of the 1970s and 1980s rests on a fundamental premise about poetry: that it offers embodied accounts of lived experience, and that it can do social, material, and political work. This argument pushes back on a tendency in literary study to variously discredit the social productivity of both lyric and experimental poetry. In her discussion of Rich's focus on human rights in her poems, Miriam Marty Clark frames this tendency in a 2009 article as "widespread scepticism about poetry's ethical and political force" (46). Clark cites a January 2005 issue of *PMLA* devoted to poetry in which Bruce Smith argues that "the conceptual categories favored in contemporary theory—material conditions, race, gender, class, ethnicity—seem to have a more oblique relation to verse than they do to novels, films, and plays" (46). Smith goes on to say that "the latter genres, in the eyes of many critics, bear a stronger mimetic relation with social reality" (2005, 10). This is because "contemporary poetry, even in its most abstract forms . . . is identified by most readers with the individual consciousness of the poet" (Smith 2005, 10). Smith sets up a false duality between "social reality" and "individual consciousness." He assumes the former is material and political in a way the latter cannot be. Scalapino's and Rich's poems situate their speaker or speakers in urban contexts in which the competing tensions of feminism and redevelopment are evident. A reading of their work as concerned only with "individual consciousness" ignores the detailed material and political information with which they argue for the inextricability of the individual and the social.

Critical work on both Rich and Scalapino has conversely highlighted the political importance of poetry as a scene of intervention for these two poets and for feminist activism in general. Kathryn T. Flannery argues of the women's movement that "if polemic was the founding genre, poetry was the form that invited the greater quantity and range of participation" and that "women perceived poetry as affording ideological and formal room to maneuver" (2005, 19, 20). Rich in particular was essential to poetry's development as a primary channel of feminist engagement with language. As experimental poet-critic Rachel Blau DuPlessis argues, Rich's engagement with a "female poetics" is "a signal of frustration with convention as a sign of ideological dissent, a desire to rewrite culture by the critical examination of the 'natural,'" a means afforded to Rich by writing poetry (1985, 139). Poetry offers the opportunity to experiment with and rework its form, which suggests the ability to experiment with the form of the social, and draws attention to the fact that the social, like the poem, is made of language. Similarly, Amy Moorman Robbins identifies Scalapino's writing, together with that of other experimental women writers, as "itself a mode of feminist theorizing," homologous with the "ideological dissent" of Rich's poems (2015, 146). She cites Scalapino's commitment to formal experiment as a site of feminist refusal. The form of the poem for both poets is in their own words and in their critical reception a site of structural and coalitional feminist critique.

A sexual materialist reading of Rich's and Scalapino's poems reveals that they question what feminist accounts of public sexuality might look like in dialogue with the redevelopment of New York and San Francisco in the late 1970s and early 1980s. Anti-pornography feminism loses sight both of what feminist sexuality and urban space might usefully be in the absence of violence, and of the range of gendered experiences that are part of the city. What its advocacy does make clear is that the social and political work of sexuality and urban space are mutually informing and must be read together. Following the poems' logic, we cannot address public sexuality without a willingness to consider the spaces where it occurs.

Furthermore, a detailed documentation of marginal experiences of public sexuality across sexual and gendered identifications is necessary for what Cathy J. Cohen describes as "progressive transformative coalitional work" (1997, 438). Cohen asks, "How do we use the relative degrees of ostracization all sexual/cultural 'deviants' experience to build a basis of unity for broader coalition and movement work?" (453). It is on the grounds of deviance that urban residents are denied access to their cities because their use or refusal of the street, the bedroom, and the office does not conform to a vision of the city's future that puts the white, heterosexual family at its center, as in the case of the redevelopment of Times Square. And just as people seek to locate their experience of personal and infrastructural disinvestment in a shared experience of nonnormativity, scholarship and activism focused on urban disenfranchisement can draw strength from organizing around nonnormative public sexualities as they are intimately and deeply embedded with forms of economic and political disinvestment that both catalyze and follow the contours of the public and private underresourcing of urban neighborhoods and its erosion of those neighborhoods' built, sexual, and social environments.

Acknowledgments

I would like to thank Heather Smedberg and Nina Mamikunian at the Archive for New Poetry at the University of California San Diego, and Zoe Hill at the Schlesinger Library at the Radcliffe Institute for their assistance with archival research for this article. In addition, I want to thank E. Tracy Grinnell and Tom White for permission to publish materials from Leslie Scalapino's archive. I would like to extend special thanks to Francesca Russello Ammon, Charles Bernstein, Heather K. Love, Melissa E. Sanchez, and Brooke Jamieson Stanley for their feedback on earlier versions of this piece, to Ujju Aggarwal for her detailed editing of the article's final drafts, and to two anonymous reviewers for their feedback and generative suggestions.

Davy Knittle (he/they) is a PhD candidate in English at the University of Pennsylvania. His poems and critical writing have appeared in *Jacket2*, *Rain Taxi*, *Fence*, and the *Recluse*. He curates the City Planning Poetics series at the Kelly Writers House, and can be reached at dknittle@sas.upenn.edu.

Notes

1. As urban historian Samuel Zipp (2010) notes, a federal program of urban redevelopment was inaugurated by Title I of the Housing Act of 1949 and officially termed "urban renewal" by the Housing Act of 1954. Most of its programs were completed by the mid-1960s. Renewal was "initially thought of as a way to offset the deleterious effects of decentralization, an attempt to keep investment, wealth, and the middle class downtown" by means of highway development and the clearance of the inner city. It was, in short, a program of "having to destroy the city to save it" (Zipp 2010, 364).

2. According to the 1980 Census, in the census tracts along Times Square's western edge from Forty-Second to Fiftieth Streets between 18 and 26 percent of residents lived in poverty, compared to between 13 and 15 percent of residents living in poverty in these census tracts in 2000. In the census tract bounded by Eighth and Sixth Avenues and Forty-Sixth and Fiftieth Streets, the percentage of people living at or below the poverty level decreased from 32.1 percent in 1980 to 9.1 percent in 2000 (U.S. Census Bureau 1980b; 2000b). Comparatively, the poverty rate in Brooklyn increased from 23.98 percent in 1980 to 25.07 percent in 2000. The poverty rate in the Bronx similarly increased from 27.62 percent in 1980 to 30.69 percent in 2000 (U.S. Census Bureau 1980a; 2000a).

3. Lisa Duggan was a founding member of the Feminist Anti-Censorship Taskforce (FACT), which opposed anti-pornography feminism and was inaugurated in 1984. In an opinion piece in the *Washington Post*, she argued, "It is sexism and violence, not sexual explicitness, which harm women" (Duggan 1985).

4. In addition to the contribution of her time and energy to WAP, Claire Bond Potter notes that Rich, together with journalist Susan Brownmiller and author Frances Wyatt, donated $3,000 to the organization's early work (2010, 71).

5. As historian Themis Chronopoulos notes, the Bronx lost 36 percent of its housing stock and 40 percent of its population during the 1970s (2017, 935).

6. For example, 1979, the year of the WAP protest in Times Square, was also the height of New York City's abandoned property crisis. In 1976 the city passed Local Law 45, which "allowed the city to foreclose on property for nonpayment of taxes after one year, instead of three" (quoted in Goldstein 2017, 178). By January 1979, the *New York Times* estimated that the city was landlord of 9,500 buildings, a number that had increased to 11,700 buildings with 166,000 units by April 1979 (Goldstein 2017, 178). The city introduced programs including Tenant Interim Lease, which for several years allowed tenants to buy their buildings from the city and manage them as owner-occupied cooperatives (see Goldstein 2017, 178–181, 195).

7. A June 1979 press release announcing the opening of WAP's office at 579 Ninth Avenue at Forty-Second Street, explains that the New York group "grew out of Women Against Violence in Pornography and Media (WAVPM) . . . a national feminist organization working to eliminate pornographic images of women being raped, tortured, mutilated, and victimized for male sexual stimulation," which was founded in San Francisco in 1976 (Records of Women Against Pornography 1979b).

Works Cited

Brest, Paul, and Ann Vandenberg. 1987. "Politics, Feminism, and the Constitution: The Anti-Pornography Movement in Minneapolis." *Stanford Law Review* 39, no. 3: 607–61.

Bronstein, Carolyn. 2011. *Battling Pornography: The American Feminist Anti-Pornography Movement, 1976–1986.* New York: Cambridge University Press.

Chronopoulos, Themis. 2017. "The Rebuilding of the South Bronx after the Fiscal Crisis." *Journal of Urban History* 43, no. 6: 932–59.

Clark, Miriam Marty. 2009. "Human Rights and the Work of Lyric in Adrienne Rich." *Cambridge Quarterly* 38, no. 1: 45–65.

Cohen, Cathy J. 1997. "Punks, Bulldaggers, and Welfare Queens: The Radical Potential of Queer Politics?" *GLQ* 3: 437–65.

Delany, Samuel R. 1999. *Times Square Red, Times Square Blue.* New York: NYU Press.

Dembart, Lee. 1977. "Carter Takes 'Sobering' Trip to South Bronx: Carter Finds Hope Amid Blight on 'Sobering' Trip to Bronx." *New York Times*, October 6, 1977. https://www.nytimes.com/1977/10/06/archives/carter-takes-sobering-trip-to-south-bronxcarter-finds-hope-amid.html.

Duggan, Lisa. 1985. "The Dubious Porn War Alliance: Feminists and the Right Agree for Once, But They're Both Wrong." *Washington Post,* September 1, 1985. https://www.washingtonpost.com/archive/opinions/1985/09/01/the-dubious-porn-war.

Dullea, Georgia. 1979. "In Feminists' Antipornography Drive, 42d Street Is the Target." *New York Times*, July 6, 1979. https://www.nytimes.com/1979/07/06/archives/in-feminists-antipornography-drive-42d-street-is-the-target.html.

DuPlessis, Rachel Blau. 1985. *Writing Beyond the Ending: Narrative Strategies of Twentieth Century Women Writers.* Bloomington: Indiana University Press.

Flannery, Kathryn T. 2005. *Feminist Literacies, 1968–75.* Champaign: University of Illinois Press.

Frost, Elisabeth A., and Leslie Scalapino. 1996. "An Interview with Leslie Scalapino." *Contemporary Literature* 37, no. 1: 1–23.

Goldstein, Brian. 2017. *The Roots of Urban Renaissance: Gentrification and the Struggle Over Harlem.* Cambridge, MA: Harvard University Press.

Gotham, Kevin Fox, and Miriam Greenberg. 2014. *Crisis Cities: Disaster and Redevelopment in New York and New Orleans.* New York: Oxford University Press.

Isenberg, Alison. 2017. *Designing San Francisco: Art, Land, and Urban Renewal in the City by the Bay.* Princeton, NJ: Princeton University Press.

Kaiser, Charles. 1979. "Cleanup Unit Looks Beyond Sex." *New York Times,* November 13, 1979. https://www.nytimes.com/1979/11/13/archives/cleanup-unit-looks-beyond-sex.html.

Potter, Claire Bond. 2010. "Taking Back Times Square: Feminist Repertoires and the Transformation of Urban Space in Late Second Wave Feminism." *Radical History Review* 113: 67–80.

Records of Women Against Pornography. 1979a. "WAP Theater Benefit Press Release." Box 1, identifier 37. Schlesinger Library. Radcliffe Institute, Harvard University.

———. 1979b. "Women Open Times Square Office to Kick Off Anti-Pornography Campaign." Box 1, identifier 13. Schlesinger Library. Radcliffe Institute, Harvard University.

Rich, Adrienne. 1978. *The Dream of a Common Language: Poems 1974–1977.* New York: W. W. Norton & Company.

———. 1981. "Disobedience Is What NWSA Is Potentially About." *WSQ* 9, no. 3: 4–6.

———. 1985. "We Don't Have to Come Apart Over Pornography: A Statement by Adrienne Rich." *off our backs* 15, no. 7: 30, 32.

———. 1986. *Blood, Bread, and Poetry: Selected Prose 1979–1985.* New York: W. W. Norton & Company.

Robbins, Amy Moorman. 2015. "Affective Identification, Critical Production: Leslie Scalapino's 'hmmmm.'" *Studies in the Humanities* 41, nos. 1–2: 143–64.

Scalapino, Leslie. 1979. "Leslie Scalapino to Charles Bernstein and Bruce Andrews." May 1, 1979. Box 56, folder 9. Charles Bernstein Papers, Archive for New Poetry. Mandeville Special Collections Library, University of California San Diego Libraries.

———. 1982. *Considering How Exaggerated Music Is.* Berkeley, CA: North Point Press.

———. 1998. "Interview with Linda Russo." Box 111, folder 7, Leslie Scalapino Papers, Archive for New Poetry. Mandeville Special Collections Library, University of California San Diego Libraries.

Smith, Bruce. 2005. "Some Pre(sup)positions." *PMLA* 120, no. 1: 9–15.

Smith, Neil. 1996. *New Urban Frontier: Gentrification and the Revanchist City.* New York: Routledge.

Starecheski, Amy. 2016. *Ours to Lose: When Squatters Became Homeowners in New York City.* Chicago: University of Chicago Press.

Tolchin, Martin. 1975. "Ford Signs Aid Bill; Bankruptcy Change for City Advances." *New York Times*, December 10, 1975. https://www.nytimes.com/1975/12/10/archives/ford-signs-aid-bill bankruptcy-change-for-city-advances-bankruptcy.html.

U.S. Census Bureau. 1980a. Population for Whom Poverty Status Is Determined, Kings County and Bronx County, 1980. Map prepared by Social Explorer. Accessed April 12, 2019.

———. 1980b. Population for Whom Poverty Status Is Determined, New York County, Census Tracts 119, 121, 125 and 127, 1980. Map prepared by Social Explorer. Accessed September 7, 2018.

———. 2000a. Ratio of Income in 1999 to Poverty Level for Population for Whom Poverty Status Is Determined .75 to .99, .50 to .74 and Under .50; Kings and Bronx County, 2000. Map prepared by Social Explorer. Accessed April 12, 2019.

———. 2000b. Ratio of Income in 1999 to Poverty Level for Population for Whom Poverty Status Is Determined, .75 to .99, .50 to .74 and Under .50, New York County, Census Tracts 119, 121, 125 and 127, 2000. Map prepared by Social Explorer. Accessed September 7, 2018.

Zipp, Samuel. 2010. *Manhattan Projects: The Rise and Fall of Urban Renewal in Cold War New York.* New York: Oxford University Press.

PART VI. **CLASSICS REVISITED**

Gender Violence and the Prison-Industrial Complex

Statement by Critical Resistance and INCITE!

We call social justice movements to develop strategies and analysis that address both state AND interpersonal violence, particularly violence against women. Currently, activists/movements that address state violence (such as anti-prison, anti–police brutality groups) often work in isolation from activists/movements that address domestic and sexual violence. The result is that women of color, who suffer disproportionately from both state and interpersonal violence, have become marginalized within these movements. It is critical that we develop responses to gender violence that do not depend on a sexist, racist, classist, and homophobic criminal justice system. It is also important that we develop strategies that challenge the criminal justice system and that also provide safety for survivors of sexual and domestic violence. To live violence-free lives, we must develop holistic strategies for addressing violence that speak to the intersection of all forms of oppression. The anti-violence movement has been critically important in breaking the silence around violence against women and providing much-needed services to survivors. However, the mainstream anti-violence movement has increasingly relied on the criminal justice system as the frontline approach toward ending violence against women of color. It is important to assess the impact of this strategy.

Critical Resistance and INCITE! Women of Color Against Violence. 2006. "Gender Violence and the Prison-Industrial Complex," in *Color of Violence: The INCITE! Anthology*, edited by INCITE! Women of Color Against Violence, 223–26. Copyright 2006, INCITE! Women of Color Against Violence. All rights reserved. Republished by permission of the copyright holder and the publisher, Duke University Press. www.dukepress.edu.

WSQ: Women's Studies Quarterly 47: 3 & 4 (Fall/Winter 2019) © 2019 by Critical Resistance and INCITE! All rights reserved.

1. Law enforcement approaches to violence against women MAY deter some acts of violence in the short term. However, as an overall strategy for ending violence, criminalization has not worked. In fact, the overall impact of mandatory arrest laws for domestic violence have led to decreases in the number of battered women who kill their partners in self-defense, but they have not led to a decrease in the number of batterers who kill their partners. Thus, the law protects batterers more than it protects survivors.

2. The criminalization approach has also brought many women into conflict with the law, particularly women of color, poor women, lesbians, sex workers, immigrant women, women with disabilities, and other marginalized women. For instance, under mandatory arrest laws, there have been numerous incidents where police officers called to domestic incidents have arrested the woman who is being battered. Many undocumented women have reported cases of sexual and domestic violence, only to find themselves deported. A tough law-and-order agenda also leads to long punitive sentences for women convicted of killing their batterers. Finally, when public funding is channeled into policing and prisons, budget cuts for social programs, including women's shelters, welfare, and public housing, are the inevitable side effect. These cutbacks leave women less able to escape violent relationships.

3. Prisons don't work. Despite an exponential increase in the number of men in prisons, women are not any safer, and the rates of sexual assault and domestic violence have not decreased. In calling for greater police responses to and harsher sentences for perpetrators of gender violence, the anti-violence movement has fueled the proliferation of prisons which now lock up more people per capita in the U.S. than any other country. During the past fifteen years, the number of women, especially women of color, in prison has skyrocketed. Prisons also inflict violence on the growing numbers of women behind bars. Slashing, suicide, the proliferation of HIV, strip searches, medical neglect, and rape of prisoners have largely been ignored by anti-violence activists. The criminal justice system, an institution of violence, domination, and control, has increased the level of violence in society.

4. The reliance on state funding to support anti-violence programs has increased the professionalization of the anti-violence movement and alienated it from its community-organizing, social justice roots. Such reliance has isolated the anti-violence movement from other social

justice movements that seek to eradicate state violence, such that it acts in conflict rather than in collaboration with these movements.

5. The reliance on the criminal justice system has taken power away from women's ability to organize collectively to stop violence and has invested this power within the state. The result is that women who seek redress in the criminal justice system feel disempowered and alienated. It has also promoted an individualistic approach toward ending violence such that the only way people think they can intervene in stopping violence is to call the police. This reliance has shifted our focus from developing ways communities can collectively respond to violence.

In recent years, the mainstream anti-prison movement has called important attention to the negative impact of criminalization and the buildup of the prison industrial complex. Because activists who seek to reverse the tide of mass incarceration and criminalization of poor communities and communities of color have not always centered gender and sexuality in their analysis or organizing, we have not always responded adequately to the needs of survivors of domestic and sexual violence.

1. Prison and police accountability activists have generally organized around and conceptualized men of color as the primary victims of state violence. Women prisoners and victims of police brutality have been made invisible by a focus on the war on our brothers and sons. It has failed to consider how women are affected as severely by state violence as men. The plight of women who are raped by INS officers or prison guards, for instance, has not received sufficient attention. In addition, women carry the burden of caring for extended family when family and community members are criminalized and warehoused. Several organizations have been established to advocate for women prisoners; however, these groups have been frequently marginalized within the mainstream anti-prison movement.

2. The anti-prison movement has not addressed strategies for addressing the rampant forms of violence women face in their everyday lives, including street harassment, sexual harassment at work, rape, and intimate partner abuse. Until these strategies are developed, many women will feel shortchanged by the movement. In addition, by not seeking alliances with the anti-violence movement, the anti-prison movement

has sent the message that it is possible to liberate communities without seeking the well-being and safety of women.

3. The anti-prison movement has failed to sufficiently organize around the forms of state violence faced by Lesbian, Gay, Bisexual, Trans, Two-spirited, and Intersex (LGBTTI) communities. LGBTTI street youth and trans people in general are particularly vulnerable to police brutality and criminalization. LGBTTI prisoners are denied basic human rights such as family visits from same sex partners, and same sex consensual relationships in prison are policed and punished.

4. While prison abolitionists have correctly pointed out that rapists and serial murderers comprise a small number of the prison population, we have not answered the question of how these cases should be addressed. The inability to answer the question is interpreted by many anti-violence activists as a lack of concern for the safety of women.

5. The various alternatives to incarceration that have been developed by anti-prison activists have generally failed to provide sufficient mechanisms for safety and accountability for survivors of sexual and domestic violence. These alternatives often rely on a romanticized notion of communities, which have yet to demonstrate their commitment and ability to keep women and children safe or seriously address the sexism and homophobia that is deeply embedded within them.

We call on social justice movements concerned with ending violence in all its forms to:

1. Develop community-based responses to violence that do not rely on the criminal justice system AND which have mechanisms that ensure safety and accountability for survivors of sexual and domestic violence. Transformative practices emerging from local communities should be documented and disseminated to promote collective responses to violence.

2. Critically assess the impact of state funding on social justice organizations and develop alternative fundraising strategies to support these organizations. Develop collective fundraising and organizing strategies for anti-prison and anti-violence organizations. Develop strategies and analysis that specifically target state forms of sexual violence.

3. Make connections between interpersonal violence, the violence inflicted by domestic state institutions (such as prisons, detention

centers, mental hospitals, and child protective services), and international violence (such as war, military base prostitution, and nuclear testing).

4. Develop an analysis and strategies to end violence that do not isolate individual acts of violence (either committed by the state or individuals) from their larger contexts. These strategies must address how entire communities of all genders are affected in multiple ways by both state violence and interpersonal gender violence. Battered women prisoners represent an intersection of state and interpersonal violence and as such provide an opportunity for both movements to build coalitions and joint struggles.

5. Put poor/working-class women of color in the center of their analysis, organizing practices, and leadership development. Recognize the role of economic oppression, welfare "reform," and attacks on women workers' rights in increasing women's vulnerability to all forms of violence and locate anti-violence and anti-prison activism alongside efforts to transform the capitalist economic system.

6. Center stories of state violence committed against women of color in our organizing efforts.

7. Oppose legislative change that promotes prison expansion, criminalization of poor communities and communities of color and thus state violence against women of color, even if these changes also incorporate measures to support victims of interpersonal gender violence.

8. Promote holistic political education at the everyday level within our communities, specifically how sexual violence helps reproduce the colonial, racist, capitalist, heterosexist, and patriarchal society we live in as well as how state violence produces interpersonal violence within communities.

9. Develop strategies for mobilizing against sexism and homophobia WITHIN our communities in order to keep women safe.

10. Challenge men of color and all men in social justice movements to take particular responsibility to address and organize around gender violence in their communities as a primary strategy for addressing violence and colonialism. We challenge men to address how their own histories of victimization have hindered their ability to establish gender justice in their communities.

11. Link struggles for personal transformation and healing with struggles for social justice.

We seek to build movements that not only end violence, but that create a society based on radical freedom, mutual accountability, and passionate reciprocity. In this society, safety and security will not be premised on violence or the threat of violence; it will be based on a collective commitment to guaranteeing the survival and care of all peoples.

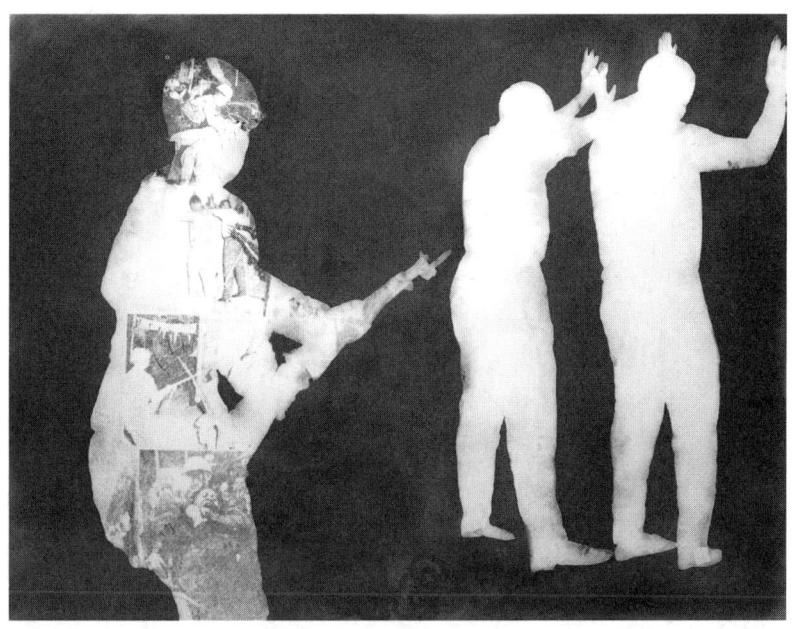

Mildred Beltré. *Newark 1967 (the men)*, 2015. Graphite, ink, and xerox transfer, 50 x 38 in. Image courtesy of the artist.

Mildred Beltré. *Newark 1967 (the women and children)*, 2015. Graphite, ink, and xerox transfer, 38 x 50 in. Image courtesy of the artist.

For Aprina, for Cierra, and for Me:
Questions and Commitment to Abolition

M Adams, Freedom Inc.

I remember where I was when I got the first call. "M, 'Prina is missin'. Her mom said she ain't heard from her. Dis ain't like 'Prina. Wat we gon' do?" At the time, I had no idea who Aprina was, but that didn't matter. This happened in October 2013 and I was twenty-eight years old. As a survivor, I had long learned that there is very little space between fear and privacy, so it didn't take long for the worry about Aprina to become my own.

I got a second phone call from the same voice at the end of the first one, a young Black stud/gender-nonconforming nineteen-year-old who I had been building with through my queer youth work at Freedom Inc. The voice cried out, "They found her. She's fuck'n dead M, they found her." And then, seconds later, "He chopped her body up and burned her! They roasted marshmallows over her M, fuck'n marshmallows," and the voice turned from a fire and rage, to a helpless plea. There were screams. There was silence. Then there was me breaking. It was more than I could take. The phone call ended for me before I hung up. I went static, offline. I didn't remember where I was for about a minute before I snapped back to my organizer *go, go, go* mode. I wiped my tears, called on my ancestors, and went to Freedom Inc. to rally the crew.

Freedom Inc. is a nonprofit and grassroots collective of Black, Hmong, and Khmer women and girls, and queer and trans folx, based in Madison, Wisconsin. Our mission is to end violence within and against low-income Black and Brown communities. We define violence comprehensively to include both systems of violence such as colonialism, patriarchy, and capitalism, and the range of interpersonal expressions such as sexual assault and intimate partner violence. In order for us to accomplish this work we are

WSQ: Women's Studies Quarterly 47: 3 & 4 (Fall/Winter 2019) © 2019 by M Adams. All rights reserved.

grounded by a set of frameworks: gender justice, queer justice, Black and Southeast Asian liberation, anti-colonialism—which are rooted in radical Black queer feminisms, Hmong and Khmer feminisms. We use these ideologies and frameworks as our compass to building movements that help to realize our mission and meet the immediate needs of our folx.

Our strategy to accomplish our mission is threefold: 1) to provide gender-, generation-, and culturally specific lifesaving services to survivors of gender-based violence, 2) to offer leadership development that focuses on and works with the same survivors to develop a sharp analysis of how their personal experiences are connected to broader issues of power and oppressions, and equips them with tools to create change around it, and 3) to develop grassroots campaigns led by survivors that uproot the root causes of violence. Some examples of our campaigns have been fighting to stop jail expansion, fighting for community control over land with the Take Back the Land Movement, fighting to stop deportations with the Southeast Asian Freedom Network, and fighting to end state violence against Black people with the Movement for Black Lives.

Given the work of Freedom Inc., we often straddle multiple issues and act as brokers to bring disjointed movements together, and in particular have really worked to help align the anti–violence against women movement with queer justice movements and prison abolition movements. We know intimately how we and our communities are failed when we don't. In our work, the praxis of building an abolition movement that centers solutions to gender-based violence as outlined in the Critical Resistance–INCITE! statement is critical (2006).

As we organize for justice, liberation, and wellness for survivors, we are continuously challenged by the penultimate questions of abolition: What do we do in real time when violence is happening that we can't stop? What to do with people who won't change and who are harming the most vulnerable among us?

Though we are faced with these questions, in many ways, we share an analysis with many survivors that the prison industrial complex—a term used to describe "the overlapping interests of government and industry that use surveillance, policing, and imprisonment as solutions to economic, social, and political problems" (Critical Resistance 2019)—doesn't actually provide constructive solutions for us. Many of the Black women we work with, trans and nontrans, have been arrested when they sought help from the police as victims of gender-based violence. Even those who have not been arrested have experienced the derivatives of the prison nation which has threatened their freedom and safety—such as child protective services and foster homes that hold their children hostage, the criminalization of mental health needs, and carceral and penal cultures that punish homeless and poor mothers.

Justice for Cierra Finkley, a campaign that Freedom Inc. spearheaded in 2015, embodies all of these dynamics. Cierra, at the time, was a twenty-four-year-old young Black woman and a mother to a five-year-old Black girl. On August 15, 2015, Cierra called the police several times as her partner attempted to harm her. The police did nothing to protect Cierra. When the partner returned another time to Cierra's home to harm her and her daughter, he kicked in the apartment door. In a fight to defend her life and her daughter's, Cierra used a knife. As a result, her partner died. As you can imagine, the same police force who would not protect her was swift and ever ready to arrest her for first-degree homicide.[1]

Freedom Inc., in partnership with others, organized a grassroots campaign led by Black queer and trans survivors of violence, to free Cierra and demand Community Control Over the Police (CCOP). Community Control Over the Police is a demand and campaign originally developed out of the Black Panther Party, based in an analysis within the Black Power Movement and organized by people like Assata Shakur, that the Black community functions as a domestic colony within the United States, and therefore the police act as an occupying force (see Adams and Rameau 2016). CCOP proposes that the fundamental reason for police violence is the colonial nature of the relationship, and therefore the solution to the violence is power. Freedom Inc. has built upon this analysis to assert that the fight to end police violence must not only focus on building alternatives in community but must also include wresting political control over policing from the hands of the state. Indeed, according to Adams and Rameau, CCOP is important because it lends people the power to "self-determine what is and how to do safety in our community" (2016, 519). We have understood this as a necessary step toward an ultimate vision of abolishing policing systems. In instances like that of Cierra Finkley, it is easy to be anti-police and anti-prisons, as we see them attack survivors and fail the needs of our communities. What we struggle with at Freedom Inc. is what to do in the infrequent instances when police and prisons "work."

Aprina Paul was murdered by a white man. He had placed an ad on

Craigslist to meet up with a woman for sex. Aprina answered the ad. The white man raped and killed her. He mutilated her body. He chopped up and burned her body in his backyard. He and his family, at some point, roasted marshmallows over Aprina's body. The father of the white man also has a documented history of racial violence.[2]

Aprina's story has stayed closely with me all of these years, and it is her story, and ones like it, that challenge me as an abolitionist in really core ways. As we fought for justice for 'Prina, frankly put, we could not figure out what justice meant. How can her mother be whole again? What is justice for those who loved her, and for the broader Black community? What does transformation mean for this society where Black women and girls are still not valued? Our current society is still formed in the crucible of white supremacy, capitalism, and patriarchy—therefore there is not institutional or interpersonal recourse for this kind of violence. I understood this, and I knew this, both cognitively and in my body; and so I knew the family's demand for prison for this white man was a decision I and Freedom Inc. had to support.

Aprina's family and loved ones wanted the white man to be locked up for what he had done. It is too shortsighted and simple to say the reason for this was simply punishment, though I am sure for many that it is a justifiable factor. Aprina's story begs the question of what to do about vertical violence. Here, vertical violence describes violence done by a group, or member of a group, who is in power, to a group, or member of a group, who is oppressed or disenfranchised. In this instance, we have a white man, who is supported by white supremacy, capitalism, and patriarchy, through law, culture, history, and various systems and institutions, who murdered a Black girl who is exploited and targeted by these same systems. Because of these realities, if a white man is not incarcerated for murdering and assaulting a Black girl, that is not a measure of abolition, it is rather a show of the power of white supremacy, capitalism, and patriarchy. I assert the true measure of abolition will not be the acquittal of white men, but rather the freeing and acquittals of Black women, girls, and trans and gender-nonconforming people from prisons, prosecution, and criminalization. An illustration of this is the use of stand-your-ground laws that protected George Zimmerman, a white Latinx man who committed an anti-Black murder against Trayvon Martin; while Marissa Alexander, a Black woman surviving violence, was incarcerated for protecting herself and her children, while harming no one, and was not allowed to use the stand-your-ground law.

Black women and girls (trans and nontrans) are often the currency of abolitionist politics. Oftentimes it is our lives that are up for bargain as demonstration for how radical or anti–white supremacist a position is. While the lives of Black women and girls hang in the balance, we have witnessed polarizing politics of abolition, and also, frankly, patriarchy disguised as abolitionist politics to determine whether or not Black women have the right to be free of harm.

In my own life, this has shown up as creating a culture of "forgiveness" for many men who have harmed women and children, without accountability or transformation. My father is an example of this. He was a very violent man. He has been incarcerated most of my life and perhaps this is the only thing that has saved me from his violence. My mother could not protect us; she could not protect herself. In current popular culture, we are watching similar dynamics happen with R. Kelly. Sympathy for him, protection of him—not the wellness of his victims—has been and continues to be centered.

Though perhaps I have been in contradiction to my abolitionist beliefs in some of my practices, I also affirm and maintain that I AM AN ABOLITIONIST. Despite the challenge in the questions posed here, and in my own experiences, I know that I must follow in the traditions of my ancestors who were visionary and radical enough to use speculative fiction—which encompasses works in which the setting is other than the real world, involving supernatural, futuristic, or other imagined elements—in their abolitionist dreams. I continue this tradition because what is at stake here is my life and the life of my children. I have a nineteen-year-old daughter and a nine-year-old son. As a person who spends a lot of time working to end gender-based violence, I teach them a lot about healthy relationships and body safety. I teach them about bodily autonomy and feminisms, everything ranging from having the right to say no, naming your body how you choose, healthy touching, appropriate boundaries, being able to be free from sexual assault, etc. Policing and prisons directly contradict these radical Black queer feminist values, however. I worry for my children's safety as I have taught them that they have the right to their bodies, and that no one has the right to harm them—no one. I worry for my Black children who are learning to be bold and unafraid and that they have the right to stand up against anyone who is going to cause them harm—and the police do just that. Policing and prisons are the antithesis of autonomy, self-determination, body positivity, gender justice—they are patriarchal systems.

The CR-INCITE! statement facilitates an important opportunity for us to understand the interrelatedness of the issues of gender-based violence and prisons. It is upon us to advance this opportunity, not only by aligning seemingly separate issues, but by reorienting how we understand the root of both of the issues. The root causes of prisons and policing are certainly white supremacy and capitalism, and it is also just as much patriarchy. If we sharpen our analysis and name prison as an institution of patriarchy, we can then better understand patriarchy as a system, and design a movement to defeat the entire spectrum of patriarchy. Imagine this: a movement not based around ending specific expressions of patriarchal violence (i.e., prisons or gender-based violence) but around ending patriarchy itself. As abolitionists, why not see ourselves as not only abolishing prisons, but abolishing patriarchy; as not only seeking to stop interpersonal harm, but abolishing patriarchy?

This analysis may provide more room to call multiple populations into the fight for abolition. To Black cis men, who are at an important juncture of being harmed by patriarchy and also using patriarchy to cause harm to others, to move into greater alignment with other Black genders and Black feminists, and deepen their commitment to ending gender-based violence. If they are, in fact, part of the same oppression, we can then conclude that prisons cannot be defeated as long as patriarchy is not abolished. To white feminists and those who believe in carceral feminisms, if we understand prisons as patriarchal, then those of us vulnerable to gender-based violence must immediately do away with carceral feminisms, despite whatever temporary relief they may provide. To the mainstream LGBTQ movement, patriarchy (along with white supremacy and capitalism) is the basis for the way gender is currently constructed along the gender binary. Patriarchy also orders sexual orientation as the relationship between genders, where cis men are dominant, women are subordinate, and heterosexuality is normal, and anything outside of this is deviant and punishable. Prisons and policing, and their institutions and related cultures, are fundamental to maintaining the punitive power of harming and keeping LGBTQ, queer and trans folx, in check. Therefore, it is also imperative upon the mainstream LGBTQ movement to abolish prisons, for prisons are patriarchal and act as primary aggressors of anti-LGBTQ violence.

As a Black gender-nonconforming, female-assigned person, I know that I will never be free of harm, as long as any patriarchal systems exist. I know that it won't be long until the system turns its gaze on me. Let us rise to meet the challenge of our time. We must confront the violence of patriarchy—and all its institutions, cultural and political systems, economies, and individual actors—as a primary oppression. The imperative of this time is to abolish white supremacist, capitalist patriarchal violence!

All Black Genders Unite! All Feminists Unite! All Workers Unite! All Queers Unite!

M Adams is a community organizer and co–executive director of Freedom Inc. Adams has developed and organized for a strong intersectional approach in numerous important venues and campaigns. Adams is a leading figure in the Movement for Black Lives and in the local movement in Wisconsin for Black community control. M is also a proud hubby and Baba. Adams can be contacted at madams@freedom-inc.org.

Notes

1. See Manjon, Sager, and Buckingham 2015, and Rivedal 2015 for more information about Cierra Finkley.
2. See Shabazz 2013 and NBC15 2013 for more information about Aprina Paul.

Works Cited

Adams, M, and Max Rameau. 2016. "Black Community Control Over Police." *Wisconsin Law Review* 2016, no. 3: 515–39.

Critical Resistance. 2019. "What Is the PIC? What Is Abolition?" Critical Resistance (website). http://criticalresistance.org/about/not-so-common-language/.

Critical Resistance and INCITE! Women of Color Against Violence. 2006. "Gender Violence and the Prison-Industrial Complex." In *Color of Violence: The INCITE! Anthology*, edited by INCITE! Women of Color Against Violence, 223–26. Durham, NC: Duke University Press.

Manjon, Liam, Gretchen Sager, and Alex Buckingham. 2015. "We Want Justice for Cierra Finkley." Socialistworker.org. August 24, 2015. https://socialistworker.org/2015/08/24/we-want-justice-for-cierra-finkley.

NBC15. 2013. "UPDATE: Man Gets Maximum Sentence for Burning Woman's Body." NBC15. Last modified June 18, 2014. https://www.nbc15.com/home/headlines/Police-look-for-missing-teen-229921881.html.

Rivedal, Karen. 2015. "Madison Woman Set Free in Fatal Stabbing after DA Declines to File Charges for Now." *Wisconsin State Journal.* September 24, 2015. https://madison.com/wsj/news/local/crime-and-courts/madison-woman-set-free-in-fatal-stabbing-after-da-declines/article_cf8f642a-42c7-5b2b-93d4-4c6fcf0d16d7.html.

Shabazz, Alix. 2013. "Justice for Aprina Paul." Socialistworker.org. November 19, 2013. https://socialistworker.org/2013/11/19/justice-for-aprina-paul.

Youthalizm

BreakOUT! We Deserve Better Campaign Committee

Our mission at BreakOUT! is to end the criminalization of lesbian, gay, bisexual, transgender, and queer (LGBTQ) youth to build a safer and more just New Orleans. Building on the rich cultural tradition of resistance in the South, we build the power of LGBTQ youth ages thirteen to twenty-five directly impacted by the criminal justice system through youth organizing, healing justice, and leadership development programs. All of BreakOUT!'s programming and campaigns work in tandem to move us closer toward our vision of creating a city where all people can move down the street without fear.

The We Deserve Better Campaign is BreakOUT!'s first and oldest campaign. Formed in 2011, BreakOUT! began working with the Department of Justice (DOJ) and other community stakeholders to bring attention to the experiences of the LGBTQ community in New Orleans—and in particular African American transgender women and LGBTQ youth — impacted by the criminal or juvenile justice system. The federal investigation of the New Orleans Police Department (NOPD) that resulted named discriminatory policing toward the LGBTQ community as an area of top concern, and was the first time the DOJ had gone so far as to outline concrete measures to address profiling and discrimination against our community. This moment marked an unprecedented victory for the LGBTQ community, which experiences discriminatory policing. Since then, our campaign has worked to end discriminatory policing practices against LGBTQ youth of color and address "feeders" into the criminal justice system. These "feeders" include the conditions that contribute to LGBTQ youth homelessness as well as the oversurveillance of and police harassment in areas frequented by LGBTQ youth of color.

WSQ: Women's Studies Quarterly 47: 3 & 4 (Fall/Winter 2019) © 2019 by BreakOUT! We Deserve Better Campaign Committee. All rights reserved.

Fighting the criminalization of LGBTQ and nonbinary youth in New Orleans—the largest city by population in the state of Louisiana, which boasts the highest rate of incarceration in the United States (if you don't include people awaiting to be sentenced [O'Donoghue 2019])—positions BreakOUT! at the intersection of multiple movements including youth, gender, sexuality, immigration, prison abolition, poor people's movements, and more.

Context matters to what these intersections mean and Louisiana's progressive organizations are facing crucial fights this year. These fights include:

— A heartbeat abortion law which would outlaw abortions as early as six weeks, or as soon as a fetal heartbeat is detected (Frazin 2019), which is being challenged by Women With a Vision, local partnerships, collaborations and coalitions of legal, service, and community organizations;

— The continual rise of surveillance, as exemplified by the Citywide Public Safety Improvement Plan, which invests millions of public dollars toward the 24/7 surveillance and monitoring of our city under the slogan of not only making New Orleans safe, but making it *feel safe* (Maris Jones 2018);

— The Crimes Against Nature Law (CANS), which dates back to the nineteenth century and equates adult consensual sex that is not "heterosexual" as "against nature." A crime against nature is described in Louisiana state law as either of the following: (1) The unnatural carnal copulation by a human being with another of the same sex or opposite sex or with an animal, except that anal sexual intercourse between two human beings shall not be deemed as a crime against nature when done under any of the circumstances (described in R.S. 14:41, 42, 42.1, 43); or (2) The marriage to, or sexual intercourse with, any ascendant or descendant, brother or sister, uncle or niece, aunt or nephew, with knowledge of their relationship.[1] Although the law was amended in 2016, the amendment is not retroactive for individuals who were unlawfully impacted, meaning there are still significant numbers of Black trans women and Black women sex workers who are still on the sex offender registry list for having consensual sex. The law is being challenged by the CANScantSTAND campaign;

— The continual rise of immigration raids and detainments which is being challenged by the Congress of Day Laborers/Congreso de Jornaleros and the New Orleans Workers' Center for Racial Justice (Burns 2019), who have recently brought attention to the advanced collaboration of local law enforcement with Immigration and Customs Enforcement (ICE), the use of technologies of warfare, and the documented excessive use of force, lack of due process, deprivation of right to counsel, and retaliation against individuals who attempt to defend their rights during the arrest;

— The city's proposed prison expansion, which particularly targets individuals struggling with mental health, and reflects a growing national trend of expanding incarceration; the Orleans Parish Prison Reform Coalition (OPPRC) is leading the fight against the proposed expansion in New Orleans (Sledge 2019); and

— The anticipated exit of the City of New Orleans from the Consent Decree, which is being challenged by many organizations and people locally. As part of our We Deserve Better Campaign, BreakOUT! worked with the Department of Justice and other community stakeholders to issue new police policy, specifically dealing with the treatment of members of the lesbian, gay, bisexual, transgender, and queer/questioning (LGBTQ) community. The policy includes protocols for stopping and searching transgender individuals and mandates that officers be trained on issues pertaining to the LGBTQ community. However, despite the New Orleans Police Department's Policy 402, adopted in 2013 and revised in 2017, which states, "Officers shall not use an individual's actual or perceived gender identity, or sexual orientation as reasonable suspicion or probable cause that an individual is or has engaged in any crime," the NOPD's treatment of African American and Latinx trans, nonbinary, and LGBTQ communities has not improved.

No single organization can address all of these fronts alone. Nineteen years ago, INCITE! and Critical Resistance came together recognizing the same (2016). We build upon their work to bring together the multiple fronts of struggle that shape our lives; and to create and develop collaborative working spaces that hold intersecting identities as vital to this work.

Below, we describe some of our best learning lessons from our work to build these spaces and long-term trusting partnerships:

Being that we are youth-led with an intergenerational strategy, we seek to create that link from our ancestors to community in order to shape a future of accountability and integrity.

Youth voices are often sought out in movement spaces that are not equipped to support different experiences and provide the bridges needed to build connection. This type of inclusion functions as a performance of political standards designed to create an illusion of decision-making power, or what some call tokenism.

When we go to these movement places people stare at us, and we feel dismissed or unwanted. Whether it is constant misgendering in the media, harassment from police, or overcoming our experiences being invisible in movement spaces, we have had to build a model for ourselves that embodies who we are as individuals and as community.

Some practices, tools, and principles that we implement and need include:

— Healing justice and restorative justice are practices that MUST be used in all movement spaces. When they are known and consistently practiced they create roads to building trust within the movement.
— Story circles are a necessary tool to understanding and creating visibility for each other in the movement.
— Commit to not assuming someone else's gender. These assumptions are dangerous and come across as disrespect of the legacy of trans and nonbinary organizing. Everyone involved in movement work has something to learn.
— We have to develop practices that help us identify when we (as movements) are judging each other instead of listening and adapting to each other.
— And most importantly, youth are not your property—we are not meant to be handled as property by whomever it is beneficial for or for how other people want us to be seen in their eyes. Youth aren't anyone's except their individual self-property. "Take me as I am or stop denying me the space I hold."

Building spaces that hold intersecting identities and with the intention of long-term trusting partnerships takes time. Living in New Orleans, our lives are plagued with violence rooted in white supremacy, making our work all the more challenging. As we work toward this vision, we work to create the world we want to live in inside the walls of our own spaces. As part of that model we have developed House Agreements for BreakOUT! that we use at all meetings, and bring with us into coalition spaces. These agreements are crafted from the knowledge of our membership and other agreements that are used throughout the movement. We share these as an example of the trust and agreement that can be built across community.

Where we begin.

If we work together to commit to making our space a safe space for all of us, we'll have no need for weapons here. Some of us are on probation, struggle with substance abuse, are in recovery, or are under drinking age. We commit to keeping the office and our spaces substance-free. If you use, do it off the property.

Throw no shade.

Don't talk badly about each other or book each other, even if they're not here. If you have serious problems with someone, ask for help from staff.

R-E-S-P-E-C-T.

Respect for ourselves, for each other, and for our ideas. We are all beautiful, valuable beings worthy of love, support, and self-care. We keep open minds and recognize that we all have things we can learn from one another.

Say my name, say my name.

Don't make assumptions about who people are or where they are coming from. Call people what they want to be called. Use the pronouns people ask you to use. NO MATTER WHAT!

This is a place of solidarity.

So many things in the world separate us and keep us from building community. We agree to not let issues divide us and keep us from organizing together. We are stronger when we are together. We agree not to make judgments about each other, including whether we engage in *sex work* or *how we dress*. We agree not to let *religion* separate us. We agree not to let *HIV status* separate us (and to keep things confidential when asked). Lastly, we agree not to let ourselves be divided by *how we identify* and *who we love*.

Stay engaged.

While we build power together we ask that folx do what they need to stay engaged. Let's try and put down phones, refrain from social media for a bit, and focus on building community together.

KIT-KAT.

We understand that sometimes we may need to have hard conversations as we struggle together. In times where things get tense, or rough, or we just need a break, anyone in the room can call a 5–15 minute KIT-KAT, or break. KIT-KATs are always proposed with a suggested time, and an activity to bring us all back together when we reconvene.

Don't yuck my yum.

As individuals we don't have to like what every other individual also likes and we support lifting one another up. Practicing ways to celebrate our differences moves us through hard moments and conversations, encouraging clarity and understanding.

Assume no shade.

Create personal relationships with each other and check in with folx, especially when we notice changes in how they show up. Take accountability for ourselves and our actions.

ELMO (Enough, let's move on).

Conversations can also begin to circle and cycle. When it is keeping us off of our task we can declare ELMO to move us back into focus.

One mic.

All voices should be heard, all of our voices are important! We make space, we encourage each other to move up and move back, pushing ourselves to create space for both those of us who speak often and those of us who do not.

BreakOUT! seeks to end the criminalization of lesbian, gay, bisexual, transgender, and questioning (LGBTQ) youth to build a safer and more just New Orleans. We build on the rich cultural tradition of resistance in the South to build the power of LGBTQ youth ages thirteen to twenty-five and directly impacted by the criminal justice system through youth organizing, healing justice, and leadership development programs. BreakOUT! envisions a city where transgender, gender nonconforming, and queer youth of color can live without fear of harassment and discrimination.

Notes

1. To read more about the revised Crime Against Nature law, see LA Rev Stat § 14:89 2016.

Works Cited

Burns, Julien 2019. "Press Release: Federal Judge Delivers Blow to ICE in Fight with New Orleans Community Group over Race-Based Immigration Raids Program." New Orleans Workers' Center for Racial Justice. March 14, 2019. http://nowcrj.org/2019/03/14/press-release-federal-judge-delivers-blow-to-ice-in-fight-with-new-orleans-community-group-over-race-based-immigration-raids-program/.

Critical Resistance and INCITE! Women of Color Against Violence. 2006. "Gender Violence and the Prison-Industrial Complex." In *Color of Violence: The INCITE! Anthology*, edited by INCITE! Women of Color Against Violence, 223–26. Durham, NC: Duke University Press.

Frazin, Rachel. 2019. "Louisiana Lawmakers Advance 'Heartbeat' Abortion Bill." *The Hill*, May 7, 2019. https://thehill.com/policy/healthcare/abortion/442515-louisiana-latest-state-to-advance-heartbeat-abortion-ban.

Maris Jones, G. 2018. "It Is Time to #StopWatchingNOLA with Surveillance Cameras | Opinion." Nola.com, July 3, 2018. https://www.nola.com/opinions/2018/07/crime_cameras.html.

O'Donoghue, Julia. 2019. "Is Louisiana Still the Incarceration Capital of the U.S.?" *Times-Picayune*, April 29, 2019. https://www.nola.com/politics/2019/04/is-louisiana-still-the-incarceration-capital-of-the-us.html.

Sledge, Matt. 2019. "Advocates Urge New Orleans to Abandon Jail Expansion Plans, Call for Rehab Instead." *New Orleans Advocate*, March 26, 2019. https://www.theadvocate.com/new_orleans/news/courts/article_cf2d2504-5026-11e9-8177-276b4a93804d.html.

Almost Twenty Years Later: Lessons Learned from Critical Resistance and INCITE! on Building an Organizing Framework to Tackle Violence at the Nexus of State Violence, Gender-Based Violence, and Structural Islamophobia

Darakshan Raja, Justice for Muslims Collective

The late Rose Braz, one of the cofounders of Critical Resistance, stated, "Even though the goal we seek may be far away, unless we name it and fight for it today, it will never come" (Berger, Kaba, and Stein 2017). Braz's words describe the integral role Critical Resistance–INCITE!'s "Statement on Gender Violence and the Prison-Industrial Complex" played in laying out a powerful mandate for social justice movements to "develop strategies and analysis that address both state and interpersonal violence" outside of the carceral system (2006). This mandate was particularly important given the ways mainstream anti-violence and social justice movement strategies and analysis excluded women of color survivors. Working-class, immigrant, Black, Brown, and indigenous survivors of color didn't fit the problematic constructions of the ideal victim and were often forgotten by movements, disposed of, and had organizations turn their backs on them when they needed their support. In other instances, the very movements that survivors entered to attain justice re-created systems of abuse that further pushed them out of movement spaces. Certain groups of women like Muslim women were rarely mentioned within these circles, and still continue to face gendered forms of Islamophobia from mainstream social justice and anti-violence movements.

In 2001 INCITE's statement offered a critical intervention to warn against the long-term impact on survivors of color, given the mainstream anti-violence movement's decision to collaborate with the criminal enforcement system, particularly as a result of the Violence Against Women Act of 1994. While VAWA has undeniably played a critical role in meeting the needs of many survivors of interpersonal forms of violence, and serves

WSQ: Women's Studies Quarterly 47: 3 & 4 (Fall/Winter 2019) © 2019 by Darakshan Raja.

as a key funding stream for direct service providers, the law was part and parcel of the broader 1994 Crime Bill that further expanded mass incarceration. VAWA did disproportionately invest resources into the criminal enforcement system over community-oriented solutions. Simultaneously, as noted in the Critical Resistance–INCITE! statement, the professionalization of the anti-violence movement redirected energy from investing in mass-scale collective movements that tackled gender-based violence by addressing root causes, including holding the state accountable, to building professionalized services that were in many cases restricted by state funding sources. This analysis has been helpful as a framework for organizers and advocates who navigate the complexity and challenges of tackling state- and gender-based violence on a daily basis within communities that are facing assaults on all fronts, and are often unsupported by broader social justice movements, community, and the mainstream anti-violence movement. Without clear values and lessons from the past, we can easily replicate mistakes that hurt our ability to achieve collective liberation.

In the past eighteen years since the release of the statement, there have been inspirational efforts to actualize the vision set out by INCITE! Most notably, groups such as Survived and Punished, Project NIA, Love and Protect, Black Youth Project 100, and the work of notable scholar-activists and organizers like Dr. Beth Richie, Mariame Kaba, Dr. Angela Davis, and Dr. Kimberlé Crenshaw, alongside many others, have been central to actualizing a vision where survivors of gender- and state-based violence are centered. The collective work produced from Critical Resistance–INCITE's statement has inspired and moved me personally in my own journey, and has inspired the work of Justice for Muslims Collective in further developing a framework and praxis that organizes at the nexus of state violence, gender-based violence, and structural Islamophobia.

Before delving deeper into the work of Justice for Muslims Collective (JMC), a community-based organization I cofounded and codirect with Dr. Maha Hilal that seeks to dismantle structural and institutional Islamophobia, and the ways we are integrating the principles laid out by Critical Resistance–INCITE!'s statement through our programming, it is important to contextualize the expansion of the prison nation since Critical Resistance–INCITE!'s statement was released in 2001. At that point, it would have been hard to predict the scale at which the U.S. prison industrial complex, the military industrial complex, and the immigration industrial complex would have expanded on a global scale. The nineties witnessed the crystallization of numerous laws and policies that paved the way for the launch of the War on Terror in 2001. In 1994 the Crime Bill expanded the U.S. mass incarceration system. In 1996 the Illegal Immigration Reform and Immigrant Responsibility Act further entrenched the anti-immigration and deportation machine. In 2001 the United States passed the War on Terror to further entrench institutionalized Islamophobia.

A cursory review of the impact of the War on Terror that was recently published in the *Smithsonian* magazine by Stephanie Savell from the Costs of War Project at Brown University found the United States is actively engaged in counterterrorism operations within eighty nations on six continents, and has added $2.4 trillion to the U.S. debt (Savell 2019). While we don't have an accurate estimate of the number of casualties from the War on Terror, it is estimated that between 480,000 to 507,000 people have been killed in Iraq, Afghanistan, and Pakistan. Domestically, one of the first presidential executive orders passed by Trump and upheld by the Supreme Court was the Muslim Ban. The Muslim Ban is part and parcel of a broader assault on immigrants, refugees, and asylum seekers. Accompanied by this violence is the expansion of mass surveillance on a global scale.

A critical aspect of the War on Terror is the construction of Muslims and people racialized as Muslims as the "other" in order to expand empire and the prison nation on a global scale. Within this national security narrative, gender constructions, gender-based violence, and sexual violence are deployed as key tactics for controlling, dehumanizing, and humiliating Muslim bodies, including racialized Muslim bodies. It is also used to justify the War on Terror with the aim of liberating Muslim women and girls from oppressive Muslim men, while simultaneously killing, maiming, and criminalizing Muslim women and girls.

JMC is among a handful of organizations led by Muslim women to tackle state- and gender-based violence, particularly as it manifests under the War on Terror and more broadly institutionalized Islamophobia. Our work to combat gendered Islamophobia incorporates survivors of gender-based and state violence. Our internal working definition of gendered Islamophobia is as follows:

> Gendered Islamophobia consists of the ways the state utilizes gendered forms of violence to oppress, monitor, punish, maim, and control Muslim bodies. It includes the ways gender binaries and gender constructions are

used to prescribe negative social constructions on Muslim women and girls while erasing the existence of femmes, trans women, gender non-conforming, and nonbinary Muslims because of the assumptions that Muslims are inherently homophobic and queerphobic. These negative social constructions portray Muslim women and girls as terrorists, terrorist sympathizers, and supporters and potential terrorists, who pose a threat to the security of the state on one end of the spectrum. They also depict Muslim women and girls as cultural representatives of Islam and Muslim communities, and hence women's and girls' bodies are often the sites of control and domination. Simultaneously, Muslim women and girls are depicted as inherently oppressed and lacking of any individual or collective agency. Therefore, violence against Muslim women and girls is often seen as normal and acceptable. Gendered forms of violence that are inflicted on Muslim bodies include the use of sexual violence, torture, harassment, murder, and state reproductive control, coercion, and violence. Finally, gendered Islamophobia exists on a continuum, and is enforced and heightened through the interplay of violence that manifests at the institutional and systemic (interplay between multiple institutions) levels, as well as via nonstate actors (specifically vigilante violence in the form of hate violence), through community institutions and members, through family and interpersonal relationships, and also at an internalized level. In other words, it includes the ways the state fosters an environment of impunity that produces hate violence, use of gendered violence by state agencies, and intracommunity abuses to flourish, such as femicide, sexual assault, domestic and family violence, trafficking, harassment, and abuse. This violence is rooted in and lives at the intersection of heteropatriarchy, institutional Islamophobia, and interlocking systems of oppression that produce gender-based violence and negatively impact the quality of life for Muslim women and girls.

This working definition was formed after our collective efforts to raise awareness on the ways gender-based violence and state violence are interconnected, and through multiple listening sessions with Muslims on gender-based violence, Islamophobia, and trans- and queerphobic violence. Moreover, it is also based on our research that is documenting gendered harassment of Muslim women, femmes, nonbinary people, and trans women at airports and at the border. Further, it is shaped by our work with direct service organizations and advocacy groups that work directly with Muslim survivors.

In order to provide concrete examples, we are sharing the names and stories of a few Muslim women and girls who have been impacted at the intersection of state- and gender-based violence.

— **Noor Salman**: As an organization, we worked to draft a statement and campaign for #WeStandWithNoorSalman that was signed by over 120 organizations to demand the prosecution drop all charges against Noor Salman. We heard about Noor Salman's case after she had been held in federal prison on terrorism charges. Her only crime was being married to Omar Mateen, the shooter responsible for murdering multiple individuals at the Pulse nightclub. Rather than the state acknowledging that Noor Salman had also been a survivor of domestic violence, given Mateen had a history of abusing women, the state moved to hold her responsible. Due to media pressure and the weak case presented by the FBI, Noor Salman's charges were dropped.

— **Nabra Hassanen** was a seventeen-year-old Sudanese American Muslim teen who was sexually assaulted and murdered during Ramadan. Her father still believes that her being a visible Muslim woman played a role in her murder.

— **Yusor Abu-Salha** and **Razan Abu-Salha**: On February 10, 2015, Yusor and Razan were murdered by their white supremacist Islamophobic neighbor. Yusor and Razan were harassed by their neighbor for months. They were particularly targeted because Yusor and Razan wore the hijab. The case was never tried as a hate crime in the courts.

— **Shukri Ali** was a thirty-six-year-old Black Muslim woman whose family called law enforcement in order to get their sister support for mental health reasons. Rather than responding to Ali with care, law enforcement officers shot and killed Shukri Ali.

— **Abeer Qassim Hamza** was a fourteen-year-old Iraqi girl who was gang raped and murdered by U.S. army soldiers in Iraq on March 12, 2006. A group of U.S. army soldiers also killed her entire family.

— **Mamana Bibi** was a sixty-eight-year-old grandmother who was killed by a U.S. drone strike in Pakistan on October 24, 2012, as she picked vegetables in her family's fields.

— **Nawar al-Awlaki** was an eight-year-old who was killed in a raid personally approved by Donald Trump in Yemen.

— **Shaima Alawadi** was a thirty-two-year old Iraqi woman who was killed by her husband in a domestic violence case. Her husband tried to evade accountability by falsely framing her murder as a hate crime.

All of these cases are deeply troubling and expose the multiple systems through which Muslim women and girls experience state and gender-based violence. As we continue to build out a more robust analysis and praxis, the framework laid out by Critical Resistance and INCITE! is key in paving the road to also dismantling the military industrial complex and other carceral systems. These systems rely on one another and are strengthened by collaboration on a global scale.

However, in addition to increased levels of violence from state, the case of Shaima Alawadi represents the ways abusers within our communities will seek to exploit the existence of hate violence to evade accountability. As we have learned through our work with direct service providers who work with Muslim survivors, abusers have used the existence of the immigration enforcement system to threaten survivors with deportation if they report. In other instances, abusers have threatened to report survivors as terrorists to the FBI in order to harm survivors. This is further evidence that abusers will use the carceral system against survivors. While the criminalization of men is raised as a consistent concern when conversations on criminalization are brought up, often communities and our movements fail to acknowledge the ways abusers use the carceral system against survivors.

In reflecting back on the statement released in 2001 by Critical Resistance and INCITE!, I am reminded of the work we still need to do in order to shift attitudes and beliefs that continue to justify gender-based violence within our communities. There are key questions that I believe still need to be answered in addition to the points raised in the initial statement. This includes the following:

—How do we also center survivors of violence beyond American borders as we acknowledge that American empire is sustained by carrying out gendered violence on a global scale?
—What does it mean to hold the state accountable and its policies of violating communities domestically and abroad?
—What lessons can we learn from women resisting U.S. violence and imperialism outside of the borders of the United States?
—What does it look like for our movements to apply and incorporate a gendered lens to fighting Islamophobia and centering Muslim women and girls?

Overall, it is painful to admit that almost twenty years since the release of the statement, our broader social justice movements and communities have a ways to go before we can confidently claim that we have truly built the alternative structures of community-oriented restorative and transformative justice responses at a mass scale. As we move forward, I hope we can build and sustain survivor-led responses that prioritize the well-being, safety, and needs of survivors of gender-based violence fleeing life-threatening situations from individual abusers and families. Further, as we work to build strategies to address state and interpersonal forms of violence, it is critical to remember that our own social justice movements and organizations aren't exempt from replicating abusive structures that include forms of gender and sexual violence. This particular work at this juncture is some of the least resourced, most isolating, and at times extremely exhausting work. Community organizers, advocates, and direct service providers who are also often survivors of gender-based violence are constantly navigating difficult spaces, including targeting from the state and opposition from the status quo internally within their own communities. Yet, we continue to hold steadfast onto powerful visions of the alternative world we seek to build, a world where violence in all of its forms doesn't exist.

Justice for Muslims Collective works to dismantle institutional and structural Islamophobia through raising political consciousness, community empowerment and organizing, and movement building through coalition-building focused on the Greater Washington Region. JMC envisions a world where radical inclusion leads to collective liberation for Muslim communities and beyond.

Works Cited

Berger, Dan, Mariame Kaba, and David Stein. 2017. "What Abolitionists Do." *Jacobin*, August 24, 2017. https://www.jacobinmag.com/2017/08/prison-abolition-reform-mass-incarceration.

Critical Resistance and INCITE! Women of Color Against Violence. 2006. "Gender Violence and the Prison-Industrial Complex." In *Color of Violence: The INCITE! Anthology*, edited by INCITE! Women of Color Against Violence, 223–26. Durham, NC: Duke University Press.

Savell, Stephanie, and 5W Infographics. 2019. "This Map Shows Where in the World the U.S. Military Is Combatting Terrorism." *Smithsonian*, January 2019. https://www.smithsonianmag.com/history/map-shows-places-world-where-us-military-operates-180970997/.

PART VII. **PROSE**

Dei's World

Kawika Guillermo

1: Canyon

I flew with my arms out like an airplane, through the corner window of the ancient American White House. Inside, brown-robed monks shouldered boom boxes, their asses releasing frosted wind.

"Aren't we supposed to be learning about Churchill?" I said to Sarah, my meld partner. I spotted her sitting on an oscillating chandelier made of peacock feathers.

Sarah tilted her sunglasses down, that blaze of black hair whisking in a whirlwind. "So then what happens?"

"Then," I said, levitating above the dancing monks, "salt water pours in through the windows." CRASH! The monks fell like heaps of dirt. Electric sparks flew from their stereos. "The White House is the *Titanic*," I said as the entire stone structure tilted. Men in suits poured out screaming.

She gave a light chuckle. "You're vile. Such a travesty, the *Titanic*."

"So what should I conjure next?" I said with a grin. "Lead the way, Dei."

Sarah smiled when I called her by that name, the name she was not allowed to speak. "Well," she said, "how about a flood! Can you do that?"

My mind communicated a new code, speaking the machine's language, and we levitated together through the rooftop and watched the White House float like abandoned cargo in an endless sea.

"Life begins anew," I said. "The end of mankind!"

—*Children.*

Dei's body somersaulted in midair laughter. "Killed by their own technology—"

—*Children!*

WSQ: Women's Studies Quarterly 47: 3 & 4 (Fall/Winter 2019) © 2019 by Kawika Guillermo.

I awoke from the mind mesh, sweating, my heart beating in my neck.

"Children," our caretaker said again. She stood near the canyon-wall chalkboard, her frail body hugged by a burlap dress, her wooly gray hair poking out in all directions from a blue bonnet blocking the sun. "Who is the good student? Who listened to all of Sir Churchill's speech, and can recite the last lines?"

My eyes followed the small black wire from my forehead to the fist-sized meld machine and then to Sarah, a girl whose body shone with a heavy sweat that seeped through her burlap dress. We sat on red stones at the bottom of the great canyon that protected us from the toxic gray fog above. I heard that small black creek running nearby, indifferent to our lesson.

My eyes met hers. We smiled at each other like we were being chased. Annoyed, the caretaker called on someone else.

Two years before, her people emerged from the fog on the northern edge of our canyon. They wore industrial gas masks and carried all their belongings in wagons and wheelbarrows. Hundreds of them had escaped the chaos of the subterranean mounds, only to spend weeks journeying through the fog, never pulling off their masks except to drink radish and pea soups cultivated from their underground farms. We, the canyon people, had only heard of their kind, the mound people, from our scouts. We gave them space to camp on the higher edges of the canyon, closer to the fog.

My eyes first met her defiant gaze in class, while the caretaker was leading our weekly singalong:

Who is who is who is
going to get eaten
by the fog fog fog fog
Who?
All the mountain people!
And?
All the island people!
And?
All the mound people!

I felt embarrassed, knowing that some of our classmates had just come from the mounds. But the other children sang with fervor, even the new refugees. I moved to the back of the classroom and found one other child singing like me, in small whispers. It was all the breath she could muster. Somehow, our skin was the same tint of brown. Her arm looked like mine, and seemed just as smooth to touch. I volunteered to be her partner in the meld machine, a virtual world where we learned about all of human achievement. I was supposed to help her adjust. We were supposed to use the machine to observe and honor the world before war scorched the planet. Before the fog took all the men.

But Sarah only used the machine for play. And with my unrestrained imagination, we defiled every honorable historical figure. Newton choked to death on that fallen apple. Confucius gave up wisdom when he learned to surf. Saladin got drunk and fell off his horse. And in that world she used her own name, the name that our caretakers had banned because it was too hard to pronounce. Dei, she called herself. Dei, her mound people's name. And it was Dei's world where anything could happen, so long as we had the will.

"Dei," I whispered into the small crevice. It was the last sultry summer night that mankind would ever live through. For the first time I had crossed the steep riverbank separating our peoples, for the first time saw her motley folk encamped on the slope, dotting the canyon like lichen. How did they survive?

I heard my echoes bounce through the tunnels of our canyon, to the other side of the demarcation, where Sarah's family dwelled. "Dei. Can. You. Hear. Me?"

An echo bounced back: "Yes. Is that you?"

"Yes. It's me."

"I'm sorry."

"I'm. So. Sorry."

Silence. I wondered if she had heard the same announcement, only days before, that our food rations were insufficient. That supporting refugees was a privilege we could not afford. That a barrier was to be erected. That the people of the mound, if they wanted to survive, had better head back to where they belonged.

"Please. Tell me. That. You're. OK."

My echoes bounced. I heard sounds, perhaps unformed words, perhaps sobs.

"Dei," I said. "Can. I. Kiss. You. Where. It. Hurts?"

Silence. Then: "Yes," she said. "You. Are. Kissing. Me."

2: Exodus

Horns blared from atop the canyons. Gray obelisks drifted from the fog in shapely rows like ghosts bearing their own gravestones. They came down to us in streaming elevators, setting down within our canyon walls. At the edge of starvation, we followed the smell of rice porridge and baked potatoes that wafted through the canyons, hailing us to come aboard.

The gods had sent a divine race to save us. The Jucs. Broad-shouldered, their bodies shaped like tall lamps, their pose always stiff. We followed a red-lighted line through the ship's hallways and encountered hordes of them staring us down with their menacing yellow eyes. Some of them carried signs in our language:

Shame on those who destroy their planet
You do not deserve us
Keep your disease away

We were brought to a bright room that had to be dimmed before we could see each other. We faced a dark screen that our caretaker told us was a window to outer space. "Those are stars," our caretaker said, pointing to the lights twinkling in the distance. "And one of those stars is Earth. And those floating ships beside us"—she pointed to the rectangular obelisks, gray and tall like the Washington Monument—"those are our saviors. Every ship now is full of humans from all around the world."

I cried in a torrent. "What about the mound people? Where are they?"

"You're lucky to be here," my caretaker said, dour-faced. "Do you even know how lucky you are?"

For years we lived under the Jucs' parentage. My body grew thick in their passing delights. My friends Pea, Cherry, and I rode our automatic bikes through the ship's gray corridors, wavering past those tall gods like street signs. We parked in front of the mountain people's triage wing, our tires barely touching the yellow demarcation border where mechanical devices were forbidden, to respect the mountain people's belief in naturalism.

Three of their old-timers met our gaze. They held water-stained books and wore colored cotton cloth that hung over their shoulders.

Cherry revved the engine she made in our mechanical engineering class. "Hey, mountain people!" she baited. "Why don't you get a job or something?"

"Loafin' around all day," Pea joined. She spat a thick wad across the yellow border.

"No mountains here in space," I said. "Your venerable Buddha is back at home, kissing your holy cows!"

I laughed as the other girls sped away. My engine sputtered; the blue lights blinked on and off. The three mountain people lunged toward me just as the motor churned on, and I whizzed down the halls, past those Jucs with their menacing stares, smoke billowing from my bike.

We regrouped at the canyon people's demarcation line.

"There's something wrong with you," Cherry said, wiping black dust from her yellow floral patterned dress.

"You think that kind of talk is funny?" Pea joined, as they departed to their dormitory rooms.

I sank into the bustle of the market, passing diamond-patterned skirts and petaled suit jackets. One person, I thought, would have found it funny.

In my last year of education, I still would not meld like the other children.

In the last virtual dream of our class, I sat with Cherry in the crowd of black, brown, and white people, listening to that man on stage talk about having a dream.

"What if," I said, leaping into the air above the humid crowd, "Cleopatra woos the good doctor?" I sent code to the machine and the Egyptian queen appeared, gold headdress and all, massaging the man on stage. "The good doctor lets loose his passions—"

"That is filthy!" Cherry yelled from inside the crowd. "I'm trying to focus on what he says."

"You *know* what he says," I said, bashing away the onstage fellatio with the wind of my arm stroke. "We have to memorize it every year, just to recite it for those stupid lampshades."

"How are you so talented in here, but in the real world you can barely unscrew a bolt?"

"It's more fun in here!" Mark 14 torpedoes whizzed out of my fingers, flying through the air like air was water, leaving a trail of bubbles behind them.

"I'm glad we're graduating. I won't ever need to meld with you again."

The bombs made a circle and soared toward Cherry in the crowd. "Better think of something quick!" I taunted.

"These torpedoes cost real human lives," Cherry said as the missiles rocketed closer to the dispersing, panicking crowd. "Have some respect."

The bombs exploded. Mass casualties. The Washington Monument fell, revealing Amelia Earhart's stashed carcass.

Cherry burst out of the rubble, livid. "What is wrong with you? This is *sacred*, don't you get that?"

"You really don't enjoy any of this?"

"What kind of person would?"

3: Ships

For six years more we remained aboard the Jucs' ship. In that time, the mountain people were moved into our triage zone. At first they refused to cross, and we would not take them in, until the Jucs took one of their children, and then one of ours.

"They'll do far worse soon enough," Cherry told me as we watched the mountain people brush wool into yarn.

"They called it a 'coup,'" said Pea, the girl most literate in the Jucs' language. "It means their crazies took over. Remember them, the ones with those signs telling us to go back to Earth? The ones who tell us to go eat fog? They're in power now."

"So what?" I said. "We've already been prohibited from ever setting foot on a planet again. We're a near-extinct species. What more could they do?"

That night we were taken to the gas rooms. The gas, they told us, mimicked the fog we left behind on Earth. They saved us from it, so it was their right to put us back whenever they pleased. The lampshade-looking Jucs assaulted us with flashlight beams in our eyes, then checked our teeth and took photographs of our nude bodies. I was the last of my crew to enter the interrogation office.

"Who is Thomas Edison?" a pacing lampshade asked in a calculating voice.

"An inventor," I said, my arms bound behind my back. "Nineteenth century, I think."

"And what do you think of inventors like Edison?"

"I don't know. I was taught to call them heroes."

"What do you think of your people's atomic bomb?"

"I was told nuclear energy had potential."

"And what do you say to that?"

"It's hard to accept, I guess."

"What about your men? Do you accept that your technology killed them?"

"You mean the fog?"

"Your inventors created the fog. Your wars let it cover your planet. In nature, any species without balance goes extinct. Do you not see the perversion of staying on?"

"I think I see it. Yes."

"So then. Do you wish to re-create human technology?"

"I just don't care. I wish it would just end. We're done."

"Is this your bike?" Two lampshades pulled out my blue bike. The outside was caked in a layer of black soot.

"Yeah, that's the one."

The Jucs looked it over. "But it barely works. We tried it. It won't even start."

"Yeah, I know."

"Aren't you going to repair it?"

"To be honest, I have no idea what to do with that piece of garbage."

"I see."

When I was sent back to the canyon people's triage grounds, there were few children left. The remaining adults wandering about the pen were either pregnant or drunkards. I waited for days but no one else came. Pea and Cherry, gone. Anyone capable of ever re-creating human technology, disappeared. And just to make a point, days later our melding devices were torn apart and laid out at the demarcation line, their parts stacked in neat pieces for us to see.

The Jucs liked to gloat. They had executed anyone with the knowledge to put our machines back together. But they gave us the parts, knowing that we survivors had no idea what to do with them. All the knowledge of human history and achievement, spread out in front of us, with no tangible way to re-create it.

Our colony grew as we were shoved into other ships with other groups of humans. Mountain people, mound people, island people, canyon people, all brought into the same triage centers. Most were too young or too broken to care. As one of the oldest survivors from the Grand Canyon, I was more interested in the other young adults. Over the course of my youth I met others who preferred to be drunk on Juc wine. One sip was enough to get drunk—four, enough to kill yourself. With no jobs, no schooling, no caring for our future, I cruised from woman to woman.

For my first love, I wrote a poem about prefabricated two-story homes inhabited by samurais in pantyhose masks.

"Who would find this funny?" she said. "None of this goes together."

For my second love, I sang about Archimedes basking in a pool, wife-swapping with Louis XVI.

"You're disgusting," she said. "Can't you just be normal?"

For my third love, I painted a canvas of equidistant cannons, all beige, riding on top of rows of Steppes mules, exploding in New Year fireworks.

"Don't show that to anyone," she said. "And keep it away from me."

For my fourth love, I drew a picture of enchanted harpsichords bouncing upon hijra bellies as they imbibed pipes of rubber and formaldehyde.

"Just be normal, please. It was cute, but you need to stop."

I could never love them, those women with iron bubbles. After a while even romance became dull. For years we were sent from ship to ship to integrate with new people, only to see so many of them get called into interrogation and never return. Or else they took four gulps of the Juc wine and crawled into their beds, never to wake. I breezed through women like wind through the open windows of a house, until numbness and isolation were the only refuge left.

During my interrogations I gave obscure answers to my captors, and was possessed by laughing fits. They kept me alive, sparing me as madmen are spared. When, after every interview, the Jucs integrated us with a new group of humans, I looked for her. When I forgot her fake name I remembered her real name was Dei. When I forgot what her face looked like I still remembered the way her black hair tossed about in the wind. When I felt so very sullen, so lonely in my fantasies, I remembered the world we made together, Dei's world, a world without judgment, with only the names we chose. We did more than preserve, more than eradicate the pain we felt. When I began to forget exactly what we did there, I remembered the feeling of not being alone.

4: Harbor

I had lost count of my age when the Jucs underwent another regime change, and we humans were integrated with another colony. Finally the interrogations stopped, and we were left some autonomy inside of a moon-sized space harbor. By then we had no distinctions. So many years had passed since any of us had seen a mountain, an island, a mound, or a canyon.

When our clans merged, the healthiest of us were chosen to form the policies that would guide our combined society. We gathered in a circular theater.

"The new Juc regime is in need of resources," said a blond woman, her voice echoing across the chamber. "To prove our loyalty, we must send humans to work for them. Who will it be?"

"Give them the lamp-humpers," said someone in a colorful gown. "They love the Jucs so much, let them live among them, as pets!"

"No, no—give the Jucs our lowest-scoring students," said another, face impassive. "Those rotten apples will be satisfied with labor anyway."

"Just give the Jucs the infertile," said another. "No chance of mixture there."

I resigned myself to the back of the chamber, sitting in the balcony's last row. There I spotted a woman at the corner of the aisle, tucked snugly inside a Jucs foldable chair, just large enough to frame her nestled body.

"Do I know you?" I whispered, as if through an echo chamber.

"I don't think so." Her eyes floated to mine, her face in that forced smile, the only kind we humans were capable of. "Do I know you?"

"I don't know."

"Sorry," she said, leaning her head into her palms. "It's just my blood pressure. They are keeping it low." A bluish bruise marked her inner elbows, a dark pool in the muddy brown of her skin.

We listened to the new human leadership debate on our new divisions—the Juc-lovers, the low-scorers, the infertile. Soon others emerged. The criminal. The drunk. The perverse. They called a vote to decide who would be condemned, and who would be spared. All that court and convocation, all that vested authority.

"I can't do this," I said.

The woman shook her head. "Come, help me walk out."

We sat together on a metal bench, observing the stars through a thick glass. We watched the empty space, where humans were forever banned. With the station's slow rotation, a green-and-blue planet came into view. A place where we could never step foot. A place without fog, and without us.

I told her of the purges I had lived through. The scattered machines that no one could re-create. She told me the Jucs shot her tribe through with some chemical that her own kind had developed in the mounds. It kept them docile and desperate for Juc guidance. High blood pressure when they refused to work. Low pressure, brittle nerves, when they spoke of revolt.

"How have you survived?" I asked.

"How did you?"

"I don't know. There was nothing special about me. What were you like back on Earth?"

"I don't remember that anymore. I chose to forget it."

"Me too."

We sat in silence.

"Sometimes I like to pretend," she said, "that on Earth, I grew up on a field of grass. Somehow the fog was not there. Just me."

"And no toys?"

A tear fell onto her cheek. "No toys," she said. "Every now and then, wind would come."

"And toss your hair up?"

"Yes."

Her arms shook as she pulled back her black hair. I remembered her. A girl laughing in levitating somersaults.

"You know, I grew up in a jungle," I said.

"Really?"

"Yes. Somehow, the fog was not there."

"No monkeys in those trees?"

"No. But there was a hill I would climb."

"Yes," she said. "I remember that hill. It was steep—"

"But it had a great view."

"Yes."

Somehow, a smile emerged between us. The kind humans were incapable of.

"I remember I met a girl on that hill," she said. "In her world, anything could happen."

Knowing that a kiss couldn't change anything, I took the chance that there were still roots left to pull.

Kawika Guillermo is an assistant professor in the Social Justice Institute at the University of British Columbia. He is the author of *Stamped: An Anti-Travel Novel* and *Transitive Cultures: Anglophone Literature of the Transpacific*. He can be reached at kawikaguillermo@gmail.com.

Dear Reader

Harmony Neal

Author's Note: "Dear Reader" was inspired by and written down on Dakota and Ojibwe land. I would like to pay my respects to the Dakota and Ojibwe and their elders past and present. Thank you for your stewardship of this land and for your survivance, which I believe will save us all. Since the writing of this story, I have learned that towns similar to Sunlight have already existed here.

For Danielle:
I created Sunlight for you most of all.

I am so glad you're here! I've created the most beautiful story I could, the most amazing, alluring world. I can hear you asking for the catch, because there's always a catch, isn't there? Fiction is conflict, is pain, hopefully with redemption, or at least a bit of understanding or possibility. Yes, I'm afraid there is a catch, but try not to let it trouble you. For now, please, come closer to see what I've made for you, for me, for all of us.

There are over five dozen birds speaking to each other in the trees that line my porch. I've invited them all, along with the grunting, chirping squirrels and the raccoons I never see during the day, but whose prints I witness in the snow, and the feral black-and-white cat watching me warily from behind the gnarled leafless tree with twisting spines. She sniffs the top of a strawberry I've left as an offering, as sustenance for all my friends, big and small, mammal, bird, bug. I give freely all my scraps and more. I go back inside and open a can of food meant for my fat orange-and-white cat, take it outside, dump it gently on a mound of ice for my feral friend,

WSQ: Women's Studies Quarterly 47: 3 & 4 (Fall/Winter 2019)

hoping she won't come back in spring and beat up my old tabby cat, who's not much of a fighter.

Have you ever listened to Reiki music? Indian flute music? Japanese koto? Celtic instrumentals? Burundi drum music? There is much that blends the human soul with its flora and fauna kin, with the elements themselves. Find something you like now. If you're in the mood for nature noises minus human touch, a nice track of birdcalls blended with waves or rivers or rain would serve nicely too. Anything that bridges the gap between you in a building, in a vehicle, near roads, near human noise of industry and longing. Anything that puts you outside, puts you within your natural context, which is a world full of sights, smells, sounds, and touches that don't originate in human acts alone.

We're about to leave so much behind to go somewhere else, somewhere where I haven't just been watching a memorial video of the seventeen people most recently murdered in another school shooting on February 15, 2018, the latest of eighteen school shootings so far this year. All of that will soon fall aside as I take you far, far away from here, to the most beautiful, wonderful place I know, where there aren't shootings or other needless deaths, no environmentally triggered diseases, not even the ones from stress. Nope. I'm taking you way away from all of that. Did you find some music you like for this adventure? I settled on Andalusian Spanish Arabic music, الأَنْدَلُس, myself. Okay. Wonderful, then let's go!

It's summer in the town of Sunlight. Flowers bloom everywhere, but no one is allergic since there's no diesel exhaust in the air to trigger delicate mammalian systems. The humid air is full of birdsong, as well as the sounds of stringed instruments, flutes, and drums, singing, and the laughter of children and adults alike—especially the older adults, who take great joy in surveying the generations at play.

I describe them as at play because there's nothing resembling what you or I might call work, which is often something no one actually wants to do, or at least, heavily involves any number of tasks we'd rather not do. Not so in Sunlight. One of the things that will likely be hard to understand about this community is that no one there has ever been coerced into doing anything they don't want to do. Ponder that for as long as you like. There are no exceptions, especially not for the children, the people we're most used to seeing coerced and coercing. That's not how things are done in Sunlight.

Sit with that information as long as you need. No coercion. Period. As you've likely already guessed, no coercion means no prisons, no borders, no police. No coercion means no bosses, no hierarchies of any sort. Each individual speaks their needs from birth and is respected.

Summer is much loved in Sunlight, which exists away from the equator, so the winters are long and snowy, spring still sees snow and ice melting and the occasional flurries, but then summer—luxuriant, wonderful summer. It rarely gets too hot, and life rushes forth in a way hard to appreciate in more even-keeled environments. Where there was snow and ice, there is green, green, green three months out of the year.

Some people are out in the terraced gardens, weeding and harvesting ripe fruit and vegetables, popping early strawberries in their mouths. Some people are digging and sculpting new homes in the outskirts, so there will always be enough room come winter. Some people are wandering home to home with toolkits, searching out things to repair. Others dance in the gardens or stroll around town with their instruments playing. Some cook large meals or tidy the outdoor communal area, pruning bushes and sweeping debris. Some engage in games of skill, wit, strength, or dexterity. Some engage in ritual movement that resembles tai chi or yoga. Some have slipped away to favored locations in the nearby woods to engage in more lusty activities.

And where are the children in all of this? Anywhere but the last places. There's a toddler trying their hand at the ritual movements to the best of their not-quite-coordinated-enough abilities, there's a six-year-old sweeping the courtyard, stopping to look at a green-and-yellow caterpillar on a downed leaf before carefully carrying the insect to nearby greens. Two tweens follow a person with their toolkit, hoping to learn how to reset off-kilter doors and fix ovens and tighten up plumbing. All sorts of children are in the gardens and helping in the kitchen, and of course, many are playing games, strange ones unfamiliar to us where there aren't any winners or losers, but a general good spirit of appreciating fantastic feats and clever twists and general increases in ability and dogged determination to keep trying whether one is naturally talented or not.

Three children have collected flowers and are taking them into homes to leave beautiful surprises for residents when they return. And out in the woods, there's a solitary child sitting on a felled tree, contemplating the mushrooms springing forth from the bark. Several have taken books from the library outside where they pore through them, sharing interesting parts with each other, and assisting when someone doesn't know a word.

Does it look like chaos to us? Do we wonder how the important things get done when no one *must* do anything? When no one is in charge? But look, everything needed for a good life is taken care of and no one is engaged in work they dislike and no one is engaged in any sort of "job" needed for "money" required to exist. The work they do is not dangerous or soul-crushing or designed to harm many for the supposed benefit of the few. No one is stressed out about anything. What would cause them stress?

Follow the path down to the river where dozens are fishing, using poles or nets, a few trying to fish like bears, reaching down into the water. They will not bring back more fish than are needed. They will not compare their catches to see who did better or best. They will admire the fish and thank them for nourishing the people of Sunlight.

Are you struggling to believe that such a place exists? Perhaps it's easier to believe in all the warring peoples of history, their atrocities, their violence, their hate and degradation, as if misery is the "natural" state of humans. Is that what you believe?

Or maybe you concede that Sunlight could exist, but you also assume that somewhere not-too-far-away there are other peoples, planning an attack. Every apocalyptic story you've consumed has primed you to believe that there must be roving bands of selfish monsters, those who would steal, snatch, murder, and enslave.

No, I think you can envision the town of Sunlight, and I think you can envision it without dangerous others nearby, waiting to descend. I think you know it already exists. The multiverse is infinite, so any place that could exist does. So here is the town of Sunlight: beautiful, lush, peaceful, content.

Take a moment and fully imagine the place. Now imagine yourself in it. Who would you be? There are endless choices. A scholar in the stacks. A builder of new dwellings. A gardener. An inventor of games. The person who cleans up common areas. One who fishes. A musician. A builder of instruments. The person who throws clay pots.

Go ahead, ask yourself: What would you do if you could do anything you wanted? What roles would you play? No one will harm you here in Sunlight. They won't mock you or coerce you or tell you who or how you're supposed to be.

There's no competition. No need to try to be the best at anything. And contrary to Western colonial belief, the lack of competition and labels like "best" produces wonderful results, genuine art and craft that is appreciated, useful inventions, and rigorous intellectual debate and curiosity. So what would you do if you lived in Sunlight? Would you learn medicinal herbs? Weave cloth? Create stories to tell?

Have a seat in the garden or at the common tables or in the woods or by the river or in a cozy home. Pick a spot you like and think about it. Perhaps you'll carve birds from deadwood or play your flute beautifully. Or turn sand to glass panes, happily teaching anyone else who wants to learn. Or turn fat and herbs to soap. You could be the person to discover which plants repel biting insects and help the gardeners protect the perimeter and intersperse the plants throughout the town, then help the soap makers make repellent soaps and sprays.

What would be your contribution? Your joy?

Humans enjoy being useful, something most of us aren't often allowed to be in the ways we crave. In Sunlight, you get to be useful, appreciated, and loved.

Speaking of love, imagine the friends you would have. The hugs and smiles and jokes and games. The meals eaten together. The stories you'd tell. Do you want them here with you now? They will come and share your joys and sorrows. Your relatives too, blood and by choice. Look, here come Twilight and Bearcub now, who have enjoyed and loved and indulged you since you were barely toddling around. They have graying hair and weathered skin, but their bodies are still strong and their love for you only grows stronger and stronger still. They are happy to sit with you and comb your hair and listen to your thoughts while you go through the options.

Perhaps you prefer a lover's insight. Sunlight has many lovers, no one owing anything or feeling owed, just respectful interested persons coming together in the ways that please them. One or more of them are happy to sit with you too, or fish with you or garden or play a game if any of those are the ways you do your best thinking. There is no rush, after all. You can decide to do whatever you want, whenever you want, and your friends, family, lovers, and neighbors will all find it good, a perfect contribution.

Don't worry, you're not locked in for life, whatever you choose. You can change, grow, and try new things. Just look at Twilight, who was originally from the plains, a hunter, who traveled alone three seasons before settling in Sunlight. Twilight can navigate anywhere by stars and sun alike, and later in life learned to weave and dye beautiful fabrics, and is currently learning all there is to know of medicinal herbs.

Bearcub has never lost their childish love of play, the good-natured twinkle in their eye. Bearcub invented several beloved games that have spread out from Sunlight to other towns, and helps organize activities for each year's several festivals, and also enjoys cooking and cleaning, and has woven a halo of flowers for you now.

Your life follows the rhythms of nature instead of the demands of capital. You do less in winter when sunlight and energy are low and more in summer when there's longer days and so much nature to enjoy. The only deadlines are the ones nature imposes to follow planting and harvesting seasons and fish migrations. Only useful and beautiful things surround you. No clutter and no scarcity.

Have you imagined it fully? Does it feel amazing? Are you eager to fill your days with nature, meaningful projects, community, and solitude in the proportions that make sense for you? To breathe the fresh air and eat real food that's made with love and not full of poison?

Are you ready?

I am so ready.

So then, what's the catch? I said there would be one. You're certainly expecting one. A tortured scapegoat? An AI rendition that is mere illusion? It was all a dream or a sociological experiment that's run out of funding? Are you expecting some sort of devil's bargain was made for Sunlight? You've been trained by the stories before this one that it must be so. There is always a catch, and anything that seems better than what you have now will reveal itself to be worse.

The catch is that Sunlight exists, but we cannot go there. Even if we could travel to the parallel universe where Sunlight, and thousands of towns like it, exist across the globe, we should not go. They have everything they need, and while they would welcome us, because that is their way, we do not know how to behave like the people of Sunlight, how to give and receive and take no more than is needed, and speak our needs. Yes, I do think we would mess it up, so we shouldn't go there, even if we could. But that is no cause for despair.

We have much we can do to bring Sunlight to where we are. Imagining it is always the first step, isn't it?

The squirrels that share a yard with me love avocados. Can you believe it? I was surprised too. They're not as picky as I am, so I take out the skins with flesh still left inside, the bruised parts, sometimes the whole thing, and I leave the halves on my porch railing, and they come and eat them.

I put out old apples too, and sometimes a fresher one if I haven't given much recently. It's the darndest thing. They eat the apples a bit at a time and always leave them sitting right where they found them. I look out and see the apple several times a day, always getting a little smaller, always sitting in basically the same spot, a communal resource that none of the squirrels tries to hide or take away.

I've been lied to so much about so many things in my life. Yes, by people with devious intent, but also by people who already thought they knew how everything works, so they only saw what they expected to see. So many people I meet expect the worst from other people, expect that is how humans are, even if they themselves aren't that way. But like the apple shared by the squirrels, I've seen the moments of compassion and coming together, even among strangers. I see the light and love in people's eyes, the craving for a safe place, a better way to be, connection, trust, love, mutual benefit, usefulness. These are basic human needs that we're told we cannot have.

That is not the nature of reality. Our real needs could be fulfilled. We all want the same basic things and are all capable of providing them to each other.

Sunlight is real. It exists. Of that I am certain.

Harmony Neal was awarded a 2018 Minnesota Artist Initiative Grant to develop new models of storytelling grounded in human and nonhuman flourishing. "Dear Reader" is a direct result of that funding. She/he/they can be reached at happyepsilon@gmail.com.

PART VIII. **POETRY**

The Witness Plays Dodgeball

Kelly Fordon

A ghazal in honor of the Survivors Network of those Abused by Priests.

On an April day dense with wounded weather
Tom got hit on the full; down he went. *The Witness*

emerged from the office two hours later. No
memory of the door or the knock. *The Witness*

missed the dive and the final elimination.
He missed first and second lunch. *The Witness*

turned into the wimp on the line who drops
or punts; who knows no bounds. *The Witness,*

the kid no one wants on his side, the one who
would rather kip than compete. *The Witness*

is a mark now. He never dodges the blow.
He's always first man out. *The Witness*

had *not a scratch on you* that day. Now,
he'll never be the same. His last thoughts

on a continuous loop through the drop and
the shock and the moment he awoke

WSQ: Women's Studies Quarterly 47: 3 & 4 (Fall/Winter 2019)

covered in grime, to his friends calling
his name: *Tom, Tom, Tom.*

Gaslighting

Kelly Fordon

I didn't hit you, that was a spank.
    You hit me.
That was barely a slap.
    You hit me.
You're crazy.
    You hit me.
I'm sorry for my part in it.
    You hit me.
You're always so dramatic.
    You hit me.
Don't be ridiculous.
    You hit me.
I can't believe you are my daughter.
    I don't want to suffer any longer.
That's exactly the way I feel about you.
    You are going to end up alone.
Good.

Kelly Fordon's novel-in-stories, *Garden for the Blind*, was chosen as a Michigan Notable Book, among other awards. Her poetry collection, *Goodbye Toothless House*, was published in 2019, and a new short story collection, *I Have the Answer*, will be published by Wayne State University Press in 2020. She can be reached at www.kellyfordon.com.

Promesa

Mónica A. Jiménez

This, too, is a kind of legacy:
my family broken apart slowly.
At times, I touch my face to remember
my brother, now dead for six years.
The ocean, his unyielding,
reclaiming the ash of his body daily,
even as our island collapses into itself.

I am moved to see what I cannot name,
the undoing of what I most love,
stormy with a debt unpaid.

Children are merely birds, I think.
Reptilian and savage:
my daughter's teeth
against my swollen breast.
I stick my finger in her mouth,
Feel around her first teeth, searching.
If what I have made is decay, let me
touch it directly, finger it shortly.

Mónica A. Jiménez is an assistant professor in the Department of African and African Diaspora Studies at the University of Texas at Austin. Jiménez can be reached at majimenez@utexas.edu.

WSQ: Women's Studies Quarterly **47: 3 & 4 (Fall/Winter 2019)** © 2019 by Mónica A. Jiménez.

The Intellectuals of Mongolia and Their Influence on Modern Art

Jennifer L. Knox

Please stop <u>stealing</u> my vegetables, says the cardboard sign
in my neighbor's zucchini patch, a zucchini patch that only exists
because I planted zucchini last year and seeds blew into his yard—
actually the no-man's-land between our yards—I could probably find
a property map showing where the vines cross into our yard.

The zucchini are enormous—about two feet long, five pounds each,
and there are at least twenty of them out there. They will rot
on the vines because the neighbor's an idiot—he doesn't even know
what they are, which is why his sign doesn't say *Please stop <u>stealing</u>
my zucchini.* I saw him mowing the lawn once (his lawn is very
mowed)—a young white man wearing a red polo shirt, tan pleated pants,

and wrap-around black sunglasses that made him look like a cyborg.
The curtains in his house are always drawn, which makes me think
he's making meth in there, and the American flag hanging next to his
front door makes me think he's racist. I'm going to make a sign and lay it
over his sign: *They're <u>zucchini,</u> asshat, and the only reason you'd need
that many, that big, is if you're swapping them out for sex toys.* Then
I'm going to write the word *<u>micropenis</u>* on his car with a Sharpie
just because.

I've been perusing privacy fences online. There are many kinds.
Some are quite creative. I miss New Yorkers' fear. If Iowans worried
100% more about getting beat up, there'd be no more signs,
and they'd tailgate less, too—that shit'll get you shot in New York.

WSQ: Women's Studies Quarterly 47: 3 & 4 (Fall/Winter 2019) © 2019 by Jennifer L. Knox.

I considered sharing my rage about this on Facebook, but they're all on Facebook—posting pictures of their grandkids and talking about Jesus—and it's too long for Twitter, but I had to tell someone, so I decided to hide it in a place they'd never look.

Jennifer L. Knox is the author of four books of poems; her fifth is forthcoming from Copper Canyon Press in Fall 2020. Her poetry has appeared in the *Best American Poetry* series as well as in the *New York Times*, the *New Yorker*, and *American Poetry Review*. She teaches at Iowa State University and is currently at work on a culinary memoir. She can be reached at jenniferlknox@gmail.com.

Cairo Divorce Twice Told

Ellen Sazzman

(1952 Nasser's purge of foreigners, 2011 Arab Spring)
after Lucette Lagnado, daughter/author of Man in the Sharkskin Suit

Dreaming of manicured boulevards as yet unbarricaded,
lined with mansions still pristine in their neoclassicism,
I float above courtyards lush with trees of rose-gold apricots.

In senescent sun, I ascend effortlessly to the terrace
of Shepheard's Hotel. My father, shiny in his white sharkskin
suit, is busy dealmaking, post–World War II, but not too busy

to ask if he may dance with my mother. They waltz
under Orion's winking belt at L'Auberge des Pyramids,
King Farouk's ballroom. At our apartment I hear my mother

discuss French classics she once studied at Bibliothèque Cattaoui
before marriage and children curtailed her curiosity.
Her mother prepares the Shabbat meal. Hidden

behind the window's silk drape I watch the sinuous streets
of Tahrir Square swell with men clutching velvet pouches,
discreet holders for prayer shawls and skullcaps,

as they walk to Gates of Heaven, the corniced temple where
my parents wed, and I spy the bronzed-umber boy I adore.
At dinner the family chews cinnamon-spiced lamb

WSQ: Women's Studies Quarterly **47**: 3 & 4 (Fall/Winter 2019) © 2019 by Ellen Sazzman. All rights reserved.

and braided challah glazed with the sweetness of apricots
cooked into syrupy marmalade and sealed in tins
soon to conceal jewels and gold coins carried to Brooklyn

where I wake struggling for breath in an airless room
and mourn the dissipating aroma of apricots, a winey incense;
the feel of their downy nap, conjoined hemispheres

cupped in my hand; and their flavor, honeyed musk
of nascent love; so seductive to my senses as to entice
a return sixty springs later to the Square where I search

for baskets of ripened apricots carried by young women,
their cursive lips coated with commingled words
of Christian, Muslim intellects. Instead I find men's

flanks and shoulders pressed flesh to flesh, bruised raw
to the pith. Crimson stains pavement and streaks banners.
I struggle to break free, bow my head and recite Kaddish

for the second exile. I retell of apricots in absentia,
the whisper of ferment, burst of juice, broken caress
of cleft globe upon my palate, a description more finite

than what I want to express—sweetness, the taste I want
to last; sweetness, the lyric I want to hear; sweetness,
the blessing I want to give and receive, a bite please.

Reflecting Absence

Ellen Sazzman

At the National September 11 Memorial, New York City

Bronzed parapets limn the grave of nearly
three thousand, their names stencil-cut
into panels. I lean close and listen
for a whisper.
What reaches the ear is
a cascade
that describes the perimeter of the void
split into recessed pools,

a squared pair of flattened feet. Twinned
sentries and their civilian denizens
exploded into a nullity.
The ultimate miscarriage, blood
emptied out, justice filtered
through pulverized bone, mangled steel
sunk deep beneath the ground
of zero,

zero divided, an impossibility.
I was not there. It was not me shouting
but cries reverberate inside my head
from bodies trapped across bodies
of water. How to distribute their discourse,
document their words so as not
to be blown
away?

WSQ: Women's Studies Quarterly 47: 3 & 4 (Fall/Winter 2019)

Ellen Sazzman has been published in *Sow's Ear*, *Lilith*, *Beltway Quarterly*, *Southward*, *Miramar*, *Comstock Review*, and *CALYX*, among others. She received an Allen Ginsberg Poetry Awards honorable mention in 2019, was shortlisted for the 2018 O'Donoghue Prize, and was a 2012 Pushcart Prize nominee by *Bloodroot Literary Magazine*. She can be reached at ellensazz@gmail.com.

A Prayer for the Precariat

Laura Sweeney

who resides in the academy, escaping
corporate life, reviving the dying
dialectic lost to the reality

of mediocre tv; while minions
and mortgagers make away with murder
she struggles to commit a social science;

displaced by recession-suppression-excession
retreats to the underground and scrawls "peace"
on the whiteboards in adjunct hell; in the margins

without easy answers she wonders how
she missed the neon glaring signs; swearing
she's not a pathetic-ascetic-heretic but in this

culture of division, an experiment
gone awry, an indignation is like an elegy
to the diseased elm tree, or a country

in precarity—an endless slammer, endless
bummer; and in this bastion of freedom, she is
the ars poetica, dancing in the hallways,

singing about the self-exiled, subsisting in America.

WSQ: Women's Studies Quarterly 47: 3 & 4 (Fall/Winter 2019) © 2019 by Laura Sweeney. All rights reserved.

Five Research Analysts on the Verge of Precarity at the Social Behavior Institute

Laura Sweeney

were glorified factory workers,
clocking in clocking out. We couldn't
sign our names without shaking while

the woman in the corner office
gaslighted the truths we sleuthed
in graduate school. But we resisted

kissing the sterling silver skeleton ring,
panopticon red eye glaring. We chanted
to the beat of the black sorority's

cane dance: I am not your kiddo! You
are not entitled! We dolled up in red
lipstick and wanderlust, discovered

the key to bust out of our slammer. We
hung Kabuki masks on our cubicle walls,
spoke French, drank Portuguese wine.

And when we read books: the poets
of protest, the essayists, the female Beats,
we vowed to one day write our truths

and call for a new paradigm.

WSQ: Women's Studies Quarterly 47: 3 & 4 (Fall/Winter 2019) © 2019 by Laura Sweeney. All rights reserved.

Laura Sweeney facilitates Writers for Life in central Iowa. She represented the Iowa Arts Council at the First International Teaching Artist's Conference in Oslo, Norway. Her recent poems appear in numerous journals. Her recent awards include a residency at Sundress Publication's Firefly Farms, and an MFA scholarship to attend the 2019 Sewanee Writers' Conference. She can be reached at lauraswny@hotmail.com.

PART IX. **ALERTS AND PROVOCATIONS**

Black Latina Womanhood: From Latinx Fragility to Empowerment and Social Justice Praxis

Zaire Zenit Dinzey-Flores, Hilda Lloréns,
Nancy López, and Maritza Quiñones,
on behalf of Black Latinas Know Collective

On April 29, 2019, the Black Latinas Know Collective (BLKC) published its website and statement (Black Latinas Know Collective 2019). The BLKC Statement, shared below, reflects our thinking as Black Latina scholars in the United States, Latin American, and Caribbean academies. First we expound on the context and motivations that led to the formation of BLKC.

The Collective and Its Goals
The academy replicates the very inequities that exist outside of it. Like society, the U.S. Latinx academic community shows a preference for white Latinx individuals and their scholarship. A quick survey of the Latinx academy reflects these patterns. The small number of Black Latina scholars, the lack of recognition—past and present—of the scholarship produced by Black Latinas, the continued failure to center Black Latina experiences, the lack of recognition of our intersectional social locations and how race-gender shapes Latinx academia, all make the Black Latinas Know Collective (BLKC) necessary and crucial.

BLKC emerged out of the recognition of our commonly shared experience of exclusion, which for years we whispered about on the sidelines of graduate school halls and academic conferences. Latinx academics, often shrouded in the protective blanket of "brownness" or "people of color," fail to see the ways in which they reproduce anti-Black Latinx rhetoric and practices.

Many conference panels are organized without regard to the race or gender composition of panelists. Calls for "no white-and-male-only"

WSQ: Women's Studies Quarterly 47: 3 & 4 (Fall/Winter 2019) © 2019 by Zaire Zenit Dinzey-Flores, Hilda Lloréns, Nancy López, and Maritza Quiñones. All rights reserved.

panels have not been fully assimilated by Latinx organizers. And an erasure of Black Latinidad carries through Black and Latinx conference circles when panels remain racially and ethnically homogeneous/reductive, even if in Brown, even if in Black panels. As the successful Cite Black Women campaign has exemplified, the work and original ideas of Black Latinas are similarly underrepresented in citational practices. *We have each witnessed a pattern of scholars borrowing generously from our work without attribution.* At the same time, our theories and versions of race are often questioned, challenged, and dismissed; at times they are framed as reactionary, at others as inconsequential, and even as wrong. *These injustices are not simply about theoretical debates and disagreements, but they have material, physical, and mental consequences that negatively impact our well-being as individuals, families, and communities.*

BLKC emerged because, even as we produce important scholarship, that scholarship tends to adorn rather than become the axis of scholarly production on relevant topics. *With BLKC we aim to make prominent our presence and scholarship, and to highlight our versions of the world and our particular epistemological perspectives that center Black Latina womanhood.*

Why Now?: Anti-Blackness and World Events

In understanding twenty-first-century conversations about Blackness in Latin America, the Caribbean, and among U.S. Latinxs, three events that have given voice to anti-Blackness and racism are relevant: the 2001 World Conference against Racism, Racial Discrimination, Xenophobia, and Related Intolerance in Durban, South Africa; the International Decade for People of African Descent (2015–2024), both events organized by the United Nations; and the U.S. #BlackLivesMatter movement, addressing the legacy of police impunity and the crisis of racial injustice, which became a unanimous symbol of the injustices against the Black community in the United States, Latin America, the Caribbean, and globally.

Historical and contemporary conversations engendered by Black individuals in Latin America, the Spanish-speaking Caribbean, and the Latinx U.S. have centered anti-Blackness and the attendant social consequences of racism. Though feminist and womanist critiques have also been central in conversations about anti-Blackness among Black Latinas, *we insist that gender bias, misogyny, and violence against Black women must be directly confronted and acknowledged as a critical component in the fight against racism, social and economic inequality, and injustice.*

In the second decade of the twenty-first century, a host of political conditions have sparked and heightened protests in the Americas and the Caribbean, including the global impact of the #BlackLivesMatter movement and continued anti-Black violence in the United States, the assassination of Marielle Franco (a young Brazilian politician who defended women, the LGBTQ community, and the poor), as well as gender-based violence, inequality, and sexual abuse of girls and boys in our communities. *For BLKC it is clear that active resistance—in our everyday lives, in the classroom, on social media, and in our critical and public scholarship—against widespread anti-Blackness and misogyny is a significant way to contribute to the arduous, but worthy, project of building a more just world for current and future generations.*

We aim to mark our presence in the academy, to stake a claim to our existence, to challenge and acknowledge perspectives that are discordant with our views, to remind the academy that we have a voice and a presence. *Together, our scholarship highlights the intellectual field of Black Latina womanhood.* Additionally, our interventions will be made visible in monthly blog posts, panels, and publications showcasing our thought, experiences, epistemologies, ontologies, and engaged scholarship.

Self-Implicating Reflexivity and Shifting Epistemologies

The Black Latinas Know Collective underscores the epistemological shifts necessary for intersectional justice, equity, and liberation. Critical and self-implicating reflexivity is a necessary first step in dismantling Latinx (white) fragility and discomfort about discussing the realities and consequences of the color line. BLKC engages in ongoing critical and self-implicating reflexivity about the meaning of race and gender in our lives and the ensuing relationships of power.

We believe that epistemological shifts demand answering questions that speak to positionality, reflexivity, and the structural dimensions of knowledge production. The following questions may lead to innovations in knowledge and policies that center Black Latina lives:

— What are the master- and counternarratives about race and gender within Latinx studies and other fields?

— How do hardened concepts and tropes such as "raza cosmica," "cuatro pisos," "rainbow people," "racial democracy," "mixed-raceness," "black behind the ear," "¿y tu abuela, a donde está?," and "Black-Brown coalitions" circulate, and insist upon particular visions of race and gender?

— Who are the authors of race narratives and theorization, what are their positionalities, and what racial, personal, everyday, and social forces shape their concepts?

— How do scholars "know" about race in Latinx studies? What are the conditions and sources of racial knowledge(s)?

— What are the controversies, debates, paradoxes, and ethical dilemmas in researching race and gender within Latinx communities?

— What is the role of ongoing critical and self-implicating self-reflexivity about one's own social, class, racial, and gendered locations within structural inequities?

— How can we resist color- and power-evasiveness in knowledge production against the backdrop of neoliberal logics operating in academia, funding agencies, and think tanks?

— How can we consider the simultaneity and nonequivalence of race, gender, ethnicity, sexuality, nativity, documentation status, and other systems of inequality and resistance in Latinx communities?

— What are innovative and even alternative ways of conceptualizing, rethinking, and measuring race at multiple levels (e.g., individual, interpersonal, institutional, structural, and on local and global scales)?

— Under what structural conditions is research on "race" within the Latinx community viable in academia, global and national government agencies, grant agencies, think tanks, policy-making bodies, corporate media, and law?

— How do governmentality and its institutions affect the lives of Black Latinx individuals and communities in terms of access to voting, housing, employment, education, physical and mental health, law and justice, immigration, and other policy-relevant arenas?

— How might we form conceptualizations of race and gender that are inclusive of Black Latina knowledges?

— What practices and forums might center the experiences of Black Latinas, and forge opportunities for centering their/our voices?

— How do we leverage Black Latina knowledges to make for greater justice and equity?

These are only a few of the myriad questions that BLKC considers and addresses. They mark the kind of reflexivity necessary within an academy that has not reconciled our thinking. If we are truly to address racial justice, these are questions important for all. We collectively thread our scholarship and our mission with these questions, and urge others who are allies in the fight for racial justice to consider them too.

BLKC Statement

WE ARE . . . a collective of Black Latina scholars, producers of innovative and important intellectual contributions to the intersectional study of race within Latinidad and Blackness. We acknowledge that our Black womanhood and scholarship intersect to offer a particular view of race, our disciplines, and society, which is intimately tied to our own experience.

WE KNOW . . . that all scholarship comes from particular personal experiences. Our scholarship is informed by our intimate experiences with Black Latina womanhood. From early experiences of having our Latinidad and Blackness questioned, to dealing with white Latinx standards of beauty that exclude us, to being rendered invisible, to being designated as incapable of occupying our places as professors, intellectuals, and knowledge producers, our insights are important and irreplicable.

WE ARE THINKERS . . . and our thinking is crucial to the conversation on race. Scholarly dialogues about racial inequality have to make space for our thought, knowledge(s), and epistemologies. Scholarly conversations about race, racism, and anti-Blackness result from the work of pioneering Black thinkers and activists who often risked their lives to denounce oppressive systems and ideologies. Those who have been directly affected by racism opened the path we now walk on. Further, anti-Black narratives and practices, even those that manifest within the process of scholarly production, directly affect us. Perspectives that exclude our Black Latina thought are by definition incomplete.

WE CENTER . . . Black Latina voices as crucial sources of knowledge to understand how race works within Latinidad. Our voices are seminal and indelible to the production of intersectional scholarship on race and gender in Latina/o/x studies. An overrepresentation of white and mesti-za Latinas/os/xs in scholarly accounts of race reproduces the very racial exclusions that the scholarship claims to address. Overlooked in this dis-tancing are questions of racialized pain, privileges, opportunities, penal-ties, and distribution of power, life chances, and inequalities. At best these accounts are incomplete, at worst they reproduce race-based stereotypes. In part, this is due to a lack of lived experience, but more often what these accounts show is a lack of engagement with our scholarship.

WE RESIST . . . being silenced, overlooked in the knowledge production of our very own experience and knowledge base. Scholarship on Latinas/os/xs and race is increasingly highlighting the role that race plays in pro-ducing unequal conditions. Yet time and again, neither Black Latinas nor our knowledge production is embraced by scholars who benefit from our work and our experiences. Conceptual and theoretical models of race among non-Black Latinxs claim to have an insight into the Black experi-ence based on a "we are all mixed" and, by extension, "all Black" version of race. We reject translators, ventriloquists, and/or representatives in con-veying our view of race and inequality.

WE CLAIM . . . our long-term engagement with questions of race-gender inequality within Latinidad, even when it was not popular. There is a his-tory of Black Latina thought to acknowledge that includes our own episte-mologies. We have our own thought. We have our own knowledge(s). Our experiences as Black Latinas uniquely equip us to understand, talk, write about, and engage with the issues that affect us.

WE DEMAND . . . to be heard, to be cited, to be recognized, and to be at-tributed ownership of our ideas and the scholarship that we have produced.

WE BUILD . . . a collaborative, collective community of BLACK LATINA knowledge production. We stand together to name Black Latina women as central to the popular and formal scholarship on race within Latinidad.

WE WRITE . . . scholarly and popular pieces that make visible who we are, what we think, and what we know.

WE DO ALL . . . in service of something greater than ourselves. We aim to dismantle systems that oppress marginalized peoples at the intersections of multiple categories of social difference, including race, ethnicity, gender, class, sexuality, ability, citizenship, and language. We assert that our work is a crucial element of a manifold approach to social justice, one that includes activism and grassroots organizing, the arts, electoral politics, public policy, and others. We believe in liberation and we teach, conduct research, and disseminate our knowledge in order to engender a more just society.

Zaire Zenit Dinzey-Flores is an associate professor of Latino and Caribbean studies and sociology at Rutgers University. She is the author of *Locked In, Locked Out: Gated Communities in a Puerto Rican City*, and can be reached at zdinzey@lcs.rutgers.edu.

Hilda Lloréns teaches in the Department of Sociology & Anthropology at the University of Rhode Island. She is the author of *Imaging the Great Puerto Rican Family: Framing Nation, Race, and Gender during the American Century*, and can be reached at hilda_llorens@uri.edu.

Nancy López is professor of sociology at the University of New Mexico, where she cofounded and directs the Institute for the Study of "Race" and Social Justice. Dr. López is the author of *Hopeful Girls, Troubled Boys: Race and Gender Disparity in Urban Education* and coeditor of *Mapping "Race": Critical Approaches to Health Disparities Research*. She can be reached at nlopez@unm.edu.

Maritza Quiñones's experiences with race, gender, sexuality, and language in Puerto Rico and later at the university, in Indiana, led her to write. Her groundbreaking essay, "From Trigueñita to Afro–Puerto Rican: Intersections of the Racialized, Gendered, and Sexualized Body in Puerto Rico and the U.S. Mainland," fuses her life experiences, academic journey, and hopes for continued sharing. She can be reached at quinonesm@gmail.com.

Works Cited

Black Latinas Know Collective. 2019. "The Statement." Black Latinas Know Collective. Last modified April 29, 2019. https://www.blacklatinasknow.org/.

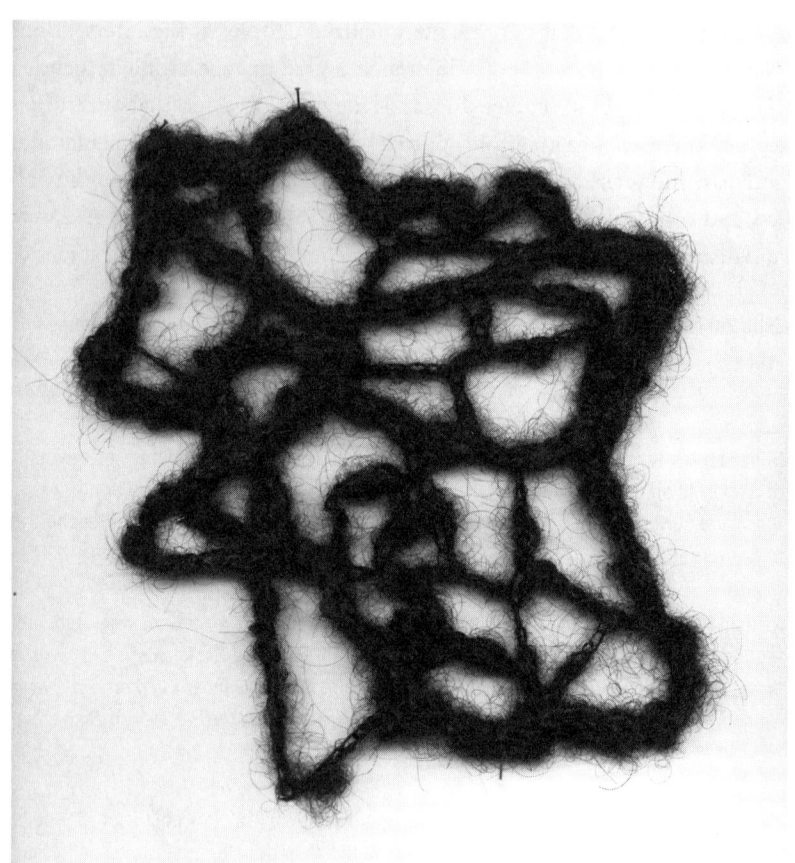

Mildred Beltré. *Constellation 3*, 2014. Human hair, approx. 3 x 6 in. Image courtesy of the artist.

Mildred Beltré is a Brooklyn-based artist, working in print, drawing, and politically engaged participatory practice. Beltré is an associate professor of art at the University of Vermont and is a cofounder of Brooklyn Hi-Art! Machine, an ongoing socially engaged collaborative art project in Crown Heights, Brooklyn. She can be reached at mildred-beltre@gmail.com.

Tulsa Studies in Women's Literature

A special forum on
Latin American Women Authors

Spring 38, No. 1

@TSWLJournal   tswl.utulsa.edu   Find us on Facebook!